The Mother & Daughter COOKBOOK

The Mother & Daughter COOKBOOK

Katherine Knight

Barrie & Jenkins London

© 1974 by Katherine Knight

Published 1974 by Barrie & Jenkins Ltd.
24 Highbury Crescent London N5 1RX
All Rights Reserved including the right
to reproduce this book or portions
thereof in any form.

Designed by Michael R. Carter.
Illustrations by John McKenna & Pat Watts

ISBN 0 214 66906 8

Printed and bound by « Les Presses Saint-Augustin », s.a.
Bruges, Belgium

For Pip, of course,
and for Richard, Alan, Peter & Robert,
who ate it all.

Contents

Before You Begin

Do you know any of the stories of Ananse, the half-man, half-spider of Ghanaian legends? Like Brer Rabbit, he almost always gets the upper hand over his enemies through trickery. One of the stories is about a magic cooking-pot, which, if one said the right words, would produce an endless stream of palm-oil soup. There is a Czech story about a similar bowl, which at command would pour out milk pudding for ever, and an old German tale of a magic table which would spread itself with a marvellous meal, provided you knew the spell to make it work. These folk-stories from different parts of the world show that people have always wanted delicious food without the bother of working for it; but something always goes wrong, to teach them not to be so greedy: Ananse's son offends the pot and spoils the magic, the milk pudding nearly drowns the old women of the village, and the magic table is stolen from its owner. Perhaps it is worth a little trouble, and safer, to make your own delicious meals.

That is what this book is about. It was written to be of help to mothers who want to share the enjoyment of cookery with their children, and to be of interest to adults as well. Some recipes have been worked out to show that it is possible for two cooks to work together without spoiling the broth.

I also very much hope that it will be used by boys as well as girls, and fathers as well as mothers. There is absolutely nothing at all sissy in cooking: some of the best chefs in the world have been men; and anyway, as eating is necessary for both males and females it is only logical that cookery should be shared. Why should women have all the fun?

Clearing Up

It is, of course, a point of honour with all good cooks of any age or sex to leave the kitchen in good order for the next session, with all washing-up done and things put away in the right places, the oven wiped down while it is still warm and the floor swept if it needs it.

Safety

Another very important thing to consider is safety, not only for yourself but for other people. This includes always washing your hands and scrubbing your nails before you touch any food; and using fresh food. Have a thick oven glove on before you touch any oven container or hot pan: a teatowel is not thick enough to protect your hand. NEVER use your apron for this purpose, because if it should catch fire you might catch fire with it. Keep long hair tied back for the same reason. Turn pan handles to a position where they can't be heated

9

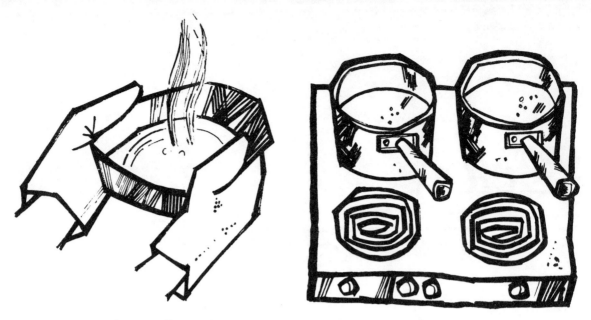

by an adjacent flame or ring, nor be knocked accidentally by anyone passing the cooker. If there are young children in your family this is doubly important. If you are young, NEVER do deep-fat frying or sugar-boiling unless you have an adult's permission and thoroughly understand what you are doing. Boiling fat and sugar are both much hotter than boiling water. Remember that knives are (or should be) sharp and make sure you are working safely when you are chopping, for instance. Work in a good light. If you drop water or grease on the floor, mop it up at once, so that no-one will slip.

Using the Book

I have chosen, invented and tested recipes with several things in mind. The recipes marked "D" are for beginners (younger daughters and sons) and are written in some detail. Many include descriptions of basic processes. They are not necessarily the easiest recipes in the book, but are the ones that I think all good cooks should know about. Those marked "M" are for more experienced cooks (parents or other adults). In these, it is taken more for granted that you know the basic terms and processes. Some of these, too, are likely to appeal more to an adult's taste.

The basic skills are described in detail at least once somewhere in this book, and essential manipulative processes are illustrated. The chapter at the end consists of bits of useful information and definitions of technical cooking terms used elsewhere. All these are indexed, as well as the recipes, so if you find an instruction somewhere such as "make a roux..." or "fold in the egg whites" and don't know what I am talking about, look up the unknown word in the index. You will then be directed to the recipe where making a roux is described in detail, or to the entry in the "Tips and Terms" chapter where folding is explained.

Using Recipes

If you are a beginner, I'd like to say something about using recipes. In this book the ingredients are set out at the beginning in a list, in the order in which they will be used, so that you can easily check through at the end to see that you haven't missed anything.

Always read through the recipe before you start, so that you can make sure you have all the ingredients and understand the method. If you spend five minutes studying the recipe you may well save yourself much more in the actual preparation.

Get the ingredients out and ready to use before you start the preparation of the dish in hand. For instance, the recipe may say "1 medium onion, chopped". This means that an onion of middling size must be peeled and chopped before you use it, and it is best to do the chopping as part of getting things ready, so you won't be held up at an important point later.

Light or turn on the oven, so that it will be heated and ready when you want to use it.

Until you are experienced, follow the recipe exactly, unless it says "optional" after any ingredient. This means that you can choose whether or not to put it in, and that the dish will be all right without it.

On the other hand, you may think I sound vague when I say "bake for about 20 minutes", or, above all, when I say "season to taste". This is because no-one can give you the last little bit of judgment needed when you cook: only you know exactly how well-done you like your biscuits, or how much salt in the soup is right for you. Another reason is that although ovens and cookers all probably start with accurate thermostats, as they grow older they develop odd quirks, just like people, and you need to know the oddities of the oven you are using before you can tell to the last minute how long, say, jam tarts are going to take to cook. If the oven is full, too, it will affect the baking time and things will take a bit longer to cook than if only one item were being baked. Even the size and thickness of your saucepans and baking dishes will affect the time that the food in them takes to be ready.

Metric Measures

Because I hope this book will continue to be useful for many years, I have given metric measures in brackets after the ingredients as well as imperial measures. There is a slight snag here: the exact equivalent of one ounce is 28.349 grams. Now unless you happen to have a chemical balance in your kitchen, this is not easy to weigh out. When metric measures come in, the equivalents must of course be rounded up or down to the nearest convenient metric weight. I have done this according to the importance of the particular ingredient in that particular recipe. For instance, if you are making soup it won't make much difference if you use 2 oz. of flour or 50 g., which is easy to measure but is really only about 1 3/4 oz. On the other hand, the missing 1/4 oz. might be vital in a sauce. In such a case I have either given the equivalent as 60 g. or adjusted the quantities of other ingredients to keep them in the correct proportions. Do not be dismayed, therefore, if you find different metric equivalents given for the same imperial weight or volume.

Teaspoons and tablespoons are standard measuring ones. If you want to convert, 1 level teaspoon = approx. 5 ml., and 1 level tablespoon = approx. 20 ml. Double these quantities for rounded spoon measures.

Garnishing

Always pay attention to the way you present food. Digestion starts in the eye of the beholder! Colour and neatness are important. On the other hand, there can be too much parsley; and in my opinion time spent doing little fiddly garnishes is time wasted. Try to achieve a colourful and appetizing effect boldly and simply. Food, I think, should look like food, rather than like a pattern for an embroidered cushion cover. This point is especially important for hot foods. Get them quickly to the table, and provide really hot plates. You can, if you like, have more fun with cold foods, though no dish should have the much-handled appearance that comes from over-garnishing.

Menu Planning

After a lot of thought, I decided not to include any set menu suggestions. In my own experience I have found that when it comes to the point, I have never had the time, money or ingredients to carry out other people's notions of ideal meals.

However, when you plan your own meals in advance, which will save you time, effort and money, there are several rules to help you.

Try to achieve a balance between starchy and protein foods.

Include fresh vegetables, salads and fruits as often as possible.

Use plenty of milk, at least 1 pint per day per child especially.

Never have a fried, pastry or sloppy-textured main course followed by the same sort of pudding. The dreadful combinations I have in mind are, for instance, fried fish-and-chips followed by fritters, or steak-and-kidney pudding with apple dumplings to follow, or stew sluiced down by rice pudding.

Always include something crisp at some point in the meal.

Balance a cheap first course with a more expensive pudding if you can afford to do so, and vice versa.

To make the best use of the housekeeping money and of the raw foods you buy with it, you need a little knowledge, experience and a developing palate. I hope you will acquire all these quickly and happily, and that you will get as much fun out of cooking with this book as I (and my daughter Pip) have had in testing and writing it. An interest in good food and cooking can repay you with health and pleasure at every meal in your life.

Stocks & Soups

First of all, may I tell you a story that I heard when I was young?

An old soldier, discharged from the wars, was walking his way home through the countryside. It was evening, the wind was veering east, and purple clouds were swinging above the dark forest that he must soon cross. As he marched along, looking uneasily at the sky, he stubbed his toe on a pebble lying in the road. He stopped to pick it up. It was a pretty stone, brown as bread and streaked with butter-yellow. It reminded him how hungry he was, and how very far from home, but he put it into his pocket.

Then he saw a light behind a hedge. It was glinting through the kitchen window of a farmhouse. At once the soldier left the road and tapped on the kitchen door.

"Have you shelter for the night for an old soldier, please?" he asked the farmer's wife.

"We are too poor to offer anything," replied the woman, and began to cry. "There is nothing to eat at all."

The soldier peered past her into the kitchen. It was true that the table was bare, with only a ham-bone on a plate in the centre, but the fire burnt warmly. A flurry of sleet against his neck made the warmth even more inviting.

"May I at least sleep beside your fire until the morning?" he asked, and the good woman let him in. When he had warmed himself a little, and talked to the children, he looked around the kitchen. There was a pot near the fire but it contained only water. Suddenly the soldier had an idea.

"I have a wonderful stone in my pocket," he told the woman, "given to me as a reward for courage. It is a magic stone; it need only be boiled in a pot of water to make a splendid broth, enough for everyone."

In a moment, of course, the coloured pebble was in the pot of water and set upon the fire.

"It would do no harm to flavour the soup with that old bone on the table," said the soldier. So that went into the pot as well.

"I see that there is a carrot or two left in the bottom of this basket—yes—and a turnip, and a big onion. Now onion always makes the stone work quicker." So the vegetables went into the pot to join the ham-bone and the pebble. The broth began to give a delightful smell.

"There are a few potatoes left in the cellar," said one of the children excitedly. "Would they make the stone work quicker, too?"

"Indeed they would," replied the soldier gravely, and pretty soon there were potatoes in the pot as well as the ham-bone, the other vegetables and the pebble.

"Could that be a piece of smoked sausage hanging on the nail in the chimney?" asked the soldier when the pot had been bubbling for some time. "A slice or two of sausage is just the thing to make the stone finish the magic—we mustn't wear it out, of course." In a minute there were some thick slices of sausage in the pot along with the ham-bone, the root vegetables and sliced potatoes—and, not least, the pebble. By now the soup smelt so good that they could wait no longer. There was enough for a good big bowl of broth for everybody, much to the wonder of the farmer's wife. Everyone slept well that night, especially the soldier, rolled in his cloak by the fire.

In the morning he washed the wonderful stone and gave it to the farmer's wife in thanks for her kindness. "Remember," he told her, "the stone will always make soup for you. It needs only a bone to keep it company, some vegetables cut small to hasten it, and a slice or two of meat or sausage to stop it losing magic." He waved goodbye to the family and set off happily through the green forest in the morning sun. Soon he came to a streamlet which slipped through ferns on a bed of shining pebbles. The old soldier picked up a pocketful of the roundest ones he could find, and went homeward whistling.

I don't know what other kinds of soup he made on his way back to the place where he lived. There are hundreds of different ones he could have tried: clear ones, thick ones; elegant consommés for formal dinners as well as peasant soups that are the whole meal; vegetable ones, creamy ones, meaty, fishy, fruity ones; steamy-hot or cold, with rolls or toast or crusty bread.

Anyway, here are some recipes for you and your mother to try, even though you may not have any magic pebbles handy. But if you possibly can, do make some stock for your soups, because this is very close to magic in the difference it makes to the taste.

1 STOCK

Stock does take time to prepare, though the hours that it spends simmering on the back of the stove don't count, as you need not watch it. The old recipes which started with "Take 4 lbs. fresh shin of beef and a fowl..." are no longer practicable for most households because of the expense and waste of meat left to be thrown away when all its flavour has been extracted. Still, if you can manage to make a batch of stock sometimes for your soups, sauces and gravies you may well come to agree with me that it is worth the trouble. If you really can't make any, even with vegetables, there are many kinds of cubes available everywhere for you to make instant stock, which is certainly better than plain water.

D Brown Stock (or bone stock if made without meat)
3 pints (1 1/2 litres very approx.)

INGREDIENTS
2-3 lbs. beef bones (1-1 1/4 kg.)
2 carrots
2 onions, peeled
1 small leek if available
2 stalks of celery
1/4 lb. minced lean raw beef, or more (optional) (100 g. or more)
2 rashers lean bacon (optional)
1 teaspoon black peppercorns
1 level teaspoon salt
1 blade mace
4 cloves
dried bouquet garni or bundle of fresh herbs if possible
3 pints cold water (1 1/2 litres, good measure)
Oven: V. Hot, Reg. 8, 450 °F.

METHOD
1 Ask the butcher to chop the bones for you when you buy them if they are very large. Put them in a meat tin and brown them for half an hour in a very hot oven, Reg. 8 or 450 °F.
2 Meanwhile prepare the vegetables by washing them and cutting them up roughly. Take a spoonful of fat from the browning bones, or use dripping, and quickly brown the vegetables in a frying pan.
3 Put the browned bones and vegetables into a large saucepan or flameproof casserole, leaving the fat behind. Pour the fat out of the meat tin (it is useful dripping), dissolve any brown sediment in a little water and add this to the pot.
4 Add all the rest of the ingredients. Bring slowly to the boil. When at boiling point, take a tablespoon and draw it across the surface to scoop out any brown froth that appears. This is called "skimming".

5   Reduce the heat until the stock is barely simmering, cover the pan with a tightly-fitting lid, and cook for 1 hour. At the end of this time scoop out the vegetables and discard them. Continue to simmer the stock for a further two hours at least.

6   Strain the liquid off the bones etc., first through a coarse strainer, then through a scalded tea-towel spread above a strainer over a basin. (To scald the cloth, boil it in a saucepan of water for 10 minutes. Allow it to cool, wring out and use quickly.)

7   Put the stock in a place where it will cool quickly, uncovered but protected from dust and flies. Skim off every trace of fat when it is cold.

8   Store in the refrigerator. Boil it up every two days in order to prevent it going bad, and use it within a week. If you have no refrigerator, store it in a cool place and boil up every day.

NOTE: You may use vegetables as available, but do not try much parsnip nor any potato, as they make the stock cloudy and also are inclined to go sour quickly.

D   White Stock

This is made in the same way as brown stock, BUT use veal bones if possible, and don't brown either bones or vegetables. Put them straight into the pot with cold water and flavourings.

D   Chicken Stock

Instead of beef or veal bones, and minced beef, use the carcase, left-over skin and giblets of a previously-cooked chicken, with flavouring vegetables as above. If you have any, some mushroom stalks are a good addition. The liquid left after boiling a fowl is usually a very good chicken stock.

D   Fish Stock

Make this from the head, bones and skin of fish (about 8 oz. to a pint of water or 200 g. to 500 ml.), with carrot, onion and bouquet garni. A tablespoon of vinegar is an extra refinement.

D   Vegetable Stock

This is a good standby (much better than water) for many soups. Cut 1 lb. mixed vegetables (500 g.) into rough pieces, add two pints of water (1 litre) and herbs as available. A teaspoon of yeast extract, Marmite for example, is a good addition, but don't then put any extra salt. The water you have left after boiling vegetables can also be made use of, unless it is too salty.

II CLEAR SOUPS & BROTH

Consommé à la Royale
Serves 4   Joint recipe

M Consommé

INGREDIENTS
2 pints well-flavoured stock (1 litre)
8 oz. lean beef, minced raw (200 g.)
3 tablespoons sherry
1 egg white
1 crushed egg shell (optional)
seasoning to taste

METHOD
1   Put the stock into a large saucepan with the beef, 2 tablespoons of sherry, the egg white and pieces of shell if used.
2   Bring slowly to the boil, whisking constantly.
3   Turn down the heat and simmer without a lid for at least an hour. Do not disturb the crust that will form on the top of the pan. During this time the liquid should reduce to about half its previous volume.
4   Scald a tea towel or linen napkin in boiling water. Cool and wring it out, then spread it over a strainer with a bowl underneath.
5   Tilting the pan gently so that the liquid runs out, leaving the crust until last, pour the consommé through the napkin and strainer.
6   Rinse the saucepan. Put the strainer and cloth, which now contains the crust, over the saucepan, and strain the consommé a second time. The crust acts this time as an additional filter.
7   Very carefully skim off all fat from the surface of the consommé, and reheat it with the last tablespoonful of sherry, but do not boil it.
8   Serve hot in soup cups if possible, with a little royale garnish in each cup.

D Royale Garnish for Consommé

INGREDIENTS
2 egg yolks
3 tablespoons cream or top-of-milk
pinch of salt
shake of white pepper

METHOD
1   Grease a dariole mould or small cup.
2   Beat the ingredients together, then strain into the greased container. Cover it with a cap of foil.
3   Put the mould into a small saucepan with enough water to come half way up the side of the mould. Simmer very gently for about 30 minutes or until the egg is set. Then let it get cold.
4   Run a knife carefully round the inside of the cup or mould and turn the custard out onto a plate.
5   Cut it into slices with a sharp knife dipped in cold water, then into strips and finally into cubes or diamonds. Make them as small as you can.

NOTE: Consommé may be garnished in many different ways, and its name changes accordingly. Here are a few of them:

Consommé brunoise: small dice of assorted cooked vegetables are used as garnish.
Consommé Carmen: add a tablespoon of tomato purée to the consommé and garnish it with dice of tomato (flesh only) and tiny strips of cooked red pepper.
Consommé with pasta: vermicelli, alphabet shapes or pasta wheels or shells, cooked for five minutes in boiling salt water, may be added to garnish any plain consommé.
Consommé à la madrilène: use chicken stock reduced by half. Clear it with egg as in basic recipe. Add 1 tablespoonful of tomato purée and 1 tablespoonful of sherry only. Garnish with tiny strips of tomato flesh, red pepper and cooked celery.

M Jellied Consommé

Set the consommé in soup cups in the refrigerator. Serve very cold. There should be no need to add gelatine if enough bones were used in the original stock. It ought to set to a lightly jellied consistency.

D Scotch Broth

4-6 servings

INGREDIENTS
1 lb. stewing mutton, lamb or beef on the bone:
  e.g. neck or breast of lamb or shank of beef (1/2 kg.)
2 oz. barley soaked (overnight if possible) in 1/2 pint of water (50 g. in 250 ml.)
1 1/2 pints extra water (850 ml.)
1 rounded teaspoon salt
1/8 level teaspoon pepper
2 oz. turnip (50 g.)
2 oz. leek (50 g.)
2 oz. celery (50 g.)
3 oz. carrot (75 g.)
1 teaspoon Marmite or other yeast extract
chopped parsley to garnish

METHOD
1 Put the meat, trimmed of fat if necessary, with any bones into a large saucepan or flameproof casserole. Add the barley with its soaking water plus the extra 1 1/2 pints. Bring to the boil and skim off any grey froth that rises, using a tablespoon.
2 Add salt and pepper. Cover and simmer for 1 1/2 hours.
3 While the meat cooks, wash and peel the vegetables and cut them into neat small dice.
4 After the 1 1/2 hours' simmering, add the diced vegetables and cook gently for a further 1/2 hour.
5 Scoop out the meat and bone from the pan. Strip the meaty bits off the bone, discard the bone and all pieces of gristle and fat. Skim any fat off the surface of the soup, then return the meat, cut into small pieces.
6 Stir in the Marmite, taste and re-season the soup if necessary. Serve in generous portions, very hot, sprinkled with finely-chopped parsley.

III THICKENED VEGETABLE & CREAM SOUPS

Perhaps the most popular soups of all, these supply valuable nutrients. Cream soups in particular are a good way to include milk in the diet of both children and elderly people.

D Bean or Lentil Soup
For 4 people

This is a nourishing and filling soup—a light meal in itself or a substantial starter.

INGREDIENTS

2-4 oz. haricot, red or butter beans, or lentils, the weight depending on how
  thick you want the soup to be (60-125 g.)
1/2 pint water (300 ml.)
1 pint white, brown or vegetable stock, or water plus stock cube (550 ml.)
1 bay leaf
1 teaspoon chopped fresh rosemary, sage or thyme, or 1/4 teaspoon dried herbs
1 oz. butter or margarine (30 g.)
1 medium onion, chopped
seasoning
2-3 frankfurters or other cooked sausages, sliced

METHOD

1 Soak the beans in the water overnight to soften and swell.
2 Put the beans and their soaking water into a saucepan with the stock, bay and herb flavourings. Bring to the boil and simmer gently for 2 hours or until the beans are broken down. The time will depend on what you are cooking: small beans cook more quickly than large ones, of course. Add extra water if much boils away.
3 Remove the bay leaf and liquidize the soup, or rub through a sieve if you have no blender.
4 Rinse the saucepan, melt the fat in it and fry the onion gently until it is lightly browned and the fat mostly absorbed.
5 Pour back the bean purée, stir, add seasoning to taste and the sausages cut into rounds. Bring back to the boil and serve very hot.

M French Onion Soup
4 good portions

French onion soup is a splendid pick-me-up on a cold day and is reputed to be comforting after late parties, too. There are plenty of recipes, each different from the next in detail, but all agree that the important thing is to cook the onion very patiently to start with. It may take half an hour or more, but could you perhaps be getting on with something else in the kitchen?

The garnishing bread may be toasted, or not; the cheese on it grilled before you put it in the soup, or browned at the top of a hot oven in the tureen—or omitted altogether.

INGREDIENTS

2 oz. butter or margarine (60 g.)
2 lbs. large mild onions, sliced (900 g.)
1 oz. flour (30 g.)
1 1/2 pints white stock, or water plus stock cube (850 ml.)
1 level teaspoon sugar

seasoning to taste
4 diagonally-cut slices French bread
4 oz. cheese, preferably Gruyère (100 g.)

METHOD

1 Melt the butter in a large saucepan and put in the onions. Turn down the heat to cook very gently and stir from time to time. Continue until the onions are golden rather than brown and much reduced in volume.
2 Stir in the flour, heat for a minute, then add the stock, a little at a time, blending well. Add sugar and seasoning to taste, bring back to the boil and simmer for a further five minutes.
3 Toast the bread if you like, put on each slice a piece of cheese and brown it under the grill. (Or see my introductory remarks.)
4 Pour the soup into a hot tureen, or into bowls ready to serve, with the bread and cheese floating on top.

M   Cream of Mushroom Soup
Serves 4

INGREDIENTS
1 oz. butter or margarine (30 g.)
1/2 lb. mushrooms, roughly sliced if large (225 g.)
1 medium onion, sliced
1/2 clove garlic, crushed
1 pint milk (550 ml.)
salt & pepper to taste
1 rounded teaspoon cornflour
2 tablespoons top-of-milk
croûtons

METHOD

1 Sauté the mushrooms and onion in the butter for a few minutes.
2 Add the crushed garlic, milk and seasoning and simmer for 10 minutes, very gently, until the vegetables are tender.
3 Liquidize briefly, or pass through a sieve or vegetable mill.
4 Rinse the saucepan, return the soup and bring to the boil.
5 Thicken slightly with the cornflour mixed in the top-of-milk.
Cook for a further five minutes to remove the raw taste of cornflour, stirring all the time.
6 Serve hot, with croûtons.

NOTE: Other vegetables can be substituted for mushrooms to make other cream soups in exactly the same way.

D   Vichyssoise Soup
4 portions

A delicious chilled soup.

INGREDIENTS
3/4 lb. potatoes, peeled weight, cut into small pieces (350 g.)
6 oz. white part only of leeks, washed and sliced (175 g.)
1 pint strong chicken stock (550 ml.)
salt, white pepper, tabasco to taste

1/4 pint double cream (150 ml.)
snipped-up chives or chopped parsley to garnish

METHOD
1   Simmer the potatoes and leeks gently in the chicken stock for 3/4 hour, or until they are very well done.
2   Rub the soup through a sieve and allow it to get cold. Season.
3   Chill thoroughly. Just before serving stir in the double cream. Garnish with parsley, or, better, chives cut very small with kitchen scissors.

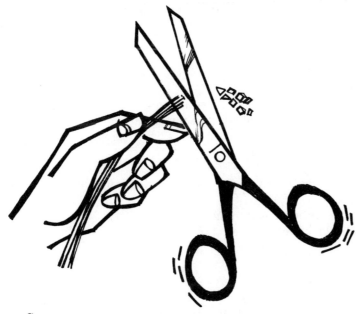

D   Tomato Soup
4 portions

INGREDIENTS
1 oz. butter or dripping (30 g.)
1 rasher streaky bacon, diced, or several bacon rinds
12 oz. ripe tomatoes (350 g.)
1 carrot
1 onion
1 pint brown stock (550 ml.)
1/4 clove garlic crushed with 1 level teaspoon salt
good shake black pepper
1 level teaspoon sugar
1 bay leaf
1 level tablespoon cornflour mixed with 2 tablespoons cold water
few drops red colouring
herb-flavoured scones or toast croûtons

METHOD
1   Melt the butter in a large saucepan, and add the bacon dice or rinds. Slice in the tomatoes, the scrubbed carrot and the peeled onion. Sauté them gently until the fat is absorbed and the tomato somewhat reduced in bulk.
2   Pour in the stock, add the garlic-salt and pepper, sugar and bay leaf. Bring to the boil, turn down the heat, cover and cook gently for half an hour, or until all the vegetables are very soft.
3   Rub through a sieve, rinse the pan and return the soup to it.

4 Stir in the cornflour and water mixture, then allow to boil again, stirring all the time for five minutes. Taste and add more seasoning if necessary. Colour a pleasant red.

5 Serve hot, with herb-flavoured scones if you like them, or toast croûtons.

NOTE: You can use different vegetables or combinations of vegetables to make many other vegetables soups by this method.

M Gazpacho
Serves up to 6
This is a Spanish soup, very good when well-chilled. No cooking is called for.

INGREDIENTS
1 clove garlic
1 level teaspoon salt
2 tablespoon olive oil
3 medium-thick slices of bread, crusts removed
3/4 lb. ripe tomatoes, skinned, and pips removed (350 g.)
3/4 pint water (425 ml.)
1 tablespoon wine vinegar
few drops tabasco
2 tablespoons sweet red pepper, raw or previously cooked, or canned, cut into dice
1/3 small cucumber, cut into dice
2 oz. small black olives (50 g.)

METHOD
1 Crush the garlic with salt.
2 If you have a blender put the garlic, oil, bread torn into pieces, tomato flesh, water and vinegar into the goblet, and switch on for 1 minute or until all is well broken down. If you have no blender, put the garlic and salt into a bowl, add the olive oil and bread, broken into pieces, then beat and mash together with a fork or wooden spoon. Add the tomatoes to moisten, a little at a time, pounding them well.
3 Finally beat in the water and vinegar and season with tabasco (or pepper) to taste.
4 Pour into a large bowl or tureen, add the red pepper, cucumber dice and olives, stir and chill thoroughly.
5 Serve in generous portions with crusty bread.

IV MEAT & FISH SOUPS

Meat soups are well-known, fish soups less so. Either makes a light meal, or a suitable beginning to a meal with a none-too-substantial main course.

M Oxtail Soup
Serves 4

INGREDIENTS
12 oz. oxtail (350 g.)
2 rashers streaky bacon
1 medium onion, sliced
1-2 carrots, sliced
2 oz. dripping or other fat (50 g.)
1 1/2 pints stock, or water plus 1 teaspoon Marmite (850 ml.)
2 tablespoons tomato ketchup or 1 tablespoon tomato purée
1/4 teaspoon curry powder
1 level teaspoon sugar
bouquet garni
1 oz. flour mixed with a little stock or water (30 g.)
salt and pepper to taste
2 tablespoons sherry or red wine (optional)

METHOD
1 Sauté the oxtail, bacon and vegetables in the dripping until they are pleasantly browned.
2 Add the stock or water, tomato flavouring, curry powder, sugar and bouquet garni. Cover and simmer for about 2 hours or until the meat is ready to fall off the bone.
3 Strain the soup, discarding bacon and bouquet garni, reserving the oxtail and rubbing the vegetables through a sieve.
4 Take the meat off the bone, cut into small pieces and return to the soup. Stir in the flour mixed to a thin cream with a little liquid, taste and add salt and pepper.
5 Return to the heat and simmer for a further five minutes. Just before serving stir in the sherry or wine if you can spare some.

D Creamy Haddock Soup
Serves 4
Fish soups are not generally popular in Britain, which is a pity. I include a very simple recipe, with a familiar taste, in the hope that it may introduce you to a new idea.

INGREDIENTS
1 pint milk (550 ml.)
1/2 pint water (300 ml.)
1/2 lb. smoked haddock (or cod) fillet (225 g.)
1 bay leaf
salt only if necessary
cayenne & dash of tabasco to taste
2 oz. butter (50 g.) mixed with 1 oz. flour (30 g.)—beurre manié
To garnish: 4 pats parsley butter and a few cooked prawns or 1 hard-boiled egg, chopped

METHOD

1 Put the milk, water, fish and bay leaf into a large saucepan. Bring to simmering point and cook gently for about 20 minutes, or until the fish begins to fall apart.

2 Strain the fish off the liquid. Rinse the pan and return the milky part of the soup.

3 Carefully remove all dark and light skin and any bones there may be. Put the flakes of fish into a basin with a little of the liquid and mash and beat with a fork or wooden spoon until it is well broken up. (It is not satisfactory to try to rub fish through a sieve; a blender, however, will do a very good job at this point.)

4 Mix the fish pulp back into the bulk of the liquid. Taste, add seasoning (probably only a very little salt needed, if any), and bring back to the boil. Drop in small knobs of the butter and flour combination, whisking all the time, and cook until the soup thickens.

5 To serve, pour the hot soup into bowls, add a sprinkling of cooked prawns or shrimps or chopped egg, and a well-chilled pat of parsley butter.

V FRUIT SOUPS

Fruit soups are an elaboration of the popular fruit juices served at the start of a meal. They may, however, be used to round off the repast, as well as at the beginning like a conventional soup. They are basically thin fruit purées, sometimes hot but more often chilled, and are particularly suitable for summer menus. If served at the start of a meal, take care not to make the soup very sweet, as sweet things give a feeling of satiety undesirable at this stage.
Here are a couple of easy recipes.

D Lemony Apple Soup
4-5 servings

INGREDIENTS
12 oz. (prepared weight) apples (350 g.)
1/4 pint dry cider (150 ml.)
1/2 pint water (300 ml.)
1 lemon
1 piece preserved or crystallized ginger, or good pinch of powdered ginger
1 1/2″ piece of stick cinnamon, or pinch of ground cinnamon
1 oz. (approx.) brown sugar (30 g.)
little whipped cream, soured cream or yoghurt

METHOD

1 After peeling, cutting up and removing the cores from the apples, weigh them and put them into a pan with the cider and water.

2 Using a potato peeler, cut off the lemon rind in thin strips, taking only the yellow part (the "zest"). Put these strips in with the apples. Add the spices too.

3 Bring to the boil, then simmer for 10-15 minutes, or until the apples start to break up. In the meantime, squeeze the juice of the lemon.

4 Rub the pulp through a sieve into a bowl. Stir in the lemon juice, add a little sugar, taste, and sweeten as you like it.

5 Chill the soup, and serve with a small dollop of lightly whipped cream, soured cream or yoghurt in each bowl.

M   Apricot Soup

4-5 servings

INGREDIENTS

1/2 pint white wine (300 ml.)
1 oz. caster sugar, or to taste (30 g.)
piece of cinnamon stick or pinch of ground cinnamon
2 cloves
8 oz. dried apricots, soaked in water overnight or until very soft (225 g.)
juice of 1/2 lemon
whipped cream or soured cream or flaky pastry sticks

METHOD

1   Bring the wine, sugar, cinnamon and cloves to the boil, boil for two or
    three minutes, then allow to infuse for half an hour.
2   Rub the raw apricots through a sieve, and stir the lemon juice into the
    resulting purée.
3   Strain the wine into the apricot purée; stir well. Taste and add more sugar
    only if needed.
4   The soup may be reheated and served hot, or, perhaps better, chilled.
    Serve with soured or slightly whipped cream, or plain accompanied by
    sticks of flaky pastry.

BREAD FOR THE SOUP

By its nature, soup is sloppy in texture, even though there may be solid pieces
in the garnish. Something crisp is needed to eat with it. To start you off, here
is a list of some of the crisp, starchy foods that you might serve with soup.

1   Pieces of fresh crusty bread such as French, wholemeal or rye; rolls or
    bread sticks, bought or home-made. Serve in a basket or bowl on a clean
    napkin.
2   Toast croûtons: cut the crusts off thin slices of toast, then cut diagonally
    into 1/4″ squares. Serve in a small bowl. Each person helps himself to a
    spoonful and sprinkles them into the soup.
3   Fried croûtons: cut the crusts off slices of bread, cut into dice and fry these
    in butter until golden brown. Serve as for toast croûtons, especially with
    cream soups.
4   Cheese straws, served with consommé.
5   Little herb or cheese scones.
6   Sticks of baked glazed flaky pastry, flat or twisted.

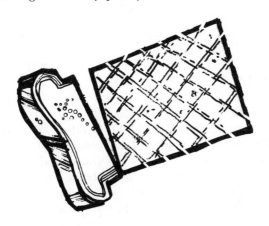

Sauces

A man once ate a whole horse
In one enormous main course;
   Then he sent for the cook
   And said "Go buy a book:
It would have been better with sauce."

Most foods, conventional or otherwise, can be made more delicious by serving them with a sauce of some kind. Sometimes it is even an essential part of the dish, as in a fricassée for instance. Especially if made with milk, sauces add to the food value of the meal. Here is a representative selection from the thousands of sauces that exist.

D I SAVOURY BUTTERS

Melted butter is the simplest sauce of all. Allow 2 oz. (50 g.) for 4 people. Melt, strain off the sediment and serve with vegetables. If you heat it a little longer it becomes nut-brown. Then stir in a little lemon juice for *Noisette Butter*.

Butter creamed on a plate with a squeeze of lemon, seasoning and chopped parsley to taste is *Maître d'Hôtel Butter*, sometimes also called *Parsley Butter*, very useful for serving, chilled, in little pats with grilled dishes.

In the same way you can add other flavourings to creamed butter: crushed garlic or anchovy for instance. These are good for making sandwiches as well as for serving with fish, eggs, potatoes and so on.

II WHITE SAUCES

D Basic White Sauce

This is to blame for a great deal of the bad reputation of British cooking. It is at the best of times a very bland if not tasteless concoction, and when it is made too thick or too watery, or is cold or lumpy, you would probably get greater enjoyment from eating a page or two out of the book. Properly made, however, it is a useful base for a sauce, to which must be added further ingredients to make egg sauce, parsley sauce and so on. If you want a white sauce, as indeed

26

you may, to serve with fish, vegetables, veal etc., please make a proper béchamel. With this warning, here are the basic ingredients and methods for a plain white sauce:

INGREDIENTS

a) *For a pouring sauce:*
1/2 pint sauce approx. (good 1/4 litre)
1/2 oz. butter or margarine (15 g.)
1/2 oz. plain flour (15 g.)
1/2 pint milk (275 ml.)
1/2 level teaspoon salt
shake of pepper

b) *For a coating sauce:*
1/2 pint sauce approx. (good 1/4 litre)
1 oz. butter or margarine (30 g.)
1 oz. plain flour (30 g.)
1/2 pint milk (275 ml.)
1/2 level teaspoon salt
shake of pepper

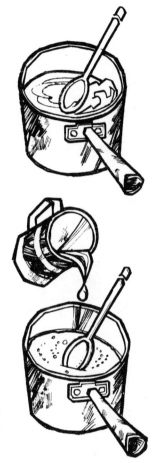

ROUX METHOD *(recommended)*
1 Melt the fat in a saucepan and stir in the flour with a wooden spoon.
2 Continue to cook and to stir over gentle heat for 2 minutes. The flour must not turn brown. This mixture is called a white roux.
3 Remove the pan from the heat. Pour in about a tablespoonful of milk and stir thoroughly until the mixture is completely smooth and well-blended. Add another tablespoonful of milk and blend again. Now you can add a little more than a tablespoon of milk—but blend again—and continue in this way until the sauce becomes quite thin, when you can add the milk more quickly still until it is all used up. The process is tedious to describe, but with practice you will find that you can do it quickly. Don't be tempted to add the liquid too fast though.
4 Add the seasonings. Return the pan to the heat, and, stirring continuously, bring the sauce to the boil. Turn the heat down a little and continue to cook and stir for at least three minutes, to make sure that all the starch grains in the flour have burst, and that there will be no raw taste left.
5 Add ingredients to make the different sauces described below.

BLENDING METHOD *(for use in a hurry)*
1 Put the flour into a small basin and add a little milk. Stir well to make a runny paste.
2 Heat the rest of the milk in a saucepan. Pour some of the hot liquid onto the flour mixture, stirring very thoroughly. Now pour the flour mixture slowly into the bulk of the milk, off the heat, stirring very well as you do so. There shouldn't be a lump in sight.
3 Add the butter or margarine and seasoning. Return the pan to the heat, bring to the boil, stirring, and continue to cook and stir for another three minutes.
4 Add ingredients to make the different sauces described below.

NOTE: First-aid for lumpy sauce: for small lumps, whisk with a hand-held wire whisk, for bad lumps, strain through a fine-meshed sieve. Remember next time that lumps are caused by impatience when blending in the liquid.

D Béchamel Sauce
1 pint approx. (good 1/2 litre)

This isn't the only recipe, or indeed the only method that exists for making this most useful and famous sauce. My recipe produces a delicately flavoured sauce without too much trouble. Use béchamel with vegetables, fish, veal, chicken and so on.

INGREDIENTS
1 oz. butter or margarine (30 g.)
2 oz. carrot, diced (50 g.)
2 oz. onion, diced (50 g.)
1 stalk celery, chopped
1 1/2 pints milk (3/4 litre)
bouquet garni
2 cloves (optional)
1 blade mace
roux made with 2 oz. butter (50 g.)
                 2 oz. flour (50 g.) for *coating sauce*
or
roux made with 1 oz. butter (30 g.)
                 1 oz. flour (30 g.) for *pouring sauce*
seasoning to taste

METHOD
1 Melt the first quantity of butter or margarine in a large saucepan. Add the carrot, onion and celery, stir, put on the lid and "sweat" the vegetable gently for five minutes, shaking the pan from time to time. The vegetables must not brown.
2 Pour in the milk and add the flavourings. Simmer all these together for 1/2 hour, with the lid tilted over the pan. The liquid will "reduce" in quantity to give a creamy-tasting sauce. Take care that it doesn't boil over though.
3 Strain the milk through a fine strainer, pressing the vegetables to extract the liquid but not so hard that they are rubbed through.
4 Rinse out the pan. Now make a roux and proceed as for basic white sauce, page 27, using flavoured milk in place of plain.
5 Taste and season the sauce carefully.

Yield on all the following: 1/2 pint (300 ml.) approx.

D Sauce Aurore
Add 2 or 3 dessertspoons of concentrated tomato purée and a large pinch of sugar to 1/2 pint basic white or béchamel or velouté sauce. Stir well. It should be the colour of the sky as the sun comes up, hence the name. Serve with meat, fish or vegetables.

D Egg Sauce
Add 1 chopped hard-boiled egg and an extra pinch of salt to 1/2 pint basic white or béchamel sauce. Especially good with fish.

D Parsley Sauce
Add at least 1 rounded tablespoonful of finely chopped parsley to 1/2 pint basic white or béchamel sauce. Good with vegetables, especially carrots, in many fish dishes and for reheating cooked chicken.

28

D   Caper Sauce

Add 3 tablespoons preserved capers and 1 tablespoon caper vinegar to 1/2 pint basic white or béchamel sauce. Serve with boiled mutton.

D   Shrimp Sauce

Add 3-4 tablespoons cooked shrimps and 1 teaspoon anchovy essence to 1/2 pint basic white or béchamel sauce. This is a special sauce for fish dishes, or can be put into little pastry cases to make party savouries.

D   Cheese Sauce

Stir 4 oz. (125 g.) grated hard cheese (Parmesan, Gruyère, Cheddar etc.) into 1/2 pint hot basic white or béchamel sauce. Season well, including a little made mustard. Often used to coat cooked vegetables to be served au gratin, such as *Cauliflower Cheese*. Also good with eggs and fish.

D   Mushroom Sauce

Add a few finely sliced mushrooms, gently fried in butter, to 1/2 pint basic white, béchamel or velouté sauce. Season well.

III   BROWN SAUCES

D   Espagnole Sauce

1 pint approx. (good 1/2 litre)

This is a classic basic sauce, the brown counterpart of béchamel. Again, the recipes and methods are legion. Here is a moderately simple version, but one of good flavour and of coating consistency.

INGREDIENTS
3 rashers fat streaky bacon, diced
1 medium onion, diced
1 large carrot, diced
2 oz. butter or margarine (50 g.)
2 oz. flour (50 g.)
1 rounded teaspoon tomato purée
1 1/2 pints brown stock (850 ml.)
few mushroom stalks or trimmings
bouquet garni
bay leaf
seasoning to taste

METHOD
1   Put the diced bacon into a dry pan and heat gently until the fat runs. Now put in the diced onion and carrot, spread them evenly over the pan and fry gently, stirring from time to time, until they turn a rich but not burnt brown. Set the pan aside.
2   Put the butter into a saucepan which has a lid, and melt it over moderate heat. Stir in the flour and cook, stirring, until it turns mid-brown in colour. This is a brown roux. Remove from the heat, stir in the tomato purée and a little of the stock. When the stock is well-blended, add a little more and stir again. Continue in this way until you have incorporated all the stock and the sauce is perfectly smooth.
3   Add the browned vegetables and bacon to the sauce. Dissolve any sediment from the vegetable saucepan in a little water and add this too, together

with any bits of mushroom available. Put in the bouquet garni, bay leaf and light seasoning—the sauce will reduce and become stronger. In particular, you can always add more salt, but can't subtract it!

4 Half-cover the pan, set it on a very gentle heat and cook, stirring and skimming from time to time, for 1 1/2-2 hours. It should simmer, not boil. If it becomes very much reduced you can add a little more stock.

5 Strain the sauce, taste and re-season if necessary.

6 Serve with beef, offal dishes, as a basis for meat hash and so on.

M NOTE: To make *Sauce Demi-Glace* add 1/4 pint (150 ml.) much-reduced brown stock to the above sauce. Blend well and reduce again to the undiluted volume.

To make *Madeira Sauce* stir in 1/2 wine-glass of Madeira to 1 pint (550 ml.) of sauce demi-glace.

D   Brown Gravy
1/2 pint (300 ml. approx.)
Usually gravy is made from the pan sediment after roasting meat, as described on page 107. Occasionally you may want a gravy to serve with something that does not provide this basis: reheated meat, for instance. That is the time to use this recipe.

INGREDIENTS
1/2 oz. dripping (15 g.)
1/2 oz. flour (15 g.)
1/2 pint stock (300 ml.)
1 level teaspoon yeast extract
seasoning
1 level teaspoon tomato purée (optional)

METHOD
1 Melt the dripping and stir in the flour. Stir over moderate heat for a few moments until the roux turns medium brown.
2 Remove the pan from heat and add the stock a little at a time, stirring well after each addition as for all roux sauces.
3 Return the pan to the heat and bring to the boil. Taste and add yeast extract, seasoning and tomato purée if liked. Continue to cook and stir for 3 minutes. Serve hot.

IV   VELOUTÉ SAUCES
"Velouté" means "velvety", which is a good description of this group of sauces. They are smooth and rich.

D   Velouté sauce
1 pint approx. (good 1/2 litre)

INGREDIENTS
1-2 oz. butter (30-50 g.)
1-2 oz. flour (30-50 g.) depending on required consistency of the sauce
1 pint white stock: chicken, veal bone or fish (575 ml.)
1/2 wine-glass white wine (optional but recommended)
seasoning to taste
3 tablespoons cream or top-of-milk

METHOD
1 Put the butter (it must be butter for this sauce) into a pan and melt it. Stir in the flour. Very carefully, continue to cook and stir until it turns golden but NOT BROWN. This is a blond roux.
2 Remove the pan from the heat. Little by little add and stir in the stock, as you added and stirred in the milk when making béchamel sauce. Stir in the wine.
3 Return the pan to the heat, bring to the boil, stirring, and simmer for three or four minutes. Taste and season. Add the cream, re-heat and taste again.
4 Serve hot, with chicken, veal or fish, according to the stock with which the sauce was made.

M   NOTE: For *Sauce Suprême* use 3 tablespoons double cream beaten with 3 egg yolks in place of the top-of-milk and add a few drops of lemon juice. This is the most delicious sauce of all to use with chicken.

D   **Onion Sauce**
Increase the quantity of butter by an extra 1 oz. (30 g.) and fry 2 medium onions, sliced or chopped, until just transparent. Then add flour and proceed exactly as for velouté or basic white sauce.

V   OTHER SAVOURY SAUCES

There are many other useful and classic sauces. The recipes that follow merely indicate some of the possibilities. After you have made these, you will I hope go on to experiment and devise your own recipes.

D   **Bread Sauce**
Serves 4
Many authorities say that you should simmer the onion and spices in milk, then strain the flavoured milk to use in the sauce. However, I prefer to leave the onion in the finished sauce. Certainly it has a knobbly texture, but also a more interesting flavour. Do try both methods.

INGREDIENTS
1 onion, chopped
1 oz. butter or margarine (30 g.)
1/2 pint milk (300 ml.)
2 or 3 cloves
pinch of nutmeg
2 slices of white bread, crusts removed, or 2 oz. white bread crumbs (50 g.)
salt and white pepper

METHOD
1 Melt the fat in a saucepan and cook the onion just until it looks transparent. Don't even let it turn gold, let alone brown.
2 Pour in the milk and add the flavourings. Simmer together for 10 minutes. Don't let it boil over.
3 Stir in the bread crumbs or cut the bread into tiny cubes and put them in. Cook the sauce, stirring, over gentle heat just long enough to make it smooth and well-mixed.
4 Taste and season carefully.
5 Serve very hot with chicken, or as a comforting "posset" for someone with a bad cold.

D Mint Sauce

This is the traditional accompaniment for roast lamb.

INGREDIENTS
a handful of fresh mint sprigs
1 rounded teaspoon caster sugar
wine vinegar

METHOD
1 Wash and dry the sprigs of mint. Strip the leaves from the stalks and throw away the stalks. Put the leaves on a chopping board in a pile and sprinkle over a spoonful of caster sugar. This makes chopping easier.
2 Using a sharp knife and care, holding above the point with your fingers as described on page 49, move the knife round in a half-circle to chop the mint very finely.
3 Put the chopped mint in a small jug and add enough vinegar to make it of pouring consistency: mint sauce means what it says.

NOTE: If you prefer a less-vinegary mint sauce, pour a tablespoon of boiling water onto the mint in the jug and add less vinegar.

D Apple Sauce

For 4-6 people
This is traditionally served with pork: it is also good with boiled bacon, grilled ham or gammon and with roast duck.

INGREDIENTS
3/4 lb. cooking apples (300 g.)
water or cider to cover
1 oz. sugar (30 g.)
knob of butter
salt and pepper (optional)
1 teaspoon lemon juice (optional)

METHOD
1 Peel, core and cut up the apples. They must be of a kind such as Bramley which will break up easily when cooked.
2 Put the apple slices into a saucepan with just enough liquid to cover them. Use cider for a luxury sauce, but you won't need much liquid in any case, as the apples themselves are watery.
3 Cook on moderate heat, half covered, until the apples are fluffy and starting to break up. Mash and stir with a fork, and stir in the sugar, butter, seasoning and lemon juice if used—taste as you go, of course. You can rub the sauce through a fine sieve and then reheat it if you like, though it isn't really necessary.
4 Serve hot.

M Curry Sauce

Rather less than 1/2 pint sauce (250 ml)
A most useful sauce for meat, fish or vegetables. Also very good with poached or hard-boiled eggs.

INGREDIENTS
1/2 oz. butter or margarine (15 g.)
1 tablespoon chopped onion

1 tablespoon chopped apple
1/2 oz. flour (15 g.)
1/2-1 level tablespoon curry powder, or to taste
1/2 pint stock or water (300 ml.)
pinch of salt
1 teaspoon lemon juice
1/2 level teaspoon curry paste (optional)
1 level tablespoon of plum or gooseberry jam, marmalade or chutney as
  available
1 oz. sultanas (optional) (30 g.)
1 level tablespoon desiccated coconut

METHOD
1 Melt the fat in a medium saucepan and gently fry the onion until golden.
   Stir in the apple and cook for a moment or two, then stir in the flour and
   curry powder. Cook, stirring, over low heat for five minutes.
2 Add the stock, a little at a time, stirring until blended before adding any
   more. Add the salt, lemon juice, curry paste, jam, sultanas if used and the
   coconut. Stir them in.
3 Simmer, covered, for about an hour.
4 A purist would strain the sauce, but I think it's a pity to do so as I enjoy the
   little bits in it.

M   Tomato Sauce
3/4 pint approx. (450 ml.)
This is a useful recipe for a very fresh-tasting tomato sauce.

INGREDIENTS
1/2 oz. butter (15 g.)
1 rasher streaky bacon cut into dice
8 oz. ripe tomatoes (225 g.)
1/2 pint stock (300 ml.)
1/2 level teaspoon sugar
1 bay leaf
2 teaspoons concentrated tomato purée
1/4-1/2 clove garlic, crushed with 1/2 teaspoon salt, and a shake of pepper
1/2 oz. each butter and flour (15 g. each) mixed to a paste

METHOD
1 Melt the butter and fry the bacon until crisp.
2 Slice the tomatoes into the pan and cook for a further 2-3 minutes.
3 Add the stock, flavourings and seasoning. Cover and simmer until the
   tomatoes are pulpy, about 20 minutes.
4 Rub the mixture through a sieve. Rinse the pan and return the mixture to
   heat.
5 Whisking all the time, add the butter-flour mixture a teaspoonful at a time.
   Cook until the sauce thickens slightly.

D   Simple Meat Sauce for Pasta
Serves up to 4 people

INGREDIENTS
1/2 oz. dripping or margarine (15 g.)
2 rashers streaky bacon, rinds removed, chopped

1 medium onion, finely chopped
1 carrot, finely diced or grated
8 oz. minced beef, as lean as possible (225 g.)
3 teaspoons concentrated tomato purée
1/4 pint stock (150 ml.)
1/2 level teaspoon fresh rosemary, chopped, or a pinch of dried
pinch of ground nutmeg
seasoning to taste
2 tablespoons top-of-milk

METHOD
1 Melt the dripping or margarine in a medium-sized saucepan. Put in the bacon pieces and fry for a minute. Stir in the onion and carrot and continue to fry, stirring, until they turn golden-brown.
2 Stir in the beef and continue to cook, stirring until it no longer looks raw.
3 Stir in the tomato purée, stock (or water), herbs and nutmeg. Simmer gently with the lid off, stirring from time to time, for 15-20 minutes, or until the meat is tender and the liquid nearly gone. Take care that it does not burn.
4 Add plenty of seasoning, tasting as you go. Allow for the blandness of the pasta with which it will be eaten.
5 Stir in the top-of-milk, re-heat a moment, then serve immediately with very hot cooked spaghetti, macaroni, noodles etc.

NOTE: The sauce can be enriched by adding 4 oz. (100 g.) chopped chicken or lamb's liver, or minced ham or pork, or 2 oz. (50 g.) liver sausage. Add any of these with the minced beef.

D   Hollandaise Sauce
For up to 4 people
This is a classic sauce, rather like cooked mayonnaise. It is splendid with fish, particularly salmon, but also very good with plainly cooked vegetables of delicate flavour such as artichokes, asparagus and kohlrabi. Many recipes call for more vinegar than I suggest, but I prefer to have a sauce only lightly sharpened, so that you can really taste the butter.

INGREDIENTS
2 tablespoons white stock, water or fish stock for fish dishes
2-3 drops vinegar
2 egg yolks
2 1/2 oz. butter, softened but not oiled (75 g.)
2 teaspoons lemon juice
seasoning to taste

METHOD
1 Prepare a double saucepan with water in the base, or if you have none arrange a pudding-basin to fit firmly over a pan of hot water.
2 Put the stock, vinegar and egg yolks into the top saucepan or basin. Using a small wire whisk or fork, stir together over gentle heat just until the mixture begins to thicken. Turn the heat off or to a mere point.
3 Now whisk in the soft butter, a small knob at a time, until the sauce is creamy and soft. It must not get very hot.
4 Take off the heat and stir in the lemon juice. Add seasoning, tasting as you go.

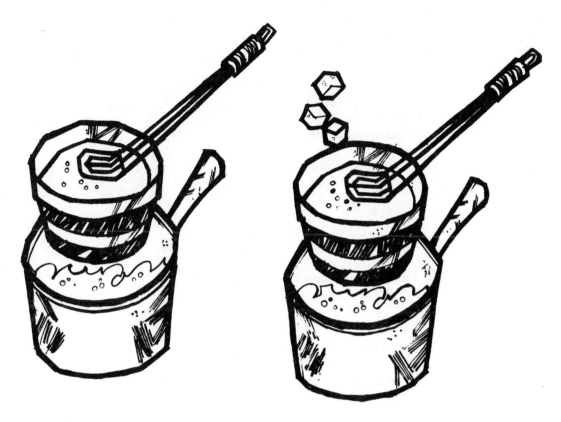

M   Tartare Sauce

4 portions

A cold sauce, very good with fish, which also gives a lift to plain salads.

INGREDIENTS

1/4 pint mayonnaise (150 ml.), preferably made with lemon juice
2 tablespoons capers, chopped, fresh or preserved, or olives, pickled gherkins
  or sweet-sour dill pickles, as liked.
few drops tabasco and Worcestershire sauce (optional)
1 level teaspoon snipped chives or finely grated raw onion (optional)

METHOD

1 Combine the mayonnaise with the capers etc. and add a few drops of
   tabasco. Taste and add more seasoning and flavouring if you think it needs
   it.
2 Serve in small quantities, as it is very piquant.

M   Lemon Sauce

1/2 pint approx. (300 ml.)

The less-sweet version of this sauce makes an unusual accompaniment for
chicken, steamed or baked fish or fish fingers. The sweeter version is very good
with baked or steamed plain sponge puddings, or cold, served with ice-cream.

INGREDIENTS

2 rounded teaspoons cornflour
1/2 pint water (300 ml.)
grated rind and juice 1 lemon
2 egg yolks
1 rounded teaspoon sugar for plain sauce, or 3 rounded teaspoons sugar for
  sweet sauce

METHOD

1 Mix the cornflour with part of the water in a small saucepan, then add the rest of the water and the finely-grated lemon rind. Boil, stirring, for three minutes.

2 Remove from heat, stir in the egg yolks beaten with lemon juice. Re-heat just to the point when it thickens, but do not re-boil.

3 Stir in the sugar and strain if desired. Serve hot or cold, according to the dish it accompanies.

NOTE: For *Orange Sauce* substitute orange for lemon: Seville orange is good for savoury dishes. Adjust the amount of sugar to taste.

VI   SWEET SAUCES

D   Sweet White Sauce
1/2 pint approx. (300 ml.)

INGREDIENTS
2 rounded teaspoons cornflour or arrowroot
1/2 pint milk (300 ml.)
1 level tablespoon sugar, or to taste
flavouring to taste, such as pinch of nutmeg, few drops vanilla, rum, brandy or liqueurs

METHOD

1 Put the cornflour or arrowroot into a basin and pour on a little of the milk. Mix well to a smooth paste.

2 Heat the milk. Pour it onto the starch mixture in the basin, stirring as you pour.

3 Return the sauce to the milk pan. Add the sugar and flavouring. Stir over gentle heat for three or four minutes past boiling-point. (Liqueurs should be added after the sauce is cooked.)

4 Serve hot with baked or steamed puddings.

D   Chocolate Custard Sauce
Add 2 rounded teaspoons cocoa, or to taste, to the cornflour and proceed as above.

D   Custard Sauce: please see *Proper Custard*, page 153.

M   Rum or Brandy Butter
For 4 people or less

INGREDIENTS
2 oz. unsalted butter (75 g.)
2 oz. caster or soft brown sugar, or icing sugar if smooth texture is wanted. (75 g.)
2 tablespoons rum or brandy

METHOD

1 Cream together the butter and chosen sugar until light and fluffy.

2 Beat in the rum or brandy. Pile into a small decorative dish.

3 This is traditionally served with Christmas pudding or mince pies, but is often appreciated as a spread on bread or semi-sweet biscuits.

D Chocolate Sauce
4 portions

INGREDIENTS
2-3 oz. plain chocolate (50-75 g.)
4 tablespoons water
1/2 oz. butter (15 g.)

METHOD
1 Put the ingredients into a small pan and stir together over gentle heat until they are blended together.
2 Serve hot with ice-cream, or warm with meringues sandwiched with cream for a party sweet.

NOTE: I also recommend *Chocolate Rum Sauce*, which is chocolate sauce with a few drops of rum stirred into it, and *Chocolate Ginger Sauce*. For the latter, stir in 1 tablespoon of syrup from preserved ginger and/or 1 tablespoon chopped crystallised or glacé ginger.

Vegetables

Once, in another country, there lived an abbot, whose abbey stood among good fields and farms. The people in the villages round about were contented and looked after their fields peacefully, knowing that the abbey was their protection and that the monks, especially Father Magnum in the kitchen, would look after them.

But when the abbot was growing old, there were two years of terrible harvests, when the wheat was crushed into the mud by storms.

"The abbot's prayers do not protect us any more," murmured the people angrily. Fewer and fewer came to the abbey to worship, but more and more came to beg food.

The abbot prayed all night; not for himself, but for the poor people. Afterwards he walked for a little in the gardens, where he came upon a novice, weeding some tuberous plants that the abbot had not seen before.

"A new plant! This may be the miracle for which we have been asking," said the abbot. "We must give some to those begging for food."

The abbot himself went to the refectory when the people came for their next meal. Snowy mounds of boiled tubers were on the tables, but, though the people were really hungry, hardly anyone had finished his helping. The old man was disappointed, especially when he heard the people muttering.

"Now the abbot gives us food fit only for animals."

"...tastes neither of meat nor of bread, neither sweet nor savoury as the herbs of the hedge."

Soon the abbot was left alone with Father Magnum, a fat monk, usually the most cheerful person in the abbey—when he wasn't asleep—but now he looked almost as miserable as the abbot, who said gently: "We may eat what the poor refuse," and cut up one of the tubers. It was tasteless, hard in the middle yet mushy outside. But it was food of a kind.

"Father Magnum, I shall have need of your knowledge, for God has sent me an idea." The abbot whispered something to Father Magnum, whose miserable face changed to sad, then to solemn, then to hopefulness, brightness and the biggest grin that the abbot had seen in a long life.

"Yes!" he exclaimed, and rushed off as fast as any man can who weighs eighteen stones in his sandals.

After that, the village people were puzzled more and more by what the monks were doing, although they would not come to the abbey any more. A big field was cleared, and then the novices planted the tubers.

"Keep away!" shouted the monks rudely. "This food is for the Father Abbot only!"

38

"*We* may get a taste—on a feast day—but you won't!" squealed one novice, and put out his tongue.

Next the monks built a hut, which they furnished with a charcoal stove, some cooking pans and a comfortable feather-bed.

"Certainly the abbot is mad," said the villagers. They came to look at the field out of curiosity, but were always chased away in the daytime. But if they came in the evening, only one monk was there: Father Magnum, whom they had once trusted. What was he doing? One evening he dug up one of the plants, washed the tubers in a bucket, then... they couldn't quite see, but there was a splendid smell floating out to the starving people in the twilight. Father Magnum ate his supper, and shortly afterwards they heard magnificent snoring from the feather bed.

"Quick," they whispered, "while he's asleep..." They crept closer, up to a pile of hot food that even Father Magnum hadn't been able to eat. Brown and crisp, slightly salty, perhaps a bit of bacon flavour? Some with butter, some spiced with nutmeg. All delicious!

The villagers smiled at each other, feeling foolish. No longer worrying about noise, though Father Magnum's snores were oddly mixed with chuckles, the men dug up potatoes and piled them into coats to take home.

Next day the abbey was full, and after thanksgiving the abbot and beaming Father Magnum gave a sackful of seed potatoes to each family and a large bagful of chips to every child who lived within smelling distance of the refectory kitchen.

I GENERAL SECTION

Choosing Vegetables

Unless you have a garden or allotment where you can go and pick your own young vegetables, you must start at the greengrocer's. Youth really does have the edge on middle age when it comes to vegetables, though young ones are more expensive to produce.

It is inevitable that many vegetables will have spent some time getting to the shop, but really stale fruit and vegetables are a waste of money. These foods are valuable chiefly because they contain vitamins and mineral salts essential to health, as well as starch, useful vegetable protein in some cases, and roughage which is needed for the proper working of the digestive tract. Vitamin C in particular decreases with staleness, so from the point of view of health as well as taste you should buy your greengroceries as fresh as possible.

Frozen vegetables are generally good, certainly better than old "fresh" foods, but still cannot quite compare with first-quality raw stuffs.

The same applies to canned vegetables, which are useful to have in the store-cupboard as a standby, but are often more expensive and less appetizing than the best fresh. Both frozen and canned fruit and vegetables do make out-of-season foods available all the time. In one sense this adds variety to your table, of course, because you have a much wider range of foods to choose from, but on the other hand one time of year can become too boringly like any other. I would advise you to use fresh foods of all kinds, not only fruit and vegetables, when they are in their best season, following the natural rhythm of the year, but to supplement them sensibly with frozen or canned foods when the fresh ones are in short supply and expensive. Don't use canned strawberries at the end of June, nor try to insist on fresh home-grown peas in February.

Quantities to Buy

Appetites and dietary needs vary very considerably with the age, size, sex and occupation of the people you are feeding. As a very *rough guide only* you will need:

1 medium-sized lettuce between 4 if it forms the main part of the salad.

3 oz. (100 g.) per person of tomatoes for main vegetable.

2 oz. (50-75 g.) mushrooms per person.

4-6 oz. per person (100-175 g.) of the solid green vegetables such as sprouts or cauliflower or cabbage for cooking.

2 oz. (50 g.) per person of cabbage for raw salads.

4 oz. (125 g.) per person of root vegetables generally.

8 oz. (225 g.) at least of peas-in-pod per person.

3-8 oz. (100-225 g.) potatoes per person, depending on what other starches are provided at the meal, as well as appetite.

Storing Vegetables

Don't is the ideal advice. But that is unreasonable when you may not find it convenient to trail out every day to the shops, or when you want to take advantage of real bargains. Here are some ideas, then, on how to prolong freshness as long as possible at home.

Salad vegetables such as lettuce, endive, tomatoes—also mushrooms are best kept in the salad drawer of your refrigerator, if you have one. They ought not to go into the main part of the fridge as this is too cold for them: they must not actually freeze. If you have no special salad drawer, put them in closed polythene bags to prevent drying out, keep as far from the freezing coil as possible and use quickly. If you have no fridge wrap lettuce in newspaper, and keep all salad vegetables in a cool place.

Leafy vegetables such as cabbage, sprouts and so on keep well in the salad drawer, but also do nicely in a cool dry place in a ventilated rack.

Root vegetables such as carrots, turnips, onions are best stored in a vegetable rack in a cool, dry, dark place. They need air circulating round them or they may go mouldy. Undo any fastenings on polythene packing or remove it completely. If you store these vegetables in closed polythene bags for any length of time you may come back to an unsavoury handful of slime.

Vegetables with stems such as watercress, celery, cucumber, parsley and other fresh herbs keep best when put into a wide-necked jar with cold water, like flowers. Cut cucumber from the flower end; the remainder can then go back into the "vase".

Fruit if soft, such as berries, may be stored briefly in the refrigerated salad drawer or a cool place, but don't keep them long before use in any case. Don't refrigerate strawberries. Stone fruit, apples and pears are best kept in the cool like root vegetables. Citrus fruits keep very well in cool dry conditions. Bananas if at all green will ripen off well at a comfortable room temperature, but if they are already ripe (i.e. freckled with brown spots) store them in a cool place. Incidentally most fresh fruit tastes best at room temperature, but pineapple and melon are nicer when chilled slightly, as are fruit juices.

Cleaning Vegetables & Fruit
You need to remove earth, dust and insects from vegetables and to wash fruits that may have been sprayed with insecticides. I find it best to clean them just before they are to be used, as if they are washed and put away again at all damp they may go mouldy quickly.

Salad & leafy vegetables: wash thoroughly several times under the running cold tap. Some people like to soak them briefly in cold salt water to make sure they are uninhabited, then to rinse them. Salad greens must be dried again before use: let them drain, then shake them dry in a clean tea towel or a salad basket. Leeks need to be slit to within 1 1/2″ of the root so that you can wash out every speck of grit between the leaves. Spinach often requires a great deal of washing too, as it is sometimes sandy. Break lettuce into separate leaves for cleaning, and cabbage too unless you want to cook it whole; if so, spread out the leaves and wash between them. Discard any yellow or decayed leaves, of course.

Root vegetables: potatoes, carrots, turnips, parsnips and so on. Keep a small brush hanging by the sink especially (and exclusively) for scrubbing these in cold or just-warm water. Cut out any damaged parts, peel and rinse again. Discard green potatoes; there is a theory that the green part contains a poisonous substance.

II METHODS OF COOKING VEGETABLES

A large part of the value of vegetables is that they provide essential vitamins and mineral salts. This is especially true of green vegetables. But vitamin C, which you need fresh every day, is spoilt by long heating, and mineral salts seep out into cooking water. There is a school of thought that maintains that the more raw vegetables you eat, the better. Other people maintain truly that there is usually plenty of vitamin C in a normal diet anyway, especially if you eat fruit too. Much depends on what you like. If you enjoy raw salads rather than cooked vegetables, may you have good health and long life! If you prefer cooked vegetables and, because their bulk is reduced by heating, can get the benefit of more than you could eat raw, then may you too have good health and long life! Most people like both. I do, and include a few recipes for salads. I'd suggest that if you can you should try to have a minimum of one salad a day.

In the meantime here are some of the ways you can cook vegetables so as to keep their best possible food value and to make them appetizing and digestible.

Conservative Method *(so called because it conserves minerals and vitamins)*
1   Put the prepared vegetables into a saucepan with boiling water to cover the pan to a depth of about 1/2″.
2   Add a knob of butter or margarine and seasoning. Cover.
3   Cook over moderate heat for 10-30 minutes, depending on the vegetable, until just cooked but not mushy. The water tends to boil away, so if you hear a frying sizzle it is time to add a little more water.
4   There shouldn't be much liquid left, but if there is any, pour it over the cooked vegetables when you serve them.

Here is a typical recipe using this method:

D Glazed Carrots
Serves 4

INGREDIENTS
1 lb. young carrots (1/2 kg.)
1/4 pint water (150 ml.)
1 oz. margarine (30 g.)
shake each of salt & pepper
1 rounded tablespoon brown sugar

METHOD
1   Wash and scrape the carrots, and cut off the tops.
2   Boil the water in a saucepan with a well-fitting lid. Put in the carrots, add the margarine and seasoning, cover and cook quite gently over moderate to low heat for 15-20 minutes, or until the carrots are just tender. Do not overcook them, and add a little more (boiling) water if they go dry.
3   Put the carrots into a hot serving-dish and keep them hot. Boil the sugar in whatever is left of the cooking liquor until there is only a tablespoonful or so left. Pour this over the hot carrots and serve at once.

Quick Boiling Method
1   Bring one-third of a panful of lightly salted water to the boil (1 level teaspoon of salt to 1 pint water).
2   Put in the prepared vegetables a little at a time, so that the water is never far off boiling. When all the vegetables are in they should just be covered with boiling water.

42

3   Boil the panful with lid on as fast as possible without boiling over. Timing depends very much on thickness and kind of vegetable: e.g. cabbage, shredded, takes 10-15 minutes, large carrots perhaps 25 minutes. Green vegetables should still be bright green when cooked; if they are brown or yellow they are overdone.

4   Drain well in a colander and add seasoning to taste. Use the liquid as vegetable stock in other dishes—hence, don't add much salt to start with.

NOTE: NEVER add bicarbonate of soda to the water—this more than anything else destroys vitamin C.

Simmering

1   Bring suitable amount of salted water to boil, as in quick boiling, and put in vegetables.

2   Cook on more moderate heat.

NOTE: This method is used only for vegetables that might be damaged by the rapid movement of fast-boiling water—beetroot and asparagus for example.

Steaming

1   Prepare the steamer with boiling water in the base.

2   Put the prepared vegetables in the top part, sprinkle lightly with salt and cover with the lid.

3   Cook for about 1 1/2 times the length of quick boiling: e.g. if you are a 10-minute sprout fiend, steam sprouts for 15 mins.

4   Replenish the base with boiling water if you are cooking vegetables that require a long time.

Pressure Cooking

A method which I highly commend because it produces very well-flavoured vegetables of high food value—*unless* you are careless: a minute too much may mean ruination. If you have a pressure cooker you will also have detailed instructions for your particular model. Do follow them closely.

Braising (Casseroling)

1   Brown the vegetables lightly in dripping or margarine.

2   Season and put into casserole (oven method) or leave in saucepan. Pour in boiling water or stock to reach half way up the vegetables. Cover with lid and cook gently in moderately hot oven, Reg. 4, 350 °F, until tender; or on medium–low heat in the saucepan. Average time about 40 mins.

3   When the vegetables are cooked, separate them from the liquid and keep them hot. Reduce the liquid by hard boiling, then pour it over the vegetables. Garnish with chopped parsley if you like. This method is particularly suitable for mixtures of vegetables such as carrots, parsnips and mushrooms.

Here is a typical recipe using this method:

D   Celery, Carrot & Mushroom Casserole
Serves 4-5

INGREDIENTS
2 oz. margarine (50 g.)
12 oz. outer stalks of celery, cut into 2″ lengths (300 g.)

8 oz. carrots, cut into rings (200 g.)
3 oz. mushrooms (100 g.)
1/2 pint stock (300 ml.)
bouquet garni
seasoning to taste
chopped parsley
Oven: Mod. Hot, Reg. 4, 350 °F.

METHOD
1 Melt the fat in a frying pan or saucepan and lightly brown first the celery, then the carrots and finally the mushrooms in it.
2 Transfer them to a casserole as they are browned.
3 Heat the stock in the pan to dissolve any vegetable sediment. When boiling, pour it over the vegetables in the casserole.
4 Add the bouquet garni and seasoning. Cover the dish with its lid and cook at moderately hot temperature, Reg. 4 or 350 °F for 30-40 minutes, or until the celery and carrots are tender.
5 Pour the liquid from the casserole into a pan and reduce it by hard boiling to a few tablespoonsful. Keep the vegetables hot meanwhile. Discard bouquet garni.
6 Pour the reduced liquor over the vegetables, garnish with parsley if you like and serve at once.

Frying DON'T USE DEEP FAT UNLESS THERE IS AN ADULT AROUND
In general, root vegetables are more suitable for cooking by this method than leafy ones.
1 Cut the prepared vegetables into medium-sized chunks. Make sure they are dry on the surface or the fat will splutter and may burn you.
2 Fry the vegetables in hot deep or shallow fat until attractively brown. Thinly-sliced vegetables may be covered with egg and crumbs before frying.

Sautéing
Previously-cooked vegetables can sometimes be finished or re-heated by gently frying in a little hot butter or other fat until they are lightly browned.

Vegetable Fritters DON'T MAKE THESE UNLESS THERE IS AN ADULT THERE
Firm pieces of cooked vegetable, or raw vegetables that only require short cooking, make successful fritters. Mushrooms are particularly good. This recipe illustrates the method:

D Mushroom Fritters
For 4 people

INGREDIENTS
Fritter batter made with 1/4 pint liquid etc. (page 146)
deep fat for frying
6 oz. button mushrooms (200 g.)
seasoned flour

METHOD
1 Make the fritter batter.
2 Prepare the deep fat frying pan by filling half-full of oil or fat. Put it to heat on a fairly low flame. HAVE READY A SAUCEPAN LID TO COVER IT IN CASE IT ACCIDENTALLY CATCHES FIRE.

3   Rinse the mushrooms if necessary and dry them on a cloth. Dip them in seasoned flour.
4   When the fat is hot enough to fry a small cube of bread quite quickly, spear a mushroom on a fork, dip it into the batter, lift it to drain for a moment, slide it off the fork into the frying basket and lower it into the fat.
5   Don't try to make too many at once, and lift the basket in order to turn the fritters over. They will need only 3-4 minutes all together.
6   Lift the fritters out in the frying basket, then drain them on crumpled kitchen paper. Keep the first ones hot as you fry the rest, and serve hot.

Grilling
1   Put the prepared vegetables on the grid of the grill-pan, or thread them on skewers. Sprinkle over a little seasoning and brush with oil or dot with butter.
2   Grill under medium heat, turning once in most cases.

Here is a typical recipe using this method:

D   Vegetable Kebabs
4 kebabs

INGREDIENTS
4 medium-sized firm tomatoes, cut into quarters
8 small mushroom caps, or 4 large ones cut in half
1 medium-sized green pepper, flesh only, cut into 1″ squares
seasoning
oil

METHOD
1   Prepare the vegetables. Blanch the squares of pepper by putting them in a colander in the sink and pouring a kettleful of boiling water over them. Allow them to drain thoroughly.
2   Thread the tomatoes, mushrooms and pieces of pepper alternately on 4 long skewers. Brush all over with oil and season them.
3   Grill under medium heat for 5-7 minutes, turning to cook on all sides. Serve hot, still on the skewers.

NOTE: You can vary the vegetables as you like, only they must be of a kind that stays firm when cooked. Try to contrast the colours, too.

Baking or Roasting
This method is especially suitable for root vegetables.
1   Put the prepared vegetables, which may be either raw or half-cooked by quick boiling and drained thoroughly, into a baking tin with dripping or oil.
2   Bake 1/2-1 hour, depending on size of pieces, whether pre-cooked or not, and position in the oven. If possible cook at fairly high temperature, Reg. 6, 400 °F, though they can also be done on the shelf below a roasting joint of meat, when they will need longer. If you are roasting meat and there is room in the tin they can go round the joint.
3   They will need basting with hot fat from the tin from time to time.

D III HOW TO COPE WITH SPECIFIC STAPLE VEGETABLES

N.B. Cooking times are suggested ones only. Tastes and vegetables vary!

Artichokes (*Jerusalem Artichokes—the ones that look like eccentric potatoes*).
Scrub. Peel as thinly and patiently as possible round their humps, using a sharp potato peeler. Drop into cold water with a little vinegar in it or they turn brown.

Cook by conservative method, or
>   quick boiling (add a few drops lemon juice to the water) about 30 mins. whole, 20 mins. for sliced; or
>   bake, or
>   sauté previously boiled slices, or
>   make fritters with them.
Plain hot artichokes can be served with melted butter, hollandaise or béchamel sauce.

Asparagus (*More a luxury, really, than a staple*)
Scrub the bottom ends. Rinse. Tie in bundles.

Cook by simmering, upright, with tips above water, 15-20 mins or
>   steam 20-30 mins.
Plain hot asparagus can be served with melted butter or hollandaise sauce, or au gratin with Parmesan cheese.
Plain cold asparagus can be served with vinaigrette dressing or mayonnaise.

Only the tender tip is eaten.

Beans, Dried. Please see recipe page 53.

Beans, French & Runner. Please see *French Beans*.

Beetroot
Rinse gently in cold water to remove soil, taking care not to damage skin.

Cook by simmering up to 1 hour, then remove skin.
Plain hot beetroot may be coated with béchamel, egg or parsley sauce.
Plain cold beetroot is cut into dice or slices and dressed with a little wine vinegar or vinaigrette dressing.

Bobby Beans, Dwarf Beans & Very Young Broad Beans
Wash, top-and-tail.

Cook by quick boiling 10-15 mins.
Plain hot beans may be coated with béchamel or cheese sauce, or tossed in butter.

They are eaten pod and all.

Broad Beans
Shell just before use or the skins will harden in air. Old beans may be blanched to remove skins.

Cook by quick boiling about 15 mins., or
>   pressure cook, or
>   casserole.
Plain hot beans may be mixed into béchamel or parsley sauce or tossed in butter.

Broccoli

Several kinds are available. It is often expensive. Prepare and cook large pieces as cauliflower, small stalks with lots of flower as asparagus. Nicest served hot with plenty of butter and seasoning.

Brussels Sprouts

Wash, and remove any yellow leaves. Cut a small cross in the stalk so that it will cook quickly.

Cook by quick boiling 10-15 mins, or
      steam 20-25 mins., or
      pressure cook.
Plain hot sprouts may be served with seasoning and butter, or with béchamel or chestnut sauce.
Raw : shred finely and use for salads.

Cabbage & Other "Greens"

Wash thoroughly. Cut in halves or quarters. Put the cut surface flat on a chopping-board then shred with a sharp knife.

Cook by conservative method, or
      quick boiling 10-15 mins., or
      steaming 20 mins., or
      pressure cook, or
      casserole.
Plain hot cabbage must be drained thoroughly and may be chopped more finely still. It may be served with butter or in plenty of béchamel or sauce aurore, or with fried breadcrumbs.
Raw : white cabbage and red cabbage in particular may be shredded very finely indeed and eaten as salad.

Carrots

If young, just scrub thoroughly and cut off the top. Scrape older ones: cut off top, put the cut surface on a chopping-board, holding firmly by the root, and scrape up and down with your sharpest vegetable knife, turning the carrot round as you scrape. Then scrape tip flat on board. Grandpa carrots may have to be peeled thinly with a potato peeler. If small, leave them whole. If larger, cut lengthwise into halves or quarters, or across into rings, or on the slant crosswise into ovals. Grate them for salads.

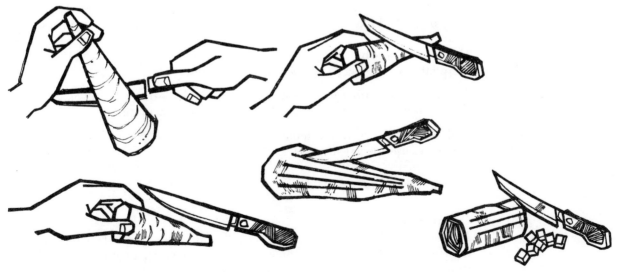

To cut into dice: hold on the chopping-board with top thick end in your left hand (if you are right-handed). Make downward cuts with a long sharp knife along the length of the carrot, almost but not quite to the end you are holding. Now give the carrot a quarter turn and cut down again at 90° to the first cuts. You should have a lot of square-sectioned strips held together at the left side. Now cut evenly across the carrot to make the dice fall away to the right.

Cook by any of the methods given, *except* simmering or grilling.
Plain hot carrots may be tossed in butter and chopped parsley, or in garlic butter, or be coated with béchamel or parsley sauce.
Plain cold carrots may be dressed with vinaigrette, tartare sauce or mayonnaise.
Raw: serve with vinaigrette, mayonnaise or cream cheese dressing.

Cauliflower
Hollow out the base of the stalk after washing, using a potato peeler, if the cauliflower is to be cooked whole. Otherwise break it into sprigs. A few leaves may be left on if you like.

Cook by conservative method, or
    quick boiling, 20-30 mins., or
    steaming, 30-40 mins. for whole cauliflower, less for sprigs; or
    make fritters with lightly-cooked sprigs.
Plain hot cauliflower may be coated with béchamel, egg or parsley sauce, or fried crumbs; or coated with cheese sauce and served au gratin.
Plain cold cauliflower, or tiny raw sprigs, may be dressed with any salad dressing.

Celery
Wash well. The heart is nicest eaten raw in salads, with cheese, or cut into 2″ lengths and stuffed with cream cheese or flavoured cottage cheese etc., as a cocktail savoury or meal starter. Outer stalks are best in soups or otherwise cooked. Remove coarse leaves; use them for flavouring.

Cook by conservative method, or
    quick boiling, about 20 mins., or
    steaming, 30 mins., or
    braising, 45 mins. approx.
Plain hot celery may be coated with béchamel, egg or cheese sauce.

Chicory *(The pale, slightly bitter-tasting plant with lance-shaped leaves)*
May be cooked like celery, but is usually just washed and eaten raw in salads.

Corn-on-the-cob
Strip off outer greenery and feathery bits inside.

Cook by quick boiling for 10 mins. or until tender—don't overcook.
Plain hot corn is best served with butter, melted or plain.

This is usually served as a separate course. Pick it up at each end to eat it, or, if finicky, use special silver picks or forks.

Courgettes Please see *Marrow*

Cucumber
May be cooked like marrow, but is usually eaten raw in salads. Don't remove the rind: its presence makes the cucumber more easily digested. Slice it very thinly, or cut into dice. Delicious in sandwiches with plenty of seasoning.

48

Dried Beans, Peas & Lentils   Please see recipe page 53.

Endive
This is very useful for winter salads. It is usually eaten raw. Wash and dry it thoroughly and break it into small pieces.

French & Runner Beans
Definitely best when young. If they are fresh they will snap in half when bent. Wash and top-and-tail only, if very young. Runner beans may need to be trimmed all the way round to remove the fibre joining the two halves. Cut in small pieces or slice slantwise if beans are large.

Cook by quick boiling, about 7 mins., or
    pressure cook, or
    braise old ones.
Plain hot beans are best tossed in butter, or may be folded into one of the "white" sauces.
Plain cold beans may be used in salads.
Raw: extremely young ones may be sliced and used raw in salads, dressed with vinaigrette.

Herbs
These are strongly-flavoured plants, used in small quantities to enhance the flavour of raw or cooked dishes.

To chop herbs: put a pile of washed leaves in the centre of a chopping board. Using a cook's knife (one with a long pointed blade) and holding just above the point with your fingertips, handle in the right hand, chop downwards, swinging the knife round in an arc so that you cover the whole pile. The point should not move much.

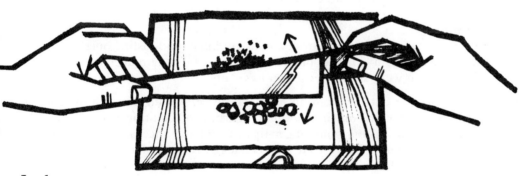

Leeks
Cut off the roots and trim the green end. Wash very thoroughly indeed, cutting in halves or quarters nearly to the root.

Cook by conservative method, 15 mins., or
    quick boiling, 10 mins., or
    steaming, 15-20 mins., or
    braising, 20-30 mins.
Plain hot leeks may be served with melted butter, or coated with béchamel or sauce aurore or parsley sauce.
Raw: may also be sliced across very thinly indeed and used sparingly in salads instead of onion.

Lettuce
There are several kinds. Commonly eaten raw after thorough washing and drying. Tear it into little pieces rather than shredding it with a knife. The

heart leaves may be used whole. It can also be cooked if, for example, you have bolting lettuces in the garden. Cooked lettuce tastes rather like spinach.

Cook by quick boiling, 10-20 mins. according to age. Drain and chop thoroughly and stir into some thick béchamel, or add plenty of butter and seasoning; or
braise, about 30 mins.

Marrow *(Vegetable Marrow, to give it its full dignity)*
When juvenile, marrows are courgettes, which are eaten skin and all. When adult they must be peeled with a sharp vegetable knife and the seeds removed. It is easier to do this cut into sections first.

Cook by any method *except* simmering.
Plain hot marrow may be served with butter and nutmeg, or coated with béchamel, sauce aurore, egg, parsley or cheese sauce, or fried crumbs.

Mushrooms
A fungus and the cook's friend. They may be used in their own right as a vegetable or as a flavouring. Large flat ones are the tastiest, tiny button ones the most decorative. Rinse them quickly. Do not peel them unless they are very old or tough. For most dishes use with stalks too, or if you must remove these use them up in stews etc. Mushrooms may be sliced, chopped or left whole, according to use.

Cook by stewing gently in a little milk or cream, or
grill, or
fry, or
bake in butter. Season well in all cases.
Raw: small mushrooms may also be sliced very thinly, sprinkled with seasoning and lemon juice and eaten as a salad.

Onions
There are several kinds. Spanish onions are huge mild-tasting ones, very good when baked. You can peel onions under water if they make you cry, and it also helps to wear spectacles if you have any.

To slice onions: cut the onion in half lengthwise, leaving the root on. Put the cut side downwards on the chopping-board, root pointing left, and held by your left hand. Using your finger-tips as a guide, slice downwards *carefully* with a sharp knife. Move your fingers back a fraction of an inch towards the root and slice down again.

To chop onions: cut the onion in half lengthwise, leaving the root on, and put the cut side down as for slices, but make cuts along the onion's length almost to the root: the root is now holding a lot of strips together. Now slice across the onion so that neat little pieces fall away as you slice. Finally discard the root.

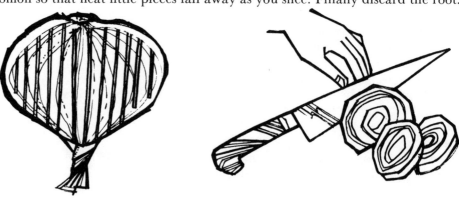

Cook by any method given. Quick boiling time, about 20 mins.,
baking, up to 1 1/2 hours.
Plain hot onions are good coated with béchamel or cheese sauce.
Raw: some people like thinly-cut (mild) onion rings, or grated onion
sparingly used in salads. Spring onions are eaten raw in salads, with the
tops trimmed.

Parsnips
Scrub and peel thinly. Cut off the top.

Cook by any method *except* simmering. Quick boiling time, about 20 mins.,
braising, about 30 mins.
roast, cook like potatoes round joint (recommended).
Plain hot parsnips are good with butter, or coated with béchamel or cheese
sauce.

Peas
Green peas may be bought in early summer in pod. Shell them just before
cooking or they get tough skins. Mangetout (= eat-the-lot) peas are eaten
pods and all, so merely top-and-tail them.

Cook by quick boiling 10 minutes, adding 1 sprig of mint and 1 teaspoon sugar
to the salted water. Remove the mint and toss in butter before serving.

Peppers *(Pimento)*
These may be green (unripe) or red (ripe). Cut off the stalk, then cut in half.
Remove the seeds and rinse. They may be stuffed and baked, but are often
used in small quantities with other vegetables.

Potatoes
Scrub. Scrape new potatoes with a small knife, peel old ones thinly with a
potato peeler: hold the potato in your left hand, peeler in your right. Practise
moving the potato rather than the peeler as it is quicker once you are expert.
Remove eyes. They may also be boiled, steamed or baked with the skin left on.
Discard green potatoes that have been exposed to light.

Cook by quick boiling, 15-20 mins. if new, with a sprig of mint. Toss in butter &
parsley. Old potatoes: put into cold water and bring to boil; cook about
20 mins., then drain and dry over low heat. May be mashed with butter,
hot milk and seasoning.
Steam, with or without skins, 30-40 mins.
Fry: see recipe for chips.
Sauté slices of cooked potato with butter and seasoning.
Roast or bake in fairly hot oven, Reg. 6, 400 °F for about 45 minutes.
Sprinkle with salt before or after cooking. Baste or turn in the fat from
time to time.

Pulses   Please see recipe page 53.

Spinach
Wash thoroughly. Put into saucepan damp, but don't add water. Then cook
quickly for a maximum of 10 minutes. The bulk reduces by a surprising amount.
When cooked, chop and drain well. Stir in lots of butter and seasoning, or
1 tablespoon cream cheese per 1/2 lb. (200 g.) spinach. May also be blended
with béchamel or cheese sauce, or puréed and served with sippets of toast
or cubes of fried bread.

Swede   Please see *Turnip*

Tomatoes
Like mushrooms, tomatoes are extremely useful and versatile. Wash them and remove the stalk at the top if necessary.

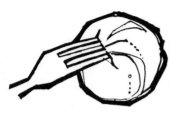

To remove skins: there are two methods. They may be blanched by pouring boiling water over them, then plunging them into cold water; or hold them impaled on a fork over the naked gas flame, twirling them so that the skin is heated equally all over. Cut tomatoes in half across the equator, or in slices or quarters for salads.

Cook by any method *except* quick boiling and steaming.
> Simmer them with only a very little water and serve all the liquid.
> Grill them with the skin left on. Cut them in half, make an incision almost to the bottom skin, season, dot with butter and cook under medium heat for about 7 minutes, cut side upwards—don't turn them over.
> Bake (with the same preparation) for about 10 minutes.

Turnip & Swede
Humble but useful vegetables, especially good in meat stews. Scrub, then peel thickly. Cut into slices or chunks.

Cook by quick boiling, about 20 mins., or
> steaming, about 30 mins., or
> pressure cook.

Plain hot turnips may be coated with a "white" sauce of some kind; so may swedes. Swedes are also good mashed like potatoes with butter and a little ground nutmeg.

IV   RECIPES FOR VEGETABLES

D   Vegetable Macédoine
For 3-4 people

This is a simple but colourful mixture of vegetables, useful as a garnish for plain-looking dishes like stew, or tossed in mayonnaise for a mixed vegetable salad.

Ingredients
2 medium carrots
2 stalks celery
1 leek or medium onion
2 oz. peeled swede (50 g.)
1 tomato, skinned, and pips removed
2 oz. peas (50 g.) or 2 teaspoons chopped parsley
3-4 olives, optional
1/4 pint mayonnaise (for salad only) (150 ml.)

Method
1   Cut the carrots, celery, leek or onion, swede, tomato and olives, if used, into small dice.
2   Heat a little salt water in a saucepan and when boiling put in all but tomato, parsley if used, and olives. Cook for 5 minutes, until just tender.

3   Drain the vegetable dice carefully and mix in the tomato, parsley and
    olives.
4   Serve hot; or mix with mayonnaise and allow to get cold.

D   Vegetable Purée
For 2
Babies and invalids may sometimes need vegetables in purée form, and they
make a change for anyone. They are very simple to prepare. This is a typical
recipe which you can adapt to most vegetables except those that won't rub
through a sieve easily.

INGREDIENTS
1/2 lb. brussels sprouts (225 g.)
salted water
seasoning
a little butter or top-of-milk

METHOD
1   Wash and cook the sprouts in boiling water according to the directions
    for quick boiling, for about 10 minutes. Make sure that they are quite
    tender, but don't overcook.
2   If you have an electric blender, put them in with 3 tablespoons of the
    cooking water and a little seasoning, adding a knob of butter or tablespoon-
    ful of top-of-milk. Don't have much seasoning for a baby, nor make the
    mixture very rich for an invalid. Switch on for long enough to pulp the
    vegetables. Rub through a sieve to remove fibres if necessary. If you have
    no blender, rub the vegetables directly through a sieve.
3   Taste to make sure the consistency and seasoning are pleasant. Reheat
    gently and serve hot (warm for a baby).

D   Pulses: Haricot Beans, Butter Beans, Dried Peas, Lentils & Others
These are a useful source of plant protein. They keep well unless allowed
to get damp.

INGREDIENTS
Beans etc.: allow 1-1 1/2 oz. (30-50 g.) per person
stock or water
bouquet garni or bay leaf
salt
butter or sauce to serve with them: e.g. béchamel or cheese
chopped parsley

METHOD
1   Soak the beans, etc. in enough stock or water to cover them, plus 1 1/2″.
    Lentils need only an hour or two to soak, the rest may be left overnight.
2   Put them into a saucepan with the soaking water and enough stock or
    extra water to cover them again plus 1″.
3   Bring to the boil. Skim. Add salt and bouquet garni or bay leaf. Simmer
    them over low heat according to the size of the pulses used: lentils cook in
    about 1/2 hour, the rest need an hour or more. Cook them until tender but
    not broken.
4   Drain the beans or whatever. The liquid may be used to make the sauce
    if you like, or used as stock on another occasion. Keep them hot until you
    are ready to serve them. They may be tossed in butter or mixed with a
    sauce of your choice. Many pulses need parsley sprinkled over to make
    them look interesting.

NOTE: Pulses make good vegetable purées after cooking in this way: see the preceding recipe.

For *Pease Pudding*, flavour the dried peas additionally with a bit of carrot and onion and a few bacon rinds, all put in to simmer with them. When cooked, rub all you can through a sieve, season well and stir in a knob of butter. Serve hot with salt beef, pork or boiled bacon.

M Peas French Fashion
Serves 4
This is a good way with older peas or frozen ones. The latter will usually cook more quickly than fresh ones.

INGREDIENTS
12 oz.-1 lb. peas, shelled weight (about 400 g.)
1/4 lettuce, preferably the heart, shredded
4 spring onions or 1 medium leek, or 1/2 medium onion, all sliced
water
1 oz. butter or margarine (30 g.)
seasoning
good pinch of sugar
bouquet garni

METHOD
1 You must use a pan with tightly-fitting lid. Boil about 1/4 pint (150 ml.) water, then put in vegetables, butter, seasoning, sugar and bouquet garni.
2 Cook covered over moderate heat for 10-15 minutes (conservative method), adding a little more water if the pan boils dry.
3 Remove bouquet garni. Serve peas on hot dish with any liquid left in the pan poured over them.

M Cabbage Austrian Fashion
4 portions
This one makes a welcome change from plain boiled cabbage—and smells much better when cooking.

INGREDIENTS
1 tablespoon oil, dripping or margarine
10 oz. red or white cabbage, washed and finely shredded (250 g.)
1 eating apple, peeled and sliced
1/4 level teaspoon caraway seeds
1 tablespoon wine vinegar
2 rounded teaspoons sugar
seasoning to taste

METHOD
1 Put the dripping or other fat into a sauté pan for which you have a lid. Heat it, put in the cabbage and stir for a minute or two in the hot fat.
2 Add the apple, caraway seeds, vinegar, sugar and seasoning. Stir again and cover.
3 Cook, over gentle heat, for about 30-40 minutes, or until the cabbage is tender. Stir it from time to time to prevent sticking, and if it becomes very dry add a little water.
4 Serve hot.

D Fried Onion Rings

For 2

These are good with steak, or for garnishing many savoury dishes.

INGREDIENTS
1 large onion
fat for frying
flour
lightly beaten white of egg

METHOD
1. Cut the peeled onion straight across into rounds 1/4″ thick and separate the rings.
2. Heat a frying pan with about 1/2″ depth of fat or oil in it.
3. Dip the rings first into flour, then into egg white beaten till frothy but not stiff.
4. Slide the rings carefully into the hot fat and fry quickly until just brown.
5. Drain on kitchen paper and serve at once.

D Juicy Potatoes

4 portions

These are good with roast meat. There isn't then any need to make a separate gravy—just stir the meat-juices from the roasting pan into the potato sauce before dishing up.

INGREDIENTS
1 1/2 lbs. potatoes (700 g.)
2 oz. dripping or other fat (60 g.)
1 oz. flour (30 g.)
1/2 pint water (300 ml.) or stock
1 stock cube if water is used
1 wineglassful white wine (optional)
bouquet garni or pinch of dried mixed herbs
seasoning to taste

METHOD
1. Peel the potatoes and slice them into 1/2″ rounds.
2. Melt the fat in a large saucepan, stir in the flour and cook over medium heat to make a light brown roux, stirring all the time.
3. Mix in the water or stock as for a sauce, little by little, away from heat.
4. Stir in all the rest of the ingredients except the potato slices. Bring to the boil stirring. Then put in the potato.
5. Cover the pan and simmer gently for 15-20 minutes, or until the potato is tender when you prod it with a pointed knife. It will need stirring gently two or three times as it cooks. Remove the bouquet garni from the sauce before you serve the potatoes (it's easy to forget).

M Duchess Potatoes

These are decorative mashed potatoes, containing egg to make them set. The mixture is useful for making a border for a special dish, or as a way of serving potatoes elaborately for a special occasion.

INGREDIENTS
1 1/2 lbs. floury potatoes, boiled (700 g.)
1-2 tablespoons cold milk

1 oz. butter or margarine (30 g.) plus a little extra to finish
seasoning to taste
1 egg or 2 egg yolks, beaten
Oven: Fairly Hot, Reg. 5, 375 °F

METHOD

1 Rub the cooked potatoes through a sieve and stir in the cold milk, butter and seasoning to make a stiff mix. Allow to cool a little if it is still hot, then beat in the egg.
2 Using a nylon forcing bag and large star pipe, make rosettes round the edge of a heatproof serving dish, or fill a dish with swirls and rosettes according to the way you will serve them.
3 Dot over the top at intervals with a little extra butter and put into a fairly hot oven, Reg. 5 or 375 °F until attractively beginning to brown.

NOTE: You may add grated cheese to vary duchess potato: the quantity depends on the strength of flavour of the cheese—and on how much you can spare! Say 4 oz. approx. very finely grated Cheddar, or 2 oz. Parmesan (Cheddar 100 g., or 50 g. Parmesan). To enhance the cheesiness, use plenty of seasoning, including cayenne pepper and a little mustard.

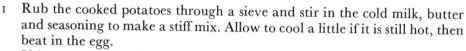

D Baked Potatoes alias **Jacket Potatoes**

INGREDIENTS
1 medium-to-large potato per person
salt or fat
filling or garnish: see below
Oven: Hot, Reg. 7, 425 °F.

METHOD

1 Scrub the potatoes well, and remove any damaged parts.
2 Using a sharp knife, cut into each potato about 1/4″ deep all round the equator. Scoring in this way will prevent a spud explosion all over your nice clean oven.
3 If you like a crisp jacket, rub the outside all over with a little salt. If you would rather have soft-skinned potato, brush it with oil, or rub with butter.
4 Bake at the top of a hot oven, Reg. 7 or 425 °F for about 1 hour. N.B. The potatoes can also be cooked at a lower temperature and/or on a lower shelf of the oven—just give them longer. I'm sorry I can't be very exact, because it depends how big the potatoes are. To find out if they are done, squeeze one gently. If cooked it will split neatly in half, and if you are still in doubt you can prod the centre with a fork.

Garnishes and Fillings for Baked Potatoes

Butter: open the potato and insert a large knob of butter. This is an occasion when margarine won't do.

Better butter: use garlic butter or maître d'hôtel butter (page 26).

Cream cheese: mix cream cheese with chopped chives and seasoning. Use about 1 dessertspoonful per potato.

Cheese: scoop out the centre of the potato. Mash it in a bowl with 2 oz. grated cheese (60 g.), seasoning, a knob of butter and tablespoon of milk. Return the mixture to the two half-potato shells, sprinkle the top with grated cheese, and if you like, raspings as well. Brown in a hot oven or under the grill. This makes a good supper dish.

M Anna Potatoes
Serves 4 people

INGREDIENTS
1 1/2 lbs. potatoes (700 g.)
2 oz. butter, or margarine will just do (50 g.)
salt & pepper
nutmeg
Oven: Very Hot, Reg. 8, 450 °F.

METHOD
1 Peel the potatoes, choosing even-sized ones, and slice them very thinly into rounds, 1/8″ thick. Leave them covered with cold water for several minutes.
2 Using about 1/2 oz. of the butter, grease a deep pie plate 7″ in diameter by 1″ deep. The butter must be very thick, especially on the bottom of the tin. Melt the rest of the fat.
3 Dry the potato slices carefully, and lay them in a spiral or circles over the base of the tin, overlapping the slices a little. When you have finished one layer, brush it over with melted butter, season lightly and sprinkle over a pinch of nutmeg as well.
4 Make another layer of overlapping slices, but this time overlap them in the opposite direction. Then brush with fat, add seasoning and so on. When the tin is full, brush finally with melted fat and if any is left sprinkle it over the top. Cover tightly with foil.
5 Bake in a very hot oven, Reg. 8 or 450 °F for 1 1/4 hours, or until the potato is tender all through and beginning to brown at the edges.
6 Run a palette knife carefully round the edge and underneath the "cake" of potato and turn it out onto a heatproof serving dish. If any slices are disarranged put them back. Return the potato to the oven for a further 10 minutes to brown on the top and sides. Serve hot.

DO NOT MAKE CHIPS UNLESS THERE IS AN ADULT AROUND
WHO KNOWS YOU ARE FRYING THEM

D Chips
For 4 people
I'm sure you have been waiting for these. Who doesn't like them? However, don't eat them often unless you are very thin!

INGREDIENTS
1 1/2 lbs. potatoes, waxy ones if possible (700 g.)
deep fat for frying
salt.

METHOD
1 Scrub, peel and rinse the potatoes. Cut them into slices 1/2″ thick or less. Put a pile of slices cut side down on a board and cut again into sticks.

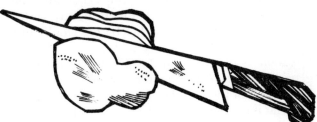

2 Put the chips into a bowl of cold slightly salt water as you cut them. Leave them to soak in the water for half an hour.

3 Dry the chips very thoroughly indeed on a clean tea towel. If you leave them wet they will make the hot fat splutter and you may get burnt.

4 Prepare the deep fat fryer with fat or oil not more than half way up the pan. Put on moderate heat and HAVE READY A SAUCEPAN LID TO PUT RIGHT OVER THE PAN IF IT SHOULD ACCIDENTALLY CATCH FIRE. TURN OFF THE HEAT BUT DO NOT ATTEMPT TO MOVE THE PAN. The saucepan lid would smother the flame.

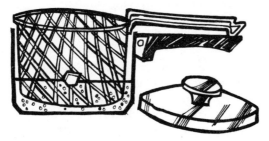 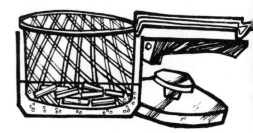

5 Test the heat of the fat by dropping a small cube of bread into it. It should sizzle as soon as it goes in. Don't overheat the fat: if there is smoke, blue or otherwise, it's too hot.

6 Put only a handful of chips into the wire basket of the frying pan and lower it into the fat. Cook on moderate heat for 3 minutes, or until the chips are softened but not brown. Lift out the basket.

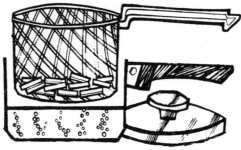 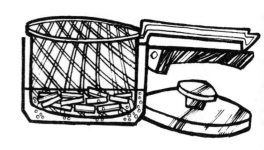

7 Now, using caution, let the fat re-heat for a minute or two. Dip the chip-basket back in. This will make the chips crisp and golden on the outside. Put them into a hot dish, sprinkle them lightly with salt and keep them in a hot place while you fry another batch. Don't cover them or they will go soggy.

8 Serve as soon as possible, but don't forget to turn off the heat under the frying pan, and leave the handle turned so that no-one could possibly knock over any of the very hot fat.

9 When the fat is cool strain it back into a suitable container to use next time.

M   Potatoes Alsace Fashion
For 4

INGREDIENTS
1 1/2 lbs. new potatoes, boiled (700 g.)
4 oz. very small onions, peeled, or sliced onion (125 g.)
2 rashers streaky bacon, diced
1 oz. butter (30 g.)
chopped parsley to garnish

METHOD
1   While the potatoes cook, prepare the onions and rashers. Fry them together gently in a shallow pan until the bacon is crisp and the onion golden.
2   Drain the cooked potatoes thoroughly.
3   Add the butter to the pan containing the bacon and onion. When sizzling, put in the cooked potatoes and stir all together gently for a few moments.
4   Serve very hot, garnished with the parsley.

V   SALADS

Excuse my asking, but are you a bit plump? Or spotty? Salads won't guarantee beauty, more's the pity, but they can help. They provide minerals and vitamins that you must have for healthy skin and hair, they are bulky, so that you feel satisfied, but they don't provide much starch and are low in calories—unless you add a lot of rich salad dressing, such as mayonnaise, which has a high count. Use yoghurt instead, if you are slimming.

The recipes that I give for the salads themselves are only a representative few of the thousands of combinations that there must be of raw and cooked vegetables. Do make up you own; but to help you on your way here are the basic rules for salads.

1   All ingredients must be fresh, clean, dry and served preferably slightly chilled. If cooked vegetables are used, do not overcook them.
2   Simplicity is best. Don't try to combine too many different vegetables or fruits as the flavours may cancel each other out. Even one vegetable on its own, properly dressed, is all right.
3   Arrange the salad neatly in a bowl or large platter or on individual plates. Try to make an artistic combination of colours: don't, for instance, put tomatoes next to beetroot, next to carrot.
4   Don't toss a salad in vinaigrette and let it stand, or it will go limp. You can prepare it a little in advance, then toss it at the last moment.

Appetizer Salads
Small portions of colourful salads, with or without tasty morsels of anchovy, sardine, pâté and so on, make good hors d'œuvres, especially for summer menus.

Main-Dish Salads
These are made with portions of cold cooked fish, eggs, grated cheese, chicken, beef, tongue and so on, arranged neatly with a harmonizing salad.

M   Mayonnaises
There is plenty of choice with these, too. Shellfish, fish, eggs and chicken are

suitable as main ingredients. Put the cooked chilled portions of food onto a wire grid and coat them with mayonnaise for coating (p. 63). Decorate them after the mayonnaise has set and brush over with aspic if you like. Then serve on a bed of a suitable simple salad.

D   Green Salad

For 4 people
Because it is plain, this salad can be perfect.

Ingredients

Select two or more of the following:
1 medium (cabbage type) lettuce
1/2 cos lettuce
1 endive plant
1 bundle watercress
1 head of chicory
1 punnet mustard/cress (or use home-grown)
also:
a few leaves of herbs, if liked, chopped or whole
vinaigrette or lemon dressing

Method

1   Wash the available saladings thoroughly and DRY them by draining, then shaking in a clean tea towel or salad basket.
2   Prepare the vinaigrette dressing in a salad bowl.
3   Put in the salad, large leaves torn with the fingers into small shreds.
4   Toss together with salad servers or forks, so that each green leaf gets coated with dressing. Serve at once.

NOTE: Many people think a green salad incomplete without a little garlic. There are several ways you can introduce it:
a) cut a clove in half and rub the cut surface round the bowl before you make the dressing (mild taste); or,
b) crush part of a clove and spread it on a quarter crust of bread. Toss the crust with the rest of the salad (medium-strong taste); or,
c) use part or whole clove of garlic, crushed in the dressing itself (strong taste).
Another variation appreciated by some is to dice and fry a rasher of bacon until crisp, then include these little pieces, especially if you have endive as one of the ingredients.

D Mixed Salads

For 4 people
These usually have lettuce as their main ingredient, though endive or finely shredded cabbage may be used instead.

INGREDIENTS

Select 3 or 4 of the following or similar ingredients:
1 green salad plant such as lettuce or endive, torn into small shreds
2 large tomatoes, skinned and sliced
1 small bunch watercress
a few radishes
a few spring onions
1 small cooked beetroot, diced or sliced
2 carrots, grated
1/2-1 blanched red or green pepper, cut into strips or dice
a few celery stalks taken from the heart
1 hard-boiled egg, shelled and cut into slices or quarters
also:
vinaigrette or lemon dressing

METHOD
1 Having washed and dried the ingredients and prepared them as directed, you may toss the greenstuff with the vinaigrette or serve a dressing separately if you prefer.
2 Arrange a neat mound of greenery in the middle of a salad bowl or platter.
3 Plan a colour scheme and design with the remaining ingredients. Perhaps you can follow the shape of the dish, or place straight lines across the green by dropping grated carrot, for example, from the edge of a palette knife. Keep the design bold and not fussy. Radishes and spring onions are often left whole so that one can avoid them when serving if they are disliked.
4 Serve very soon after arranging.

M Cool-Cucumber Salad

4 to 6 portions
This recipe started in Arabia. It is just the thing for really hot weather.

INGREDIENTS
1/2 large cucumber
1 × 5 oz. carton plain low-fat yoghurt
1 tablespoon lemon juice
1/4 teaspoon salt
shake pepper
1/2 teaspoon caster sugar

METHOD
1 Slice the cucumber very thinly, using a razor-sharp knife.
2 Mix together the rest of the ingredients. Turn the cucumber slices in this dressing until they are evenly coated.
3 Serve quickly, as the cucumber gets flabby if it is allowed to stand for long.

D Apple & Walnut Salad *(Waldorf Salad)*
Serves 4

INGREDIENTS
1/4 small white or red cabbage
3 dessert apples

1 oz. chopped walnuts (30 g.)
1 oz. sultanas, optional (30 g.)
2-3 tablespoons mayonnaise, preferably made with lemon juice
chopped parsley

METHOD
1 Wash the cabbage and shake it dry.
2 Using a very sharp knife, shred the cabbage very finely indeed. Pile it on a platter or put it into a salad bowl.
3 Peel and core the apples and cut them into slices, or dice them if you prefer. Put them into a bowl with the walnuts, sultanas and mayonnaise. Turn these together gently in the bowl until the apple is well coated with mayonnaise and the walnuts and sultanas are evenly mixed through.
4 Pile the mayonnaise mixture in the centre of the cabbage. If you have used white cabbage the salad will look anaemic, and needs a garnish such as chopped parsley.

NOTE: If you prefer, the apples need not be peeled. Red apples make a very pretty salad.

VI SALAD DRESSINGS

D Mayonnaise
Yield: 1 pint maximum (550 ml.)

INGREDIENTS
2 stardard egg yolks
1/4 level teaspoon white pepper
1 level teaspoon salt
1 level teaspoon made mustard
a few drops piquant sauce, e.g. Worcestershire. This you may vary.
1/2-3/4 pint olive oil (300-425 ml.)
2 tablespoons approx. wine vinegar or lemon juice

METHOD
1 Mayonnaise can be made in a bowl using a fork, wire whisk or rotary beater, but it is easier if you have a food-mixer powered by electricity. Put the yolks in the bowl and beat in the seasonings.
2 The oil should not be cold; use it at room temperature or a little warmer. Add it to the yolks literally a drop at a time to start with. Beat well between each addition.
3 Gradually the mixture will become stiff, almost solid, and then the oil may be added in a *very thin* trickle. Stop adding oil at once if the mayonnaise starts to lose its smoothness. (If the mixture does curdle, start again with two more yolks and add the spoiled mayonnaise as if it were oil, drop by drop again.)
4 Thin down the very thick mixture with vinegar or lemon juice.

NOTE: Some people add just a drop or two of vinegar to the yolks before adding oil.
    You may also add a tablespoonful of hot water to the complete mayonnaise if you want a slightly thinner but not more acid mixture.

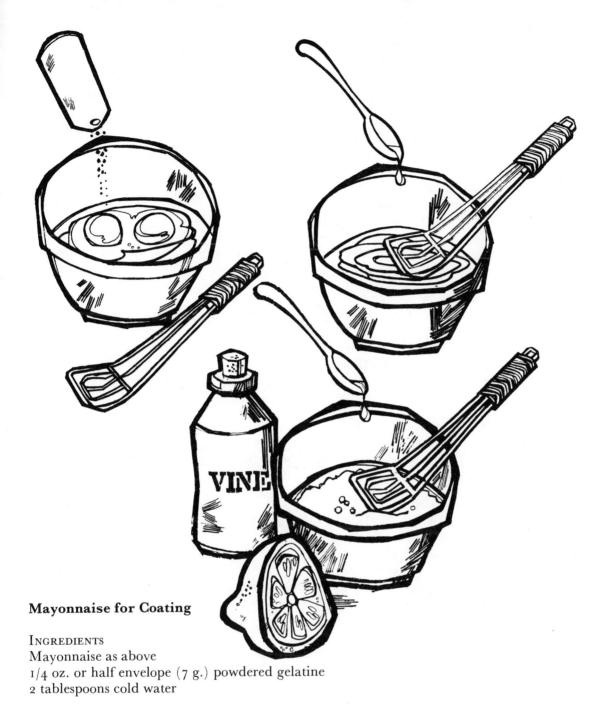

Mayonnaise for Coating

INGREDIENTS
Mayonnaise as above
1/4 oz. or half envelope (7 g.) powdered gelatine
2 tablespoons cold water

METHOD
1 Soak the gelatine in the cold water for five minutes, then melt it over gentle heat.
2 Mix the gelatine thoroughly into the prepared mayonnaise.
3 Cool the mayonnaise thoroughly and use at setting point to coat pieces of chicken, eggs, fish and so on for the mayonnaise type of salad or buffet dishes. Place the food on a wire rack before spooning or pouring the mayonnaise over evenly. Any excess will drip off the food instead of setting in a wodge round the bottom. You may garnish the pieces of coated food with little squares, strips or diamonds of such things as peppers, black olives, green olives, cucumber rind and so on. Dip these in aspic (p. 189) to make them stick. The whole lot may then be brushed over with aspic to give it a sparkle.

63

M   Aioli Sauce

This is mayonnaise strongly flavoured with garlic. Crush 2 cloves or more with the salt, add this to the egg yolks and carry on as for plain mayonnaise.

Serve it particularly with any cold poached fish that is inclined to be insipid, or with vegetables.

D   Vinaigrette (or Lemon) Dressing

For 4 or more

INGREDIENTS

4 tablespoons olive oil
2 tablespoons wine vinegar or lemon juice, or to taste
small piece of clove of garlic, crushed with a pinch of salt (optional)
1-2 level teaspoons chopped herbs, such as sage, mint, rosemary (optional)
seasoning to taste

METHOD

1   Put the oil and vinegar or lemon juice and garlic, if used, into a small basin or cup.
2   Whisk with a fork until well mixed and slightly stiffened.
3   Stir in the herbs if used, and seasoning.
4   Use at once. If allowed to stand the oil and vinegar will separate; but you can always whisk them together again.

M   Cream Cheese Dressing

About 1/4 pint (150 ml.)

This is pleasant with any salad, but especially good with root vegetables and celery.

INGREDIENTS

4 rounded tablespoons cream cheese
1 tablespoon top-of-milk or cream
1 tablespoon lemon juice
1 rounded teaspoon sugar
2 level teaspoons finely-grated onion, or snipped chives
chopped parsley or other herbs, optional and to taste

METHOD

1   Put the cream cheese into a bowl and stir in the top-of-milk or cream. Then stir in the lemon juice, blending well.
2   Mix in the rest of the ingredients.

Cheese, Eggs, Pasta & Rice

I CHEESE

All over the world, wherever people have kept animals for milk, they have also made cheese. It is a splendid food, having more protein in it than meat has, weight for weight, and being rich in calcium. It is as bland or as potently-flavoured as you like to choose: think of cottage cheese first, then of Roquefort.

That reminds me: do you know how "blue" cheeses are said to have been discovered? Once there was a poor shepherd boy, who looked after a flock of sheep in the barren limestone hills near his home. Every day his mother would give him a lunch of hard rye bread and a little piece of white cheese made from sheep's milk, which was all they had. Then off he would go to pasture the lean sheep on whatever patches of grass he could find. When he found a bit of grass he would put his lunch in a cleft of rock to keep it out of the sun, or on a ledge in one of the many caves that there were in the district.

One day, he was sitting outside the cave where he had just put his lunch away when he noticed a stray dog coming close to the sheep. At once he leapt up with his stick and drove the dog away, but the sheep had panicked; they rushed upwards over the hill. All during the afternoon and late into the twilight the boy followed the sheep. He was exhausted, famished and furious by the time he came home, though he had not lost even a lamb from the flock. He vowed he would never go to that part of the hills again.

But it was a bad year for grass; after a few weeks the usual places were useless; the boy had to lead the flock back to the unlucky hill. It was as he was putting his lunch into a cavern as usual that the boy remembered the lunch he had not had time to eat before the dog chased his sheep. He looked for it. There was the red handkerchief—just where he had left it! He unwrapped it eagerly. Ugh—the bread was a mass of mould, the white cheese veined with blue mould too. What a waste! And he was so hungry! Perhaps a corner of the cheese was still eatable? He broke off a tiny piece and tasted it.

The next day the boy and his brothers brought all the cheeses they had at home and left them in the cave. Then they took turns to stay on guard outside. After a while, they took the cheeses to market. Soon they were the richest people in the district, buying other people's sheep's milk to make their special cheese. They couldn't keep their secret for ever, of course. Then more and more of the delicious new cheeses were made, ripened in the cool limestone caves to make Roquefort in France famous all over the world. Many other countries have also produced blue cheeses: there is English Stilton, Italian Gorgonzola, Danish Blue and Norwegian Blue and many others, all delicious and good in their different ways, but, for many, Roquefort cheese is still the most splendid of all.

Cheese is made from milk basically like this. The milk, usually from cows but sometimes from sheep or goats, is turned sour by the addition of a special culture or by rennet, so that it sets like junket. Then it is cut up to make the whey run off, leaving the curds behind. The curds are salted, pressed and treated by various methods. Sometimes the cheese is eaten almost at once, sometimes it is left to ripen and change for months, even years. Cheese can be made from skimmed milk, or from whole milk, or from milk with extra cream added. Sometimes flavourings or dyes are put in, sometimes moulds are encouraged to grow on the outside of the cheese, like Camembert, or inside as with the blues.

If you want to make some cheese yourself, turn some milk sour with rennet. Put it in a jelly bag and let it drip overnight. Mix in a little salt but leave it in the bag and put the bag between two boards with a weight on top for 2 days. Then eat the cheese within a day or so. Be prepared to find you won't get much from a pint of milk.

The kind of milk used, the season, the kind of food the animals ate, the kind of land where the food grew, as well as the treatment of the milk to make cheese, all affect the taste of the finished product, which is why there are thousands of different cheeses throughout the world. Tasting some of them and finding out where they come from can be interesting, and one of the most nourishing ways of learning geography that I know.

D   Cheese Board

Cheese is often served at the end of a formal meal, or before the sweet if you are eating in French style. It can often replace a pudding at family meals and is very useful as a nourishing snack, or for lunch; Dutch people even have it for breakfast: consider that the next time you haven't time to cook breakfast before running to the bus.

Cheeses are best served at room temperature. If you store them in the refrigerator (wrapped in foil so that they don't dry out) take them out an hour or so before you serve them. Buy the softer cheeses in small quantities so that you need not store them for long.

Try to select cheeses that are different in taste and texture from one another for a cheese board. For instance, if you have Edam cheese, don't have Gouda on the same occasion. Don't have more than one blue cheese unless you are deliberately having a cheese-tasting to compare flavours. For most occasions two or three cheeses are enough to choose from.

Arrange the pieces of cheese neatly on a board, or plate if you have no board. I think myself that it needs no further decoration, but some people like to put a sprig or two of watercress or parsley among the wedges, or to put soft cheeses onto a cabbage or lettuce leaf. Each person then helps himself.

Biscuits are an obvious choice to serve with cheese, and so is crusty bread. You might like to try not only the salty and cream cracker types of biscuit but semi-sweet ones such as digestive or Marie; where bread is concerned you can let yourself go: try brown, rye, wholemeal, caraway; rolls, sticks, splits, baps; French bread, Vienna—need I go on? Celery in season, carrot sticks and apples are appreciated with cheese by many people.

Wine of almost any kind goes well with cheese, if you are allowed to have any, or (if adult) you approve. Beer goes well too, particularly with many English cheeses.

D   Cheese Pudding

For 4 people

This is a pleasant supper dish, with a texture almost like a soufflé. Don't waste crusts of bread, by the way; if you bake them slowly in a tin at the bottom of the oven when you happen to have it heated, they turn into rusks. If you then crush these with a rolling-pin you have "raspings" useful for other cheese dishes.

INGREDIENTS
3 medium-thick slices bread
2 eggs
1/2 pint milk (300 ml.)
1 oz. margarine (30 g.)
1 medium onion
a little salt if needed
white & cayenne pepper
6 oz. grated cheese of a Cheddar type (200 g.)
Oven: Fairly Hot, Reg. 6, 400 °F to start

METHOD

1 Cut the crusts off the bread, then cut the crumb part into strips, then into little squares like dice. Put them into a bowl.

2 Separate the yolks from the whites of the eggs. Put the yolks with the bread, the whites into a separate bowl for whipping. Pour the milk over the bread, give the mixture a good stir and leave it to soak.

3 Put the margarine into a small saucepan, and melt it over heat. Peel and chop the onion and fry it gently in the margarine till soft but not very brown. Stir this into the bread mix with most of the grated cheese and the seasoning. (Add salt only if the cheese is not already salt enough.)

4 Beat the egg-whites until they are very stiff and dry-looking. Fold them into the mass gently.

5 Grease a pie-dish and pour in the mixture. Sprinkle the top with the rest of the cheese and bake in a fairly hot oven, Reg. 6 or 400 °F for the first 10 minutes, then turn down to Reg. 5 or 375 °F for another 20 minutes approx. until well-risen and golden brown. Serve very hot.

M   Welsh Rarebit with Ale
For 4 people

INGREDIENTS

4 rounds of bread
butter
3 tablespoons brown ale
1 oz. butter (30 g.)
seasoning; salt only if necessary
1/4 teaspoon made mustard
8 oz. any hard cheese, grated (225 g.)

METHOD

1 Toast the bread and spread with butter. Keep it warm.

2 Put ale, butter and seasoning into a pan and bring to the boil.

3 Stir in the grated cheese and continue to heat and stir until the cheese is melted and hot, but don't let it boil or the result will be stringy and indigestible.

4 Pour the cheese quickly over the buttered toast, dividing it equally, and serve immediately.

D   Fondue
For 4, roughly

"Fondue" means melted (cheese). Cheese, of course, ought not to be cooked for long, or it becomes stringy and indigestible. You may have noticed that it is almost always added to hot sauce and not boiled.

INGREDIENTS

1 oz. butter (30 g.)
1 oz. flour (30 g.)
1/2 pint milk (300 ml.)
3 oz. Caerphilly cheese (100 g.) crumbled into little pieces
3 oz. Cheddar cheese (100 g.) grated
1 egg yolk
salt, pepper, 1/2 level teaspoon made mustard, cayenne pepper
plenty of toast cut into fingers

METHOD
1 Make a white sauce with the butter, flour and milk, by the roux method. (Refer to page 27 if you aren't sure what this means.)
2 Add the cheese and stir until the cheese has melted over very gentle heat. Do not allow the sauce to reboil once the cheese is added.
3 Remove from heat and quickly stir in the egg yolk. Add plenty of seasoning, tasting it as you go.
4 Pour into a warm serving dish and serve immediately. To eat it people dunk fingers of toast into the dish which is set in the middle of the table. Fondue is a companionable dish.

M Cheese Custard Soufflé
Serves 4
This has a slightly more solid consistency than an orthodox soufflé. It is very quick to prepare.

INGREDIENTS
4 eggs
4 tablespoons milk
1 oz. margarine (30 g.)
1 teaspoon Worcestershire or other piquant sauce
1/4 teaspoon salt if necessary
white & cayenne pepper
5 oz. hard cheese finely grated (150 g.)
Oven: Fairly Hot, Reg. 6, 400 °F

METHOD
1 Separate the yolks and whites of the eggs.
2 Stir the yolks into the milk. Melt the margarine and stir this in as well, together with seasonings and cheese.
3 Whip the whites stiffly and fold them into the cheese mixture.
4 Pour into a greased 2-pint pie dish or equivalent. Bake in a fairly hot oven, Reg. 6 or 400 °F for 20 minutes until set and well-risen. Serve at once.

M Cheese Gnocci
Serves 4 portions

INGREDIENTS
3/4 pint milk (425 ml.)
3 oz. semolina (80 g.)
6 oz. Cheddar or other hard cheese, grated (175 g.)
salt, pepper, mustard and cayenne
little butter or margarine

METHOD
1 Grease a small square tin or baking sheet.
2 Heat the milk in a large saucepan. When it comes to the boil stir in all the semolina at once. Continue to cook gently, stirring all the time, for seven minutes. You will have a very thick ball of semolina sauce.
3 Stir in 5 oz. or so of the cheese, keeping some for sprinkling on top later. Mix in plenty of seasoning, tasting as you go.
4 Spread the mixture evenly about 1/2″ thick on the prepared tin. Let it get cold.
5 Cut the solid slab into neat squares; or if you like cut out more elegant circles with a small pastry cutter. Overlap the squares or circles in lines on a greased heatproof dish.

6 Sprinkle the top with the remaining cheese, dot with little pieces of butter and grill under moderate heat for 7 minutes, or until heated through and browned lightly on top. Alternatively heat through in a fairly hot oven, Reg. 6 or 400 °F for about 10 minutes.

D Cheese Dips

These are fun for parties. They are like a cold fondue, into which you can dip sticks of carrot or celery, French bread, crispbread, biscuits, rusks, toast and even potato crisps. Here are two recipes to give you the idea, but I'm sure you will be able to think of many variations, such as adding minced ham, chopped gherkins and so on and on.

Garlic Dip

INGREDIENTS
4 level tablespoons cream cheese
4 tablespoons top-of-milk or cream
2 small cloves garlic crushed with salt
2 level teaspoons creamed horseradish sauce (optional)
1 tablespoon snipped-up or chopped chives
seasoning

METHOD
1 Put all the ingredients except chives and seasoning into a bowl and mix together.
2 When well blended, taste and make sure the seasoning is right for you. Stir in the chives and pour the dip into a serving bowl.

Blue Moon Dip

INGREDIENTS
4 level tablespoons curd cheese
2 tablespoons milk
1 egg yolk
1 oz. or more any blue cheese (30 g.)
seasoning

METHOD
1 Blend the curd cheese, milk and egg yolk in a bowl.
2 Crumble in the blue cheese and continue to mix. Add seasoning to taste. Don't make the consistency entirely smooth: leave very small pieces of the blue cheese in the dip.
3 Pour into a serving bowl.

M Party Savouries with Cheese

Spear cubes of any preferred hard *Cheese with Cubes of Pineapple* onto cocktail sticks.

Prunes & Cheese: soak large prunes overnight, but don't cook them. Cut them in half, remove stones and fill the centres with cream cheese.

Fill 2″ lengths of *Celery with Cream Cheese*, well-seasoned.

Ham & Cheese: roll thin strips of ham round morsels of cheese and impale on cocktail sticks.

Cheese Tartlets: make little tarts or boats from cheese pastry (page 134) and fill them with chopped ham or mushrooms bound with béchamel or cheese sauce.

II EGGS

Eggs are a good food. They contain protein to help you grow, some fat (in the yolk) to help keep you warm and many of the minerals and vitamins that you need for health. They don't contain much carbohydrate, so they can be eaten, in moderation, by people who want to get thinner, instead of foods of a starchy kind.

Eggs are good for making a meal in a hurry. They cook fast, and need only gentle heat; in fact too high a temperature spoils them.

Commonly the eggs used in cooking are hens', but duck-eggs (which must be thoroughly cooked), goose-eggs and bantams' eggs are also sometimes used. Hens' eggs come in various sizes and prices. The most useful is perhaps the "standard" egg, which weighs generally just about 2 oz. in the shell. "Large" ones weigh a little more, and are good as boiled eggs for hungry people, "medium" are small ones, cheaper, and can be useful on occasions when the size of the egg doesn't matter. In the following recipes I have used standard eggs.

Now let's go to work on an egg or two to make something worth getting up for.

D Boiled Eggs

These aren't as simple as you might think, because an egg straight from the hen takes longer to cook than an egg which has forgotten where it came from. A really fresh egg has a jelly-like white, and resists heat much more than a staler egg with a watery white which coagulates more easily.

So lower one to two eggs per person into a pan of boiling water and cook for 5 minutes for a really fresh egg, 3 1/2 minutes for the ordinary kind.

This ought to result in a just-set white and still runny yolk. For an *œuf mollet*, slightly harder, boil new-laid eggs for 5 1/2 minutes, shop eggs for 4 minutes.

D Hard-Boiled Eggs

Lower the eggs into boiling water and cook for 10 or 7 minutes according to your estimate of their freshness. Pour out the boiling water and leave the pan under the running cold tap until the eggs are cold. Tap them all over to break the shell and then peel them. These are used in dozens of different recipes.

D Coddled Eggs

Lower the eggs into boiling water, turn off the heat, cover the pan and leave undisturbed for 10 minutes. This gives a very lightly-set egg white and a runny yolk. These are supposed to be good for invalids.

D Poached Eggs

a) *In water*

First break the egg into a cup.

Use a shallow pan such as a frying or sauté pan. Boil water in it, adding a little salt and a few drops of vinegar. Using a spoon, stir hard until you have made a whirlpool in the middle, then slip the egg in quickly, so that the white will be wrapped round the yolk as it hardens. Cook for about 3 minutes on gentle heat, and use a fish-slice or perforated spoon to remove the egg, draining it well. Don't try to do more than one egg at once. Put the eggs onto hot buttered toast or keep them warm in a dish as they are done, and serve as quickly as possible.

b) *In steamer/poacher*

If you have one of these gadgets with small detachable pans set over boiling water, you can cook as many at a time as you have holes for, and the eggs automatically keep a good shape, though I don't think they taste quite as delicate as well-poached-in-water ones.

Grease the pans liberally with butter, break in the eggs and cook over boiling water for 3-5 minutes, until set but not hard. Serve on toast, or in a sauce as a main dish.

D Eggs "en Cocotte"

A further variation on poaching is to cook the eggs in the oven in small individual dishes called cocottes, or in ramekins. In fact, though small earthenware dishes from France are available, any small dishes you have that will hold an egg and a spoonful of sauce are satisfactory.

Grease the dishes and set them in a baking-tin of water to reach half-way up their sides. This will prevent the egg overcooking. Heat them through in a fairly hot oven, Reg. 5, 375 °F. Then put in a tablespoonful of seasoned cream or milk, or a well-flavoured soup (good way to use left-over soup) or any savoury sauce you like. Break in the egg, put a shaving of butter on top, cover with foil or greaseproof paper and bake in the water-bath for 5-10 minutes, depending on how thick the dishes are.

Serve the eggs in the dishes they are cooked in, with a salad for a quick meal, or as a homely "starter".

D Scrambled Eggs

For 2 people

One boiled egg may be enough for you, but one scrambled egg looks like a

72

meanness set on a desert of toast. Three eggs might be enough for two people, but four are better.

INGREDIENTS
1 oz. butter or margarine (30 g.)
4 tablespoons milk, or better, top-of-milk
4 eggs
salt and pepper
2 rounds of toast, crusts removed if you like, well buttered and hot.

METHOD
1 Melt the butter in a shallow pan, remove from heat, then pour in the milk, break in the eggs, shake in a little salt and pepper and beat the whole lot with a fork or whisk until it is well blended.
2 Return to gentle heat, and stir with a wooden spoon until the mixture begins to coagulate. Remove from the heat and continue to stir until the egg is set but still creamy. Do not overcook, or a watery and unappetizing liquid will ooze out. Remember that the egg will go on cooking for a few moments in the heat of the pan alone.
3 Pile the eggs immediately onto hot buttered toast and serve at once.

D   Buttered Eggs
For 2-3 people
These are similar to scrambled eggs, but richer.

INGREDIENTS
2 oz. butter (50 g.)
1 tablespoon milk or top-of-milk
5 eggs
seasoning.

The method is the same as for scrambled eggs.

NOTE: Scrambled and buttered eggs may be turned into appetizing lunch or supper dishes, simply by adding savoury morsels to the beaten eggs before cooking. Any one of the following is a pleasant addition:

2 oz. mushrooms (50 g.): slice and fry them in the butter, then add milk and egg
2 oz. shrimps or prawns (50 g.), chopped or whole
1 small onion, chopped and fried in the butter
2 rashers of bacon, diced and fried in the butter till crisp
2 oz. minced ham or chicken (50 g.)
2 teaspoons or more chopped herbs, especially parsley
a few slices of truffle (should you have any to spare!)
1 large tomato, skinned and de-seeded, then chopped, or 1 teaspoon concentrated tomato purée.

D   Fried Eggs (and Bacon)
Very often fried eggs go with bacon. Make them like this:

1 Heat the pan, on gentle heat, and cut off the rinds of the rashers with a sharp knife or kitchen scissors. If the bacon has much fat, make little snips at right-angles to the edge to stop it curling up when cooked.
2 Put the rashers into the pre-heated pan and leave them until the fat runs out. Turn and cook on the other side. Some like their bacon crisp, some like it soft—do find out.

3   Put the bacon on a hot plate in a warm place. Turn the heat down under the pan, or even off, and let the fat in it cool a little.
4   Slide the egg(s) into the bacon fat. Tilt the pan to baste the top of the eggs with a spoon or palette knife. The classic description of the yolk when cooked is that it should look like a cloudy mirror; that is, not absolutely solid white all over.
5   Slide a fish-slice or palette knife carefully under the egg, lift it and drain it for a moment over the pan. Then slide the egg onto the hot plate where the bacon is waiting for it, and serve immediately.

NOTE: If the egg has yellow transparent frills round the edge, the fat was too hot. Wait a minute longer next time before putting the egg in.
   If the yolk breaks, it may be that the egg is stale.
   If the white runs all over the pan instead of staying companionably with the yolk, the egg is certainly stale.
   If the egg comes out speckled with black, your frying pan needs cleaning. You wouldn't use dirty water to boil an egg, would you? So use fresh fat if you need more than the bacon supplies, or strain it if you have fried anything bitty beforehand.
   If you are starting from scratch, without bacon, you can fry eggs in lard, clarified dripping, butter or oil.

D   Baked Eggs (Œufs sur le Plat)
If you have a shallow heat-proof serving dish it is very simple to cook eggs in this way. A metal dish is best in my opinion, because it conducts heat quickly, but heatproof glass or earthenware will do very well.

METHOD
1   Grease the dish very thoroughly and thickly with butter or bacon fat.
2   Heat it in a fairly hot oven, Reg. 5, 375 °F for 3 minutes, then break in enough eggs to cover the bottom of the dish. Sprinkle over some salt and pepper, dot with a few shavings of butter and return the dish to the oven until the eggs are just set: about 5-7 minutes.

   This method lends itself to variation in many ways: for instance with a bed of cooked meat of some kind, or a purée of vegetables as in the following recipe:

M   Florentine Eggs
Serves 3 for main dish, 6 for a starter or snack (6 eggs)

INGREDIENTS
1/2 oz. butter (15 g.)
4-5 tablespoons spinach purée
seasoning to taste
4-6 eggs
1 1/2 oz. grated cheese (40 g.)
Oven: Fairly Hot, Reg. 5, 375 °F

METHOD
1   Spread the butter thickly over a shallow heatproof serving dish. Then put a thin layer of well-seasoned spinach purée over the butter.
2   Put the dish into a fairly hot oven, Reg. 5 or 375 °F for 5 minutes to heat through.
3   Break in the eggs, sprinkle them over with the grated cheese, return the dish to the oven for a further 12-15 minutes, or until the eggs are set.

M   Further Suggestions for Baked Eggs

Put a layer of minced ham on the greased dish, heat through, then bake the eggs.

Bake bacon rashers, rinds cut off, on the dish until nearly crisp. Break on eggs and bake.

Bake bacon rashers, as above, then cover them with very thin slices of Gruyère or Cheddar cheese. Break on the eggs and bake.

Prepare a bed of onion rings and/or mushrooms. Bake, covered, until soft. Then break on eggs, sprinkle with cheese and bake.

Main Dishes with Poached & Boiled Eggs

There are hundreds of dishes based on eggs-in-sauce. Some call for the eggs to be put in individual pastry cases, or on stamped-out rounds of fried bread (croûtes). Sometimes the eggs are put onto a bed of vegetables and then coated with sauce, sometimes hard-boiled eggs are halved or quartered and then simply mixed into the sauce. Sometimes the dish is served au gratin, sometimes plain. Sometimes—often—other ingredients are included. When making this kind of dish allow, in general, 1-2 eggs per person. Here are some examples.

D   Fricassée of Eggs

For 4 people

INGREDIENTS
4-6 eggs, hard-boiled
1/2 pint béchamel sauce (page 28) (300 ml.)
parsley to garnish

METHOD
1   Cut the eggs into halves or quarters lengthways.
2   Make the sauce and put in the eggs. Allow the eggs to heat through on a low heat for a few minutes.
3   Put onto a very hot dish, garnish with parsley, chopped or in sprigs, and serve at once. The parsley is important here, as otherwise the dish looks very pale and uninteresting.

M   Eggy Hen

For 4 people

INGREDIENTS
12 oz. cooked chicken, minced or finely chopped (300 g.)
a little chicken stock
seasoning
4 eggs, poached, or medium-boiled (œufs mollet), shells removed
1/2 pint velouté sauce of coating consistency (300 ml.)
2 oz. cooked peas to garnish (50 g.)

METHOD
1   Prepare the mince, season it well and mix with a little chicken stock. Put to heat on low flame.
2   Prepare the sauce.
3   Spread the hot mince on a warm dish, arrange the eggs on top, coat with sauce, garnish with peas and serve hot.

Further Suggestions

D   Vegetable Eggs
Serve eggs on purée of spinach or macédoine of vegetables with noisette butter. Serve hot.

M   Curried Eggs
Coat poached, or hard-boiled eggs, halved, with curry sauce and dish up in a border of plain rice. Serve hot.

D   Eggs & Tomato
Put poached eggs on a bed of hot butter beans. Coat with tomato sauce. Serve hot.

M   Cheesy Eggs
Coat eggs with cheese sauce and serve au gratin.

D   Eggs at Sea
Put poached or soft-boiled eggs, shelled carefully, on flaked cooked haddock. Coat with shrimp sauce and serve hot.

M   Eggs Suprême
Arrange poached eggs on a bed of minced chicken. Coat with suprême sauce and garnish with tiny sprigs of watercress.

D   Egg Salad
Put hard-boiled eggs on a bed of green salad and serve with mayonnaise or tartare sauce.

Omelets

There is often a lot of hoo-ha about omelets: though unless you burn one black or drop the whole thing on top of the cat an omelet is much more likely than not to be edible, even the first time you make one. The real point is not to let it cook too much, and not to let it hang about at any stage. Please read through the instructions *before you begin*, so you will know what you are going to do next without fumbling to find the page again.

Omelet pans: if possible, keep a small omelet pan or frying pan just for omelets. Don't wash it: just wipe it out with paper and then a damp dishcloth after use. If it needs scouring rub it with salt on a damp dishcloth and then rinse. If you have a new one, pour in 1/2″ oil, heat very slowly to hazing point, then allow to cool. Pour out the oil, wipe with paper and a damp cloth, then make your first omelet in it.

Notwithstanding all that, if you haven't got a special omelet pan don't deny yourself an omelet all the same. A non-stick multipurpose pan will make good omelets; remember to use matching non-stick tools so that you won't scratch it. If you have a general-purpose frying pan, make sure it is clean and as smooth as possible.

Size of pan: 2-4 eggs go nicely into a 7″ diameter pan, 4-6 eggs into a 9 1/2″ diameter pan.

Number of eggs to use: you can't make an omelet with one egg. You can make a small omelet for one person with 2 eggs. Three or four eggs are easy to handle, five or six are good, but seven eggs in one omelet are too many. How many eggs do you allow per person? This depends a great deal on who they are. A small child probably can't manage more than one egg, so must share an omelet with someone else, but a large, hungry and greedy adult might eat the whole of a four or even five-egg omelet himself. You must adjust the recipe, or make several omelets according to your commonsense.

Water: a little water is added to the eggs to make a lighter, more delicate mixture than eggs alone. Most people find 1-2 teaspoons per egg used about right.

D Plain Omelet
For 2-3 people

INGREDIENTS
5 eggs
5 teaspoons water
1/2 level teaspoon salt
good shake of pepper
olive oil or butter to fry

METHOD
1 Break the eggs into a basin and add the water and seasoning. Break the yolks with a fork and swirl them into the whites, but don't mix them completely.
2 Put a good knob of butter or 1 dessertspoonful of oil into the absolutely clean pan and heat until the butter froths or the oil begins to haze slightly. Tilt the pan so that the bottom is covered evenly with a film of fat.
3 Pour in all the egg mix and stir quickly with the back of a fork (non-stick or wooden spatula for non-stick pan). Shake and tilt the pan gently so that none of the egg sticks, and the runny egg comes into contact with the hot bottom of the pan. When the egg is nearly all set, stop stirring and continue to cook for a few seconds.
4 Starting at the handle side, fold the omelet in half if it is a thick one. (A thinner omelet is best folded into three: fold over one third from the handle side, tilt the pan and fold the other side over the centre.)
5 Turn out onto a hot dish: hold the handle of the pan with your palm upwards, then tilt the pan until it is upside down and the omelet slides out onto the dish held in your other hand. Left-handed people find it easier to hold the dish in the right hand.
6 Serve the omelet at once. It should be piping hot and just creamily set in the middle.

Flavoured & Filled Omelets

Now you know how to make a plain omelet, you can start having fun. Small quantities of flavouring may be stirred into the egg mix, larger quantities are best put in the middle of the omelet before it is folded. A savoury sauce may be used to bind together dry ingredients if you think they may fall out of the omelet, or taste better with sauce anyway. Here are a few ideas, with suggested ingredients to add to 4-5 eggs:

Omelet aux Fines Herbes

Add 2 level teaspoons or more of finely chopped herbs such as chives, parsley or sage to the egg mix.

Bacon or Ham Omelet

Cut 2 small rashers of bacon or 2 oz. ham (50 g.) into dice. Fry bacon until crisp and in either case spread the dice over the pan evenly before pouring in the egg mixture.

Cheese Omelet

Add 2 oz. (50 g.) grated Cheddar or Gruyère cheese to the eggs and, if you like, sprinkle a little more grated cheese on top of the cooked omelet before serving.

Mushroom Omelet

Allow about four medium-sized mushrooms to 4 eggs. Slice them finely or chop them and fry them in butter. Mix them with béchamel if you like. Put the hot cooked mushrooms in the middle of the omelet before you fold it in the pan.

Tomato Omelet

Cut the flesh only of at least two firm tomatoes into dice. Put these into the centre of the omelet, with or without chopped parsley as well, and fold away.

M   Soufflé Omelet

For 4 people

Some people like plain omelets filled with jam, or served with a sweet sauce. In my opinion soufflé omelets are nicer if you want an omelet as a sweet dish; though, equally, some people like soufflé omelets with savoury fillings such as the ones I have suggested for plain omelets.

INGREDIENTS

4 eggs
1 tablespoon water
2 teaspoons rum or liqueurs (optional)
butter
jam, to match the flavour of the liqueur if used
caster sugar to dredge

METHOD

1   Separate the yolks and whites of the eggs. Beat the yolks with water and rum if used.
2   Whisk the whites to a very stiff froth with a pinch of salt. Fold them into the yolk mixture.
3   Light the grill and put a little jam to warm in a small saucepan.
4   Heat the butter in an omelet or frying pan and pour in the egg mix. Smooth it evenly over the bottom of the pan. This type of omelet is not stirred.
5   Cook on moderate heat only for a minute or two. Lift the mass with a

palette knife if you want to see how the underneath is doing: it should be cooked just to golden brown.

6 Put the omelet, pan and all, under a moderately hot grill to cook the top, equally to a golden brown.

7 Make a shallow cut across the middle of the omelet so that it can be folded. Spread over a tablespoonful or so of warmed jam and fold the omelet in half. Turn out onto a warm dish, sprinkle with caster sugar and serve at once.

NOTE: For a luxury touch, fill the omelet with poached apricots and flambé with 1 tablespoon warmed rum or brandy at the table. Serve with whipped cream.

Soufflés

These are soft mixtures, savoury or sweet, which have a very thick white sauce (panada) as a basis, into which stiffly beaten egg whites are folded for lifting power. There is quite a lot of flexibility in the number of eggs in proportion to panada that can be used. My recipe is rich in eggs and holds its shape well, though there are some essential precautions to take. Don't open the oven door to watch its progress, and don't put it down with a bang when you take it from the oven; but the main thing is to get the family sitting down waiting for the soufflé: the soufflé will sit down if it is kept waiting!

D Soufflé *(Basic Mixture)*
For 4 people

INGREDIENTS
1 oz. butter or margarine (30 g.)
1 oz. flour (30 g.)
1/4 pint milk (150 ml.)
4 eggs
seasoning for savoury soufflé
2 oz. caster sugar (50 g.) for sweet soufflé
Oven: Fairly Hot, Reg. 5-6, 375-400 °F

METHOD

1 Grease a large soufflé dish if you have one, or use a 2-pint pie dish. For a sweet soufflé, sprinkle it also with caster sugar.

2 Melt the butter in a large saucepan, stir in the flour, cook, stirring, for a few moments to make a roux, then remove from heat. Stir in the milk a little at a time, blending thoroughly. Return the pan to the heat and cook for 3 minutes, stirring all the time, to make a smooth and very thick sauce (panada).

3 Take off the heat. Stir in sugar if used, and any additions suggested below. When it has cooled down a little, beat in the yolks of the eggs. Season.

4 Whip the whites very stiffly. Use an electric mixer if you have one, or a rotary beater, or wire whisk in a bowl. The whites must stand up in Himalayan peaks when you pull the whisk away.

5 Fold the whites gently into the custard mixture. (If you are in doubt as to how to do this, see page 192.) When the mixture is evenly blended, pour into the greased dish and bake at Reg. 5 or 6, 375-400 °F, a fairly hot oven, for about 30 minutes. The temperature and timing depend on the depth of mixture: a soufflé in a shallow dish needs a hotter oven and shorter time than one in a deep dish.

6 Serve hot, immediately it comes from the oven. A savoury soufflé can be served as the starter to a meal or as the main course at a light meal. Sweet soufflés make good puddings.

Additions to Soufflés

Cheese
Add 5 oz. (150 g.) grated Parmesan, Cheddar or other hard cheese to the panada. Use plenty of seasoning, including a little made mustard.

Ham
Add 4 oz. (125 g.) minced lean ham to the panada.

Bacon
Remove the rinds from 6 small rashers of bacon. Dice the bacon and fry it until crisp. Add this to the panada.

Shrimp
Add 4 oz. (100 g.) peeled shrimps to the panada.

Fish
Add 4 oz. (125 g.) any tasty flaked fish to the panada.

Vanilla
Add a few drops vanilla essence to the panada, or use vanilla sugar.

Lemon
Add the finely grated peel (zest) of 1 lemon to the panada.

Soft Chocolate
Add 3 oz. melted plain chocolate (75 g.) to the panada, and a drop of vanilla.

Dark Chocolate
Stir 1 rounded tablespoonful of cocoa powder into the panada, plus 1 teaspoon grated orange rind.

Ginger
Add 2 oz. (50 g.) finely chopped preserved ginger to the panada.

III PASTA

Macaroni, spaghetti, vermicelli, noodles, as well as lasagne and ravioli are all forms of pasta, made from finely-ground wheat mixed with water and sometimes egg. It is then shaped and dried. The wheat used contains a good amount of gluten, a protein that takes up water, turns rubbery and helps the pasta to hold its shape when cooked. Pasta is also pretty starchy, like potato, and may sometimes be served instead, plainly cooked. It is very often made up into a main dish with sauces or titbits of this and that. It isn't then necessary to serve potatoes as well.

First of all it must be cooked. Sometimes it is boiled in the soup with which it is eaten: vermicelli is often treated in this way. Or you can boil, or rather simmer, pasta in milk, to make a nourishing if unexciting milk pudding. Usually the pasta is cooked in water though, then drained and made up into various dishes. Some of the pastas you can buy have been pre-cooked to some extent, so you don't have to boil them long. Look at the packet to find out if there are any special directions.

Here is a method of cooking Italian pasta:

D   Boiled Pasta
Allow at least 2 oz. (60 g.) dry weight of pasta per person.
Boiling salt water (1 rounded teasp. salt per quart (litre) water).

METHOD
1   Use a large saucepan half filled with boiling salted water.
2   If you have long spaghetti, etc. do not break it, but hold it in a bundle with one hand. Put the end of the bundle into the water. It will begin to soften, and you can then coil it round the base of the pan until the whole length is finally in the water.
3   Give it a stir, then allow it to boil moderately rapidly for about 20 minutes for spaghetti, less for thin noodles. There should be a little "bite" left when it is cooked, rather than letting it become mushy. Stir the panful occasionally to stop the pasta sticking to itself or the bottom of the saucepan.
4   Drain the pasta in a colander. Pour some very hot water over to rinse away loose starch, then proceed as described below.
5   This is a good place to stress that pasta must be served hot, on a hot serving dish and on hot plates.

Pasta with Butter
If the cooked pasta is merely to take the place of potato, you can serve it with a big lump of butter and some seasoning, stirred together.

Pasta with Oil & Garlic
Heat 4-5 tablespoons of olive oil with from 1/2 clove upwards according to taste of finely chopped garlic. Stir this into cooked pasta: for this amount of oil about 1/2 lb. dry weight (225 g.) is about right.

Pasta with Tomato
Cook 1/2 lb. (225 g.) pasta as directed, then stir in 1 oz. (30 g.) butter and 1-2 tablespoons concentrated tomato purée, or pour tomato sauce (page 33) over the pasta spread on a dish.

Macaroni Cheese
Cook 1/2 lb. macaroni (225 g.) as directed, and make a cheese sauce (page 29). Mix the two together and put them into a greased heatproof dish. Grate another 2 oz. cheese (50 g.) and sprinkle it over the top of the macaroni. Brown under a medium-hot grill and serve hot.

Other Ideas for Pasta
You may like to invent your own recipes, ringing the changes with different sorts of pasta and different sauces. Try serving pasta with purée of tomatoes or spinach, with or without cheese, but with butter. Try some cream cheese stirred into the hot pasta. Try pastas mixed with minced ham or chicken, or even with shrimps. Try it with chopped fried mushrooms or peppers, or with fried onion.

D   Spaghetti Bolognese
For 4 people
Strictly speaking Bolognese sauce should be made with a high proportion of liver, but general usage has made it signify merely a meat sauce.

Ingredients
Simple meat sauce (page 33)
1/2 lb. spaghetti (225 g.)
4 oz. or more grated hard cheese: Parmesan, preferably (100 g.)

Method
1 Prepare the sauce according to the directions on page 33.
2 While it is cooking, boil the spaghetti as set out above. Heat a serving dish.
3 When the sauce is ready and spaghetti cooked, drain the spaghetti well and rinse away any loose starch with extremely hot water. Put it quickly into the middle of a large hot dish and pour the sauce over boiling hot.
4 Serve immediately, with the cheese handed separately.

IV RICE

As with pasta, rice dishes are numerous and varied and not yet all invented. In many parts of the world rice is the staple food, as bread is for us. The general rule for peoples who eat it so often is to serve it plain, accompanied by morsels of meat or fish and vegetables, often highly spiced and in a seasoned sauce. On the other hand, European people tend to mix up the cooked rice with savoury bits in one large dish. Both ways are very good.

Plain or nearly plain rice may be served with many meat or fish dishes in place of potato. It goes well with food that is grilled or fried, or food in a highly spiced sauce, such as curry, but not so well with foods in a bland or starchy sauce: don't for instance serve rice with a dish containing béchamel sauce.

There are several kinds of rice in the shops, some of it treated to make it cook quickly. In general, it is important to distinguish between "round" or "pudding" rice, which is highly absorbent and difficult to separate into individual grains when cooked, and "long-grain" rice, which stays whole more readily and is easier to keep in individual grains. If you overcook either, of course, you may get a sticky slush. For many savoury dishes you will choose long-grain rice, because you are aiming at lightness, but for some dishes which ought to have a porridge-like consistency round rice is the best.

For people whose main food it is, it is important to use unpolished (brown) rice, which has a thin skin left on. This contains vitamins of the B group, essential to health. If rice is eaten only occasionally the kind used is not significant.

D Plain Boiled Rice
Allow 1 1/2-2 oz. long-grained rice per person (up to 60 g.)

English Method
1 Put a kettle of water to boil.
2 Boil a separate large half saucepanful of water. Add a rounded teaspoon of salt, drop in the rice and cook quite briskly for 15-20 minutes, until no white core remains when you break a grain in half.
3 Put the cooked rice into a strainer and pour the kettleful of boiling water through to remove stickiness.
4 Spread it out on a baking sheet covered with foil. Dry off in a very cool oven, Reg. 1/4, 250 °F for 10 minutes.
5 Transfer to hot serving dish, fluffing it up with a fork.

D Saffron Rice or Yellow Rice

3-4 portions

INGREDIENTS
1 oz. margarine (30 g.)
6 oz. long-grain rice (175 g.)
1 pint stock (550 ml.)
pinch of saffron soaked in 1 tablespoon of water, or 1/2 teaspoon turmeric
   powder
1 level teaspoon salt approx.
pepper to taste
1 bayleaf (optional)

METHOD
1 Melt the margarine in a saucepan, add the rice and stir with a wooden
   spoon until each grain is coated with fat. Fry it gently for several minutes,
   stirring all the time, until most of the grains have lost their transparent
   look and have turned a more solid white. Don't let them start to brown,
   though.
2 Pour in the stock carefully, as it may splutter. Add the saffron or turmeric,
   some salt depending on how salty the stock is already, pepper and the
   bayleaf.
3 Cook over moderate to low heat, stirring from time to time, until the stock
   is absorbed and the rice tender but not mushy: about 20 minutes. Remove
   the bayleaf before serving the rice, which should be very hot.
4 This rice may be served in place of potato with highly-seasoned dishes
   especially, and see also below.

D Savoury Rice

You can make an enormously varied number of dishes from plain boiled or
saffron rice, either to accompany a meat, fish or egg dish or as a main dish in
its own right. Choose one or more additions such as these, and stir them through
the cooked rice.

4 oz. cooked green peas or sliced green beans (100 g.)
2 oz. sultanas or raisins (50 g.)
2 oz. blanched almonds, fried in butter or toasted (50 g.)
4-8 oz. mushrooms, fried in butter (100-200 g.)
4 oz. onion, diced and sautéd in butter (100 g.)
2 tablespoons diced red or green pepper
2 peeled and de-seeded tomatoes cut into dice
1 garlic clove crushed with a little salt
1-2 hard-boiled eggs, chopped
2 oz. grated cheese (50 g.)
2 oz. cooked chicken livers, chopped (50 g.)
4 oz. cooked fish such as haddock, flaked (100 g.)
3 rashers streaky bacon, chopped and fried until crisp
2 oz. chopped ham (50 g.)
etc., etc.

If the savoury rice is to be a main dish, allow two or more different kinds of
vegetable additions and at least two ounces (60 g.) per person of meat, chicken,
fish, egg or cheese. For a *Rice Salad*, use plainly cooked rice mixed with a
little vinaigrette dressing, and add cold cooked meat and vegetables. Serve
cold.

M   Chicken Pilaff
For 4-6 people

INGREDIENTS
1 1/2 oz. butter (40 g.)
2 medium onions, sliced or diced
2 oz. small raisins (50 g.)
1/2 lb. rice, long-grain type (225 g.)
1 pint strongly-flavoured chicken stock (550 ml.)
1 level teaspoon grated lemon rind
seasoning
1 small clove garlic crushed with salt
2 large firm tomatoes
1 oz. flaked almonds, or blanched almonds cut into slivers (25 g.)
1 tablespoon chopped green or red pepper (optional)
8-12 oz. cooked chicken, cut into pieces (225-350 g.)

METHOD
1   Melt the butter in a large saucepan and fry the onion gently until golden-brown. Stir in the raisins and rice; continue to stir over moderate heat until the rice begins to look opaque.
2   Pour in the stock and stir in lemon zest and plenty of seasoning. Add garlic crushed with salt, amount to taste. Bring to the boil, turn down heat to very low, cover and leave for 15 minutes.
3   In the meantime blanch the tomatoes, remove seeds and cut into dice. Toast the almonds under very low grill.
4   Add the pepper to the rice, stir, and cook for a further 5 minutes, or until the rice is tender and the liquid absorbed. Gently fork in the tomato dice, toasted almonds and chicken, and leave on low heat for a further few minutes to heat through. Serve hot.

Fish

I GENERAL SECTION

Do you know anyone who enjoys angling? Perhaps you do yourself. If so, you might like this poem:

SONG TO CHARM FISH FROM THE WATER

Silver lords of green water, I call to you.
  It is to you I speak.
Come from the coldness of your green water
  up into silver air.

Golden ladies of the clear rivers, I call to you.
  It is to you I speak.
Come from the running of your clear waters
  into calm gold sunlight.

Brothers and sisters in your strangeness of water
  I call to you:
  it is to you I speak.
Come in abundance to my nets and baskets
and forgive me, lords and ladies of the beautiful waters,
  because my child is hungry.

I hope that my hunting song will help your fishing, but if not you can always go along to the fishmonger's. What will you find there? Possibly a traditionally arranged display on a slab, with parsley and pieces of ice, possibly a deep-freeze full of packets.

Choosing Fish

Fish is a perishable food; it is at its best just after being caught, but those of us who live far from the sea or in cities inevitably must have fish that has been refrigerated if not actually frozen. Which kind you choose depends very much on what is available and what you can afford to spend. Generally, frozen food is more expensive because it has been through an extra process of preparation and packing, which must be paid for, and the choice is often very limited. On the other hand, frozen fish may well be better and more tasty finally than wilting fillets at the end of a hot day.

 Here are the standard signs of freshness in fish:

1 If the fish is whole, it should have bright eyes, red gills and a stiff-looking tail. The more scales the better on scaly fish, as these fall off when the fish is stale.
2 Fillets should look firm and not flabby.
3 Frozen fish should be solidly frozen, not starting to defrost.
4 The fish shouldn't have an unpleasant smell. This one is very difficult to detect, though, in a fish-shop full of assorted odours.

Most fishmongers will do their best for you, and I have always found that they will answer questions about their wares if there isn't a huge queue waiting. They are also usually glad to do the preparation for you if you ask: but if you have a fish filleted for you in the shop, do ask for the bones and head (for which you will have paid, anyway) because you can then make a fish stock which will most likely improve your dish no end. If you buy fillets already laid out at so much per pound this doesn't apply.

Perhaps you may have to prepare fish yourself some time. If so, these directions may help you.

Cleaning

All fish (except possibly red mullet) must have the gills and gut removed before cooking. Usually this will be done soon after being caught, or when you buy the fish: watch carefully as this is done, if you can, because the fishmonger is very skilled and you will learn a lot. Unless you want to cook the fish with the head on, cut it off using a semi-circular cut so as not to waste any edible part of the body. In any case slit down the centre line of the fish from throat to vent. Take out gills and contents of the cavity. In the case of a flat fish, make a cut under the head to remove the gut. Keep the roe if there is any—this is in a long sac, of a pale colour usually, and may be hard or soft. This is a delicacy. Use the head for stock but discard the rest of the contents of the fish. Rinse out the cavity and rub away any black skin, using ordinary cooking salt as an abrasive. Then rinse again.

Scales also need to be removed: put the fish down on some paper and scrape from tail to head with a small knife—like stroking a dog's coat backwards. Go over the fish several times if necessary. Wrap the scales in paper before you throw them away or, better still, burn them. Don't put them down the sink unless they are very small or you may block the drain.

Boning

Small and medium-sized fish may be cooked whole, on the bone. Large fish are usually cut into steaks or fillets. Even if you are cooking the fish on the bone you may like to trim off the tail and fins, using kitchen scissors or a sharp knife. This is the way to fillet most common fish:—

Flat fish such as plaice and sole: having cut off the head put the fish on a board with the tail towards you. Cut down the centre, following the line of the bone,

using the sharpest knife you have. Now, with almost a stroking movement, and keeping the blade of the knife close to the bones that divide the fish into two layers, gently free the flesh on the left side of the fish, working from head to tail and holding the filleted part with your left hand. Turn the fish the other way up so that the head is towards you and cut off the second fillet, then turn the fish bone-side to the board and continue, always cutting towards your left (if you are right-handed) until you have four clean fillets and one fish skeleton. The bones go with the head to make fish stock (page 16).

Round fish such as whiting and small haddock: the filleting of these is simply a matter of cutting through the skin to the backbone of the fish, then stroking the knife between the flesh and the bones, which in this case are curved, so that you must make little cuts, following the bones and working towards your left hand which is steadying the fish as you cut. Turn the fillets over to remove any bones that may remain.

Herrings & Mackerel: these have such a lot of little bones that another method of boning is used. Cut off the head and clean the fish if this has not been done. Continue the cut down the belly as far as the tail. Put it down with the opening spread out as far as possible on each side, then press gently all along the back-bone, using your right thumb or fingertips. Do this several times, increasing the pressure each time. Now turn it open side up, take a firm hold of the spine at the head end and pull gently. The spine should come away, bringing with it most of the side bones. Cut it off with the tail fins. Pick out as many of the remaining bones as you can: the rest you must simply learn to love.

Skinning
This can be done before or after filleting, and is also sometimes done to fish left on the bone. It is simpler to do than boning.

Whole flat fish: trim round the fish with scissors to remove the side fins, then make a little cut across the tail, just enough to start freeing the skin from the bones and flesh. Run your thumbs round the edges of the fish between the skin and flesh, then, getting a firm grip on the skin by dipping your fingers in salt, pull it off from tail to head.

Whole round fish: free the skin from either the head or tail end, whichever you find easier, depending on the particular fish, and when there is enough to get hold of, rip it off. Not all fish need to be skinned. Whole fish for baking or grilling are often slashed two or three times on each side through skin and flesh to allow the heat to penetrate evenly. This is called "crimping".

Fillets: put the fillet on the board, skin side down, tail towards you. Using salted fingers, hold down the skin with your left hand. With the knife at right angles to the length of the fillet make a slight sawing movement from side to side, keeping the cutting edge on the skin and pushing the flesh away from yourself with the knife. Gradually more and more skin is exposed, which makes it easier for you to hold it firmly. Try not to cut through the skin with the knife. Fish which is to be served in sauce should always have the skin removed. Use the fish skins (of course) as well as heads and bones to make fish stock.

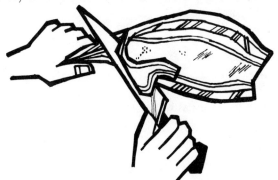

Washing

When you have completed the preparation you intend for the fish, rinse it quickly under the running cold tap and dab it dry with a clean cloth or with kitchen paper which can be relied on not to leave any bits of itself stuck to the fish. Keep the fish refrigerated until you want to cook it if you have prepared it in advance, though if the fish is very thick or frozen it is best just to let it reach room temperature before cooking. If, for example, you try to grill a thick steak of very cold fish, the centre may remain uncooked when the outside is done.

Quantities to Buy

As a very rough guide, allow:

4-6 oz. (100-150 g.) per person of fish fillets

1 lb. (450 g.) per person of whole fish to allow for weight of bones etc.

At least 2 fillets of sole or plaice per serving: 3 fillets are better.

4 oz. (100 g.) shelled prawns or shrimps per person.

Storage

Don't store fresh fish for more than a day or so. Put it in the refrigerator immediately below the cooling coil. If you put it in a polythene bag it will help to stop the smell contaminating other foods in the refrigerator, but leave the bag open so that the fish is slightly ventilated.

Frozen fish should be stored in the ice-making compartment of the refrigerator, following the star markings for your model. If there are no stars, play safe and don't store frozen fish for more than 3 days. Follow the manufacturer's instructions if you have a deep freeze.

II METHODS OF COOKING FISH

White fish is almost entirely made up of water and protein, which incidentally makes it a good choice for slimmers. The fat of such fish is stored in the liver, along with the fat-soluble vitamins A and D. Oily fish, however, such as herring, mackerel and salmon have the fat and vitamins present through the whole body.

The protein part of all fish stiffens easily in heat, much as egg-white does, and needs fairly gentle heat for only a short time to be cooked. It is therefore necessary to protect the fish from fierce heat in frying by a coating of some sort.

Deep Fat Frying — Egg & Crumbing

This is a very popular method of cooking many kinds of fish, including filleted white fish, but ONLY DO DEEP FAT FRYING IF THERE IS AN ADULT AROUND WHO KNOWS YOU ARE DOING SO.

INGREDIENTS

Prepared fillets or steaks of white fish such as cod, hake, plaice, or small whole fish

flour mixed with a little salt & pepper

egg(s) beaten

crumbs made from a two-day old loaf, grated, or perhaps raspings or even bought crumbs

deep fat for frying

METHOD

1 Some people leave on the white skin of filleted fish for frying, but I prefer to remove it unless the fish is very fragile. Cut the fish into portion sizes if necessary. Rinse and dry thoroughly.

88

2 *Prepare egg & crumb assembly line:* have a paper bag with some seasoned flour in it, a plate with beaten egg and brush, and a large piece of paper with a pile of crumbs in the middle.

3 *Egg & crumbing:* put the fillets of fish (or any other food to be coated) into the paper bag and shake to cover with flour. Shake the fillet when you take it out to remove excess. If the food is too delicate for this treatment, lay it on paper with the flour and shake the flour over by lifting the corners of the paper. Lay the floured food in the egg and brush the top over, or turn it if you prefer. Lift with tongs to let the surplus egg drain back onto the plate, then put the food down on the pile of crumbs. The kind of crumbs you use depends on what you prefer, but strictly speaking white crumbs are correct. Lifting one corner of the paper, then another, shake the crumbs all over the fish or other food. It is important to get an even coating, as this protects the food from the hot fat: it must be a seamless fatproof overcoat with no holes in it. If for some special dish you want a very thick layer of egg and crumbs, the process can be repeated, but for most purposes once is enough. Lift the finished crumbed food with a palette knife onto a board, press the crumbs in gently with the palette knife, then leave for a few minutes to set.

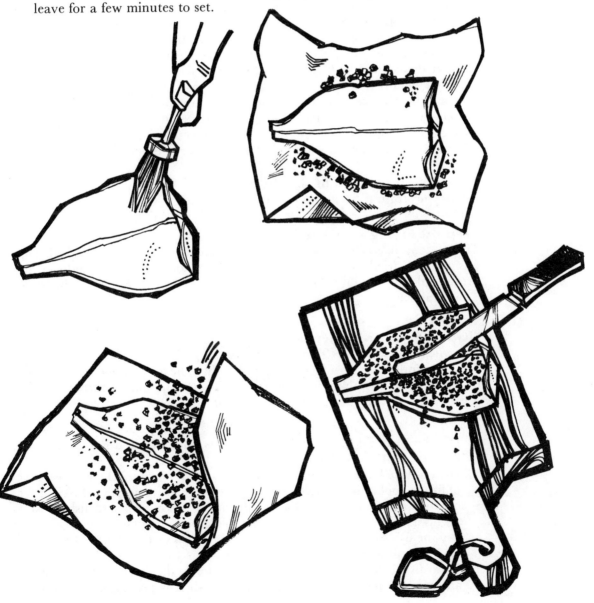

4   *Deep fat preparation:* heat some clarified dripping, lard or cooking oil in a deep fat pan with a basket. Butter and margarine are unsuitable, as well as expensive. YOU MUST PROVIDE YOURSELF WITH A SAUCEPAN LID TO COVER THE PAN IN CASE IT SHOULD CATCH FIRE: TURN OFF HEAT BUT DO NOT ATTEMPT TO MOVE THE PANFUL OF FAT. The pan should be not more than 2/3 full. Test the heat of the fat with a little piece of bread. It should sizzle when you put it in and turn brown in about 1 minute; less than this and the fat is too hot. If it does not sizzle leave the fat on the heat for a few moments more, then try again. It must be hot enough to seal the egg and crumb coating immediately the fish or other food is put in; otherwise you will get a nasty greasy concoction and a bad name as a cook. If you have a thermometer, the correct temperature for frying fillets of raw fish is 360°-370 °F, and up to 380°-390 °F for already cooked things like fish cakes.

5   *Frying:* once you are satisfied with the heat of the fat, put one or two fillets of fish into the (heated) basket. They should not touch each other. Lower the basket into the fat. Regulate the heat so that the temperature of the fat is more or less maintained. Leave the food for 2 minutes, then turn it over, using tongs, if the fat has not entirely covered it. Exact timing depends on the thickness of the fillets of fish or other food. Thin fillets of plaice may need only 4-5 minutes, thick steaks of cod as much as 10 minutes. Remove the food by lifting the basket out of the fat, then lift the food with tongs onto crumpled kitchen paper to drain. Serve it hot as soon as all the food is fried, keeping the first pieces in a warm place meanwhile.

6   Fried potatoes, lemon wedges and fried parsley all go well with fried white fish (make sure that parsley sprigs are quite dry before frying, or they will splutter dangerously). A sauce such as hollandaise, caper, tartare or maître d'hôtel butter is often served as well. Don't have small or fiddly garnishes: it's more important to serve the fish hot.

NOTE: When you have finished frying any food let the fat cool in the pan before you strain it back into a suitable container.

Deep Fat Frying — Fish in Batter
This is done in a similar way to fish that has been egg-and-crumbed. Dip washed and dried fillets of white fish such as cod, plaice or haddock into seasoned flour, then into fritter batter (page 146). Fry at once, following steps 4 and 5 above.

Shallow Frying à la Meunière
(literally, by the miller's wife's method: i.e. in flour)
This is a gentle way of frying, more suitable than the deep fat method for thick pieces of fish or for fish with a delicate taste such as halibut or turbot, though it can be used with success to cook most fish.

1   Dip the clean dry pieces of fish, or small whole cleaned fish into seasoned flour.
2   Heat a little butter in a frying pan, non-stick if possible. If you have a lot of fish to cook it is best to clarify the butter: melt it and pour the clear fat off the sediment. If you have only one or two pieces of fish it isn't necessary. Butter is by far the best fat to use because it tastes best.
3   Fry the fish quite gently on both sides until it is just golden at the surface and will come away easily from the bone, or will flake easily.
4   Put it in a hot serving dish, put more butter in the pan after cleaning out any bits left from the fish, and heat it until it is just beginning to turn

brown (noisette butter). Mix in a teaspoonful of lemon juice, pour it over the fish, and serve hot, garnished with such things as fried mushrooms, fried tomato, olives, lemon wedges and parsley: not all at once, of course.

Dorée Frying (Golden)

This is very simple indeed. Season the washed and dried prepared fish steaks or fillets and fry them in a little hot butter without flour until they are golden brown on both sides. Serve with lemon wedges.

Frying Oily Fish

Salmon is very good fried à la meunière or by the dorée method, but herrings and mackerel are perhaps best fried in a covering of seasoned oatmeal instead of flour. Remove the bones as directed on page 86, but don't remove the skin. Dip the fish first in milk, then in seasoned oatmeal and fry opened out in a lightly greased hot pan, first on one side then on the other. Serve these fish with parsley and lemon wedges.

Grilling

This method is simple and quick: again suitable for almost any fish. Shake white fish in a paper bag with seasoned flour, then dot with little pieces of butter or margarine. Lightly brush over oily fish with melted fat or oil. Slash the sides of thick fish if they are to be cooked whole.

Grill gently, turning once, until the flesh will leave the bone easily and the flakes can be separated. Serve with parsley butter or hollandaise sauce or one of those based on white sauce, such as caper or anchovy. Keep the fish moist on the outside by not having the grill too hot, and, in the case of white fish, by using a liberal amount of fat. Baste occasionally if the fish is very thick and needs a long time to cook through.

Baking

This is a method suitable for whole fish or for large fillets, and for smaller fillets provided they are rolled or folded.

If it is large and to be cooked whole, make deep cuts in the sides of the unskinned fish. Season well, brush with oil or melted butter, cover with foil or butter paper, pour in a little milk, fish stock or water and bake in a moderate oven, Reg. 4 or 350 °F for from 20-40 minutes, depending on the size of the fish: in general allow 15 minutes per pound and 15 minutes over. Large fish are sometimes stuffed. If you add further ingredients such as tomatoes, onions, bacon and so on you will have a fish casserole. Plain fillets of fish are almost always served with a sauce.

Fish is not usually baked completely uncovered or dry because the outside readily gets hard.

Here are some specimen recipes for baked fish.

D   Corny Casserole

For 4 people

INGREDIENTS
1 large can sweet corn—approx. 12 oz. (325 g.)
1 large fillet smoked cod or haddock, 1 lb. approx. (450 g.)
2 large tomatoes
1 oz. butter (30 g.)
pepper
salt only if needed
Oven: Moderate, Reg. 4, 350 °F

METHOD
1 Open the can of corn and drain it.
2 Grease a medium-sized casserole which has a lid and spread the corn over the bottom.
3 Rinse the fish, dry it and put it in one piece on top of the corn.
4 Cut the tomatoes across into thin slices. Arrange them so as to cover the fish more or less.
5 Dot all over the top of the tomato and any exposed bits of the fish with little pieces of butter. Sprinkle with a little pepper; salt may not be needed as the fish is already salted.
6 Put the lid on the casserole and bake in a moderately hot oven, Reg. 4 or 350 °F for 30 minutes, or until the fish flakes easily. The tomato will stop the top of the fish drying out.
7 Serve hot, with mashed potato.

D Baked Plaice or Sole with Sauce
For 4 people

2 large soles or plaice
seasoning
a little milk
butter or margarine
ingredients for any sauce based on white sauce, made with 1/2 pint liquid (1/4 litre)
garnishes: chopped parsley or lemon butterflies or sliced olives, etc.
Oven: Moderate, Reg. 4, 350 °F

METHOD
1 Grease a fairly small deep baking tin.
2 Fillet and skin the fish if they are not bought ready filleted. Rinse and dry them thoroughly. Sprinkle lightly with salt and pepper. Starting at the head end, roll them up tightly with the former skin side inside. These little rolls of fish are called 'paupiettes'. Alternatively, fold them in half, again skin side inwards.
3 Put the fish into the greased tin with a little knob of butter on top of each. Pour in enough milk to reach 1/4" up the sides of the fish. Cover with a piece of greased paper such as a butter paper and bake in a moderate oven, Reg. 4 or 350 °F. for 15-20 minutes, or until the fish looks opaque and is beginning to shrink.
4 In the meantime, make the sauce of your choice, reducing the amount of liquid a little.
5 When the fish is cooked, put it on a hot serving dish and keep it warm. Strain the liquid into the sauce, mix it in well and reheat if necessary.
6 Hold the saucepan handle with your palm upwards. Starting at the left side of the dish, pour the sauce in a thin trickle backwards and forwards to coat the fish evenly. You will find that with practice this way is better than pouring from the middle of the dish.
7 Garnish in any way you like, and serve hot.

NOTE: Any fillets of fish can be baked in this way.
If you make béchamel sauce for this dish, start the infusion of vegetables in the milk before you begin on the preparation of the fish. Then they ought to be ready more or less together.

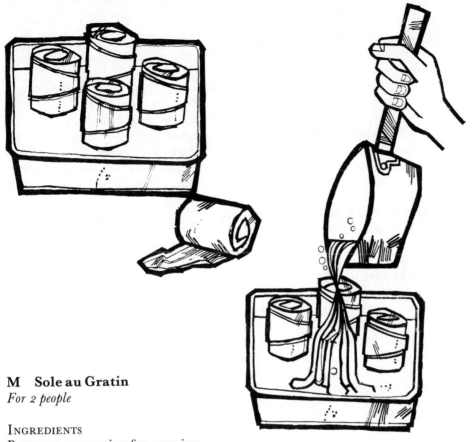

M   Sole au Gratin
For 2 people

INGREDIENTS
Butter or margarine for greasing
1 large sole
seasoning
1/2 medium onion
4 oz. mushrooms (100 g.)
a little chopped tarragon if available, otherwise use 2 teasp. chopped parsley
2 tablespoons dry white wine, or use stock
2 oz. extra butter (75 g.)
2 oz. white breadcrumbs (75 g.)
Oven: Moderate, Reg. 4 or 350 °F

METHOD
1   Thickly grease a gratin dish if you have one: otherwise use any shallow one into which the fish will fit comfortably.
2   Remove the fish head, cut off the fins all round with kitchen scissors and then remove the dark skin only. Scale the white skin, leaving the fish on the bone. Rinse and dry it.
3   Put it in the greased dish and sprinkle with salt and pepper. Chop the onion very finely and chop the mushrooms. Mix these together with the herbs and cover the fish evenly all over with the mixture. Sprinkle over the wine or stock.
4   Melt the fat in a small pan and stir in the crumbs. Spread them immediately over the top of the vegetable mixture and bake in the top of the moderately hot oven, Reg. 4, 350 °F for 25-30 minutes, or until the crumbs are nicely browned and the fish cooked (you can lift a little topping gently to find out).

Poaching
Don't ever actually boil fish because it will break up the flesh and make it tasteless. Poaching is much nearer the ideal. Many liquids can be used: court bouillon (below) is a general purpose one, or you can use wine, cider, milk,

fish stock—even water if you have nothing better. Timing in general is from 10-20 minutes for fillets, according to their thickness, and about 10 minutes per pound for larger fish.

Poaching can be carried out in a shallow covered pan on top of the stove or in a covered casserole in a moderate oven, Reg. 4 or 350 °F.

Always serve a good sauce with poached fish, using the poaching liquid to make it. Although potatoes served with poached fish are often plain boiled or steamed, try to arrange for a colourful garnish or other accompanying vegetable. Imagine how unattractive a meal of poached cod, boiled potatoes, béchamel sauce and steamed onions would look, especially on a white plate.

D General Purpose Court Bouillon
1 1/2 pints approx. (850 ml.)

INGREDIENTS
1 1/2 pints water (850 ml.)
1/4 pint dry white wine or dry cider (optional but recommended) (150 ml.)
1 tablespoon white vinegar or lemon juice (omit vinegar for salmon)
1 carrot, cleaned and chopped
1 small onion, peeled, cut in half
bouquet garni
small bay leaf
1 rounded teaspoon salt
1/2 level teaspoon black peppercorns
fish bones, skin etc. as available.

METHOD
1 Simmer all the ingredients in a covered pan for 1 hour.
2 Strain. Use for poaching fish.

Steaming
Steamed fish is traditionally given to invalids, because it is easy to digest, but it is good to eat when in perfect health, too. Thin fillets of any white fish are suitable for cooking by this method.

Fish can be cooked in steam over boiling water, but I think the following is a better method, as none of the fish juices escape.

1 Remove at least the dark skin from the fillets. Wash and dry them.
2 Grease a plate, lay the fish on it, sprinkle over a few drops of lemon juice, season lightly with salt and white pepper, and put on a shaving or two of butter.
3 Cover with a plate of matching size and put over a pan of boiling water—about half full. Keep the water boiling for 10-15 minutes.
4 Serve the fish with a little sauce and a wedge of lemon, and pay attention to garnishing, especially for an invalid, or the fish may look insipid.

III LIST OF SAUCES FOR FISH

Almost all fish is improved by a little (or a lot) of sauce. It is a good way of varying dishes too: baked cod with caper sauce, baked cod with hollandaise, baked cod with shrimp sauce—and you don't have to stop at baked cod. To show you what I mean here are some suggestions for different permutations. I don't make any claim to cover all possibilities.

1	White fish, fried in egg & crumbs	Squeezed lemon
		Maître d'hôtel or other savoury butter
		Tartare sauce
		Aioli
2	White fish, fried in batter	Squeezed lemon (probably best)
		Lemon sauce
3	White fish, shallow fried (à la meunière, dorée) & grilled	Noisette or black butter
		Any savoury creamed butter
		Caper sauce
		Sauce aurore
		Shrimp sauce
		Parsley sauce
		Hollandaise
4	White fish, plain baked, poached or steamed	Béchamel sauce
		Sauce aurore
		Egg sauce
		Parsley sauce
		Caper sauce
		Cheese sauce (au gratin)
		Fish velouté
		Mushroom sauce
		Tomato sauce
		Hollandaise
		Tartare sauce
		Lemon sauce
5	Oily fish, fried, grilled or baked	Squeezed lemon
		Lemon sauce
		Mustard sauce (i.e. fish velouté well-flavoured with mustard)

IV FURTHER RECIPES FOR FISH

M Salmon & Rice Fritters
For 4 people

INGREDIENTS
8 oz. cooked rice (225 g.)
1 can salmon, 7 1/2 oz. (200 g. approx.) size, inexpensive grade
seasoning
1 level tablespoonful chopped parsley
3 eggs, beaten
fat to fry

METHOD
1 Put the rice and salmon into a bowl. Fork the salmon evenly through the rice, breaking it into large flakes.
2 Mix in seasoning and chopped parsley. Taste to adjust if necessary.
3 Pour over and mix in the eggs to make a fairly soft mixture.
4 Heat 1/2″ of oil or other fat in a frying pan.
5 Drop in dessertspoonsful of the mixture and fry for about 4 minutes, on moderate heat, turning over once. Drain the fritters on absorbent kitchen paper and serve hot, at once.

D Fish Pie
For 4 people

INGREDIENTS
1 lb. any plain, inexpensive white fish fillets, or smoked fish, or left-over cooked fish (450 g.)
1/2 pint milk (300 ml.)
1 oz. margarine (30 g.)
1 oz. flour (30 g.)
2 hard-boiled eggs, chopped
seasoning to taste
raspings (optional)
a little grated cheese
Oven: Moderate, Reg. 4, 350 °F.

METHOD
1 If you are using raw fish, scale, rinse and dry it. Cook it by baking, grilling or poaching with a little milk taken from the half pint. This will take about 10-15 minutes.
2 Discard the skin and any bones.
3 Melt the margarine in a pan, stir in the flour and cook gently to make a roux, stirring all the time.
4 Remove from heat and stir in the liquid from the fish and the milk, little by little. When well-mixed and smooth return to the heat and bring to the boil stirring again. Boil gently for two or three minutes. Add seasoning to taste.
5 Grease a pie-dish and put in layers of fish, chopped hard-boiled egg and sauce, finishing with sauce. Sprinkle over a few raspings if you like and a little grated cheese: 1-2 rounded tablespoons is about right.
6 If the fish is already hot you can brown the pie under the grill for a few minutes. Alternatively, and if the fish needs to be heated through, put it into a moderate oven, Reg. 4, 350° until the cheese is melted and attractively coloured. Serve hot.

NOTE: Cheese sauce can be used in place of plain white sauce, in which case you may leave out the chopped egg. Many people also like some chopped parsley stirred into the sauce.

D Kedgeree
For 4-5 people

INGREDIENTS
5 oz. raw long rice (125 g.) or approx. 1 lb. (450 g.) left-over cooked rice
12 oz. cold cooked fish such as haddock, smoked cod, whiting—salmon even, if you have any to spare (350 g.)
2 oz. butter (50 g.)
3 hard-boiled eggs, whites only chopped
plenty of seasoning: salt, pepper, cayenne
nutmeg
2 level tablespoons chopped parsley

METHOD
1 Boil the rice if necessary.
2 Put the butter and fish into a sauté or frying pan, non-stick if you have one. Heat through gently, breaking the fish into large flakes. Add the rice,

plenty of seasoning, a little nutmeg and the whites of the eggs roughly chopped. Stir gently and allow to continue heating through on very low heat.

3 Sieve the yolks of the eggs, pressing with a wooden spoon to make yellow "vermicelli".

4 Turn the heated fish and rice mixture into a hot dish, smooth over quickly with a palette knife and drop bands of egg yolk alternately with bands of parsley diagonally over the top, using the blade of a long knife.

5 Serve at once as a breakfast or supper dish.

NOTE: The tastier the fish you use, the better. Most canned fish also makes a good kedgeree.

M Paella

For 4 people

This Spanish dish is called after the pan in which it is traditionally cooked and served: a large round shallow one with handles at each side. The ingredients are variable, though they almost always include shellfish, chicken (or rabbit), red or green pepper and, of course, rice. This recipe makes a substantial meal for four people, needing no accompanying vegetable dish and only a light sweet to follow.

INGREDIENTS

4 joints frying chicken
2 tablespoons (approx.) olive oil
1 medium onion, sliced
4 rashers streaky bacon, rinds removed, cut into dice
8 oz. long rice (225 g.)
1/4 level teaspoon saffron, soaked in 1 tablespoon boiling water, or 1 level
    teaspoon turmeric powder
4 oz. sliced garlic sausage (125 g.)
1 medium-sized lobster, cooked, or 1/2 pint prawns, cooked, or 8 oz. crabmeat
    or even canned shrimps (200 g.)
1 medium pepper, red or green, seeds removed, flesh cut into 1″ squares
2 tomatoes, flesh only, roughly chopped
1 small clove garlic, crushed, or to taste
3/4 pint (approx.) stock, boiling (450 ml.)
seasoning
Oven: Moderate, Reg. 5, 375 °F

METHOD

1 Brush the chicken with oil and grill under medium heat until brown, turning once. Set aside.

2 Heat 2 tablespoons oil in a flameproof casserole. Lightly brown the onion

97

and bacon, stir in the rice and cook over medium heat until the rice becomes opaque but not brown. Stir in the saffron or turmeric.

3 Take half the rice out of the pan, then arrange layers of chicken, sausage, shellfish and vegetables, finishing with the second half of the rice; but reserve a few prawns or lobster legs and claw shells for garnish.

4 Put the garlic into the stock and pour over. Season well.

5 Cover the pan with butter paper and the lid and transfer to the oven at moderate heat, Reg. 5 or 375 °F for up to 1 hour, time depending on the thickness of your casserole, until the rice is cooked. Paella should not need stirring, but add a little more stock if the dish becomes dry before the rice is cooked. Serve hot, with a garnish of shellfish or lobster legs and shells of the claws, and with lemon wedges if you like.

NOTE: Of course, if you have no flameproof casserole you can do the preliminary frying in a frying pan and transfer the ingredients to an earthenware casserole at step 3.

Skate with Black Butter   *Joint recipe*
For 4 people
1-1 1/2 lbs. skate (500-700 g.) i.e. two medium-sized wings

M   *Court Bouillon*

INGREDIENTS
1 pint water (550 ml.)
1 level teaspoon salt
2 tablespoons vinegar, preferably spiced
1 bay leaf
bouquet garni
1/2 teaspoon black peppercorns
blade of mace

METHOD
1 Rinse the skate wings thoroughly in cold water.
2 Put all the ingredients for the court bouillon into a large pan and simmer them together for 15 minutes or longer.
3 Strain the liquid, and in it poach the skate for about 20 minutes, or until the skin can easily be removed.
4 Remove the fish from the liquid. Take off the skin and, using a small fish server, free the flesh from the bones that run through the middle of the wings. Arrange it neatly on a hot dish and keep it warm if the black butter is not quite ready.

D   *Black Butter*
This is misnamed, because the butter should be a delicate brown, not burnt. Start the preparation as soon as the skate is cooked.

INGREDIENTS
2 oz. butter (75 g.)
a few capers, fresh or preserved, chopped coarsely
1 teaspoon wine or caper vinegar
seasoning
1 teaspoon chopped parsley

METHOD

1 Put the butter into a small pan and let it bubble over medium heat until it turns brown, but don't let it actually burn or it will be unpleasantly bitter.
2 Remove from the heat and stir in a few capers, the vinegar, seasoning to taste and finally the chopped parsley. Don't overdo the capers or you will overpower the delicate taste of the skate.
3 Pour the butter mixture over the hot fish in the dish and serve at once.

D   Kipper Pâté

Serves 6-10 portions

Here is an economical but delicious dish. You can serve it, cut in slices and accompanied by a crispbread or crusty fresh bread, as a starter for dinner, or with salad as a quick summer lunch.

INGREDIENTS

4-5 oz. kipper fillets (150 g.), fresh or frozen
water
2 oz. butter (60 g.)
1 oz. flour (30 g.)
1/4 pint milk (150 ml.)
1 bay leaf
1 rounded teaspoon chopped fresh herbs: parsley, sage, thyme or rosemary
   etc. as you like
white & cayenne pepper
Oven: Cool, Reg. 2, 300 ºF

METHOD

1 Poach the kipper fillets in a little water to cover them for about 7 minutes, or until they are easily flaked.
2 While the kipper is cooking, prepare a very thick white sauce, or panada, by the roux method: see page 27 if you are in doubt how to do this. Leave it to cool slightly. (There is extra butter to give a good flavour to the pâté.)
3 Grease a small pie dish and put the bay leaf in the bottom.
4 Flake the kipper, removing as many small bones as possible without waste. Mash it in a basin, adding the panada and herbs and pepper to taste. Make sure that the herbs are distributed evenly through the mixture.
5 Turn into the greased pie dish, smooth over the top with a knife, cover with foil and bake at Reg. 2 or 300 ºF, a cool oven, for 1 1/2 hours.
6 Cool the dish. Keep the pâté in the refrigerator before use and eat within a few days of making.

M   Fish Mousse

For 4 people or more

A fish mousse makes a good starter for a dinner party, as it can be prepared well in advance. Any strongly flavoured fish can be used: e.g. finnan haddock, salmon or buckling.

INGREDIENTS

1/4 oz. gelatine (7 g.) or 1/2 envelope
2 tablespoons water
8 oz. cooked fish (225 g.); weight after removing bones & skin
1/4 pint fish stock (150 ml.)
1 oz. butter (30 g.)
1 oz. flour (30 g.)

1/4 pint soured cream (150 ml.)
1 tablespoon mayonnaise and a little crushed garlic, or use aióli
seasoning to taste
2 egg whites, whipped stiffly
cucumber, watercress, etc. to garnish
crispbread or French bread to accompany

METHOD
1 Soak the gelatine in the water.
2 Flake the fish and put it into an electric blender goblet if you have one.
  Otherwise pound it in a suitable bowl.
3 Strain the fish stock. Make a panada with the butter, flour and stock and
  put this with the fish. Heat the gelatine gently.
4 Add the soured cream, mayonnaise and garlic, and seasoning to fish.
  Blend together until very smooth and homogeneous. Fold in the stiffly
  beaten egg whites and the gelatine which should be hot but not boiled.
5 Pour the mousse into a suitable dish. Put in a cool place and garnish when
  it has set. Serve with some crisp kind of bread.

Meat

I GENERAL SECTION

A long time ago there was a quarrel among some cannibals on the beach of their island.

"Roast! I tell you, roast!" shouted the chief

"Nonsense!" said his wife. "He's much too thin. May be young, but look how stringy! Casserole is the only way."

"In my opinion," butted in the head warrior, "pot roast would do."

"I wanted him fried," sobbed the chief's favourite daughter, "with onions."

"Minced and moussed, minced and moussed," chanted the other children, dancing up and down.

They turned to look at the dinner again. But the only thing lying in the sand was a tract, carrying the title "Gluttony", while the lean young missionary was a mere dot on the sea, paddling towards the sunrise in the head warrior's second-best canoe.

In fact, though I'm glad the missionary escaped (and lived to become a bishop), there is some point in being concerned about the best method to cook any particular joint of meat. What will make one cut succulent and delicious will make another—even from the same carcase—dried up, tough or tasteless. Meat is a favourite food for many people, and provides valuable protein, fat, and some vitamins and mineral salts, but it is very expensive and deserves great care in cooking.

Choosing Meat

Buying meat is perhaps one of the most difficult things to do until you have some experience. Even if you have a chart in front of you showing which cut is which, you may not recognise the joint if it is boned and packaged in plastic. In supermarkets, though, meat is always labelled with the name of the cut, and if you are buying from a real live butcher, you will be likely to find him helpful and able to recommend the best way to cook your particular piece of meat.

Here are some of the ways in which you can tell good-quality meat for yourself.

Beef ought to be bright red, not dark, with creamy coloured fat. Joints for roasting are good if they are marbled through the red with fat rather than having a thick layer round the outside. There should not be very much gristle apparent.

Mince should be fairly bright red. If it is pale it means that there is a lot of fat in it.

Veal should be pale pink, mostly lean or with a little whitish fat. The bones are slightly pink.

Mutton ought to be a dull red, with hard white fat.

Lamb should be deep pink, also with white fat.

Pork ought to be pink in the flesh, with white fat. Good joints have quite a lot of fat, but see that it isn't excessive.

Boiling bacon has deep pink flesh, not too much fat though you usually get some: this varies of course with the cut. There should be no yellow or green spots in the fat, but don't confuse this with the normal golden colour of a smoked surface.

Offal must be fresh-looking with no unpleasant smell.

Poultry Chicken should have a plump breast. A pliable breast-bone indicates a young bird—but if it is frozen you can't tell by this method. It should have smooth skin, be fresh-looking and have no unpleasant smell.

How Much to Buy
It is impossible to do more than give a very rough guide without knowing the people, but in general I'd recommend:

Medium/large joints: about 6-8 oz. (about 200 g.) including bone per person. So a 4 lb. joint (1 3/4 kg.) should be enough for at least 8 portions, even with large bones.

Small joints: allow a little more if there is a lot of bone. Small joints also seem to shrink more in cooking.

Chops and cutlets: 1 medium to large per person, or 2 small chops.

Steaks: very variable according to appetite. Say 4-8 oz. (100-200 g.) per person.

Stewing meat without bone or much fat or gristle: 4 oz. (125 g.) per person.
Offal: about 4 oz. (125 g.) per person
Cold cooked meats: minimum 2 oz. (60 g.) per person
Chicken: 8 oz. per person (200 g.) to allow for bones. If in portions, 1 piece per person.

Storage
Meat should always be kept in a cool place, preferably a refrigerator, but allow it to reach room temperature before cooking. Let frozen meat defrost before cooking: it will do this gradually in the body of the refrigerator.

Unwrap all meat and put it in the coolest part of the refrigerator into which it will fit. Joints ought to keep for 4 days or so, thinner things like steaks for 3 days if under the cooling coil. Use cut-up meat within 2 days. Mince, sausages, offal and bought sliced cooked meats should be used not more than 1 day after buying, better still the same day. The rule is that the more cut surface of meat there is exposed to air, the less time it will keep fresh.

Deep freezing is another matter. Follow the instructions if you have a freezer.

Once any frozen food has defrosted USE IT AT ONCE. It tends to go bad quickly. NEVER REFREEZE ANY DEFROSTED FOOD OF ANY KIND, let alone meat.

Cooked meat should be put in a cool place protected from flies until it is cold. Then wrap it in foil or paper to stop it drying out and store it in the fridge. Re-heated meat must be kept at boiling point for several minutes to kill bacteria which may have grown in it.

Using Cold Cooked Meat

A platter of assorted cold cooked meats, sliced continental sausages, thin slices of ham and so on are quite good enough for a party if they are served with salad and pickles, relishes or chutney, and plenty of crusty fresh bread. Pâtés can be a gourmet's delight. If they are good enough for a party, they are good enough for family meals. Most of the resistance to cold meat comes, I think, from people's memories of dried-up and tasteless meat used without any imagination; or, worse, from being faced with shapeless slices of gristle and fat—enough to put anyone off.

If you are serving cold meat then, try to have one piquant kind among the plainer ones: delicatessen sausages are invaluable here. There are French garlic sausages, ham sausages, liver sausages and pâtés in variety, Italian mortadella, German beer sausages, and so on for the length of several shop counters. You need only a small quantity of them to cheer up a lot of plainer meat. They also make good hors d'œuvres for more formal meals. If you are buying cooked meat you may find roast beef, pressed tongue, salt beef, brawn (made from pig's head), jellied veal and others including ham, carved specially for you perhaps, from the large ham on a high white china stand.

If you have cold meat cooked at home, carve it in thin neat slices and remove any large wodges of fat. These can be rendered down in the oven to make dripping. Garnish the plate of meat with bright things such as tomato wedges, parsley sprigs, stuffed olives perhaps, and also provide a dish of chutney or pickle, preferably home-made. Try to serve a salad of a suitable kind for the meat: for instance a Florida salad with rich meat, a Waldorf salad with lean beef. Many people enjoy hot vegetables with cold meat—jacket potatoes, for example, go very well with cold beef.

II HOW TO COPE WITH VARIOUS CUTS OF MEAT

The more the muscles of the animal were used in its life, the tougher the meat will be. Older animals are tougher than young ones. Tender cuts, which are the most expensive, usually taste good—but so do the much cheaper ones, provided they are properly cooked; in fact some people find them tastier. From a nutritional point of view, provided that the food can be digested, protein is protein from whatever part of the animal it came.

Before you can decide on the best way to cook any piece of meat you must know how tough it is likely to be. Although the details of butchering vary from country to country, even from county to county, the different cuts of meat can be grouped into three categories, as follows:

A   Tender Cuts

These often come from the middle of the animal's carcase, near the "waist", and are the most expensive. Cook them by ROASTING, or if in smaller pieces by FRYING or GRILLING.

Beef: middle, top and forerib; sirloin, wing rib, undercut, fillet steak, entrecôte steak, T-bone steak, porterhouse steak; rump, rump steak; minced steak (not mince).

Lamb & Mutton: shoulder; best end of neck, cutlets, rib chops; crown roast; loin, loin chops, saddle; chump, chump chops; leg of lamb, gigot chops.

Veal: shoulder; breast; loin; fillet, escalopes; leg.

Pork: (most of animal) spare ribs, spare rib chops, bladebone; hand and spring; foreloin, chops, cutlets, hindloin, loin chops, loin; fillet, chump chops; leg. Also ham; bacon rashers, gammon and bacon "chops".

B Intermediate Cuts

These generally come from either side of the middle of the carcase, and are often a problem for beginners. If the animal was young and of prime quality, ROASTING, GRILLING OR FRYING may be satisfactory, but meat coming from a tougher individual may need slow, liquid cooking such as STEWING. A compromise is often adopted by POT ROASTING or BRAISING it; or methods of tenderizing used, such as beating steaks to break down the fibres, cooking with wine or other acid liquid, or marinading before cooking, all of which help to soften toughish meat. There are also commercially prepared meat tenderizers, whose active ingredient is papain. Papain occurs naturally in the sub-tropical papaya fruit, and it pre-digests protein to some extent. Pineapple juice, if raw, is said to have the same effect.

Beef: chuck, leg-of-mutton cut; middle, top and forerib of older animals; some rump and rump steak; brisket; aitchbone; silverside, topside and buttock steak of good quality; thick flank perhaps.

Lamb & Mutton: second-quality best end of neck; breast; leg of mutton.

Veal: best end of neck, neck cutlets.

Pork: some specimens of spare rib, bladebone; belly, streaky pork.

C Tough Cuts

These come from much-used muscle, such as the weight-bearing ones in the legs, and the neck, and must be tenderized by long and slow cooking with liquid: i.e. cooked by BOILING, STEWING, making into SOUPS or CASSEROLES, or prepared for PIES. These are the cheapest cuts, and economical.

Beef: neck, clod, sticking piece; blade and chuck; flank, skirt; top rump, thick flank; silverside, round, topside, buttock steak; leg and shin; "stewing steak", mince; salted and pickled joints.

Lamb & Mutton: scrag end of neck, middle neck; shank or knuckle end of leg.

Veal: scrag end; hock, knuckle; "pie veal".

Pork: knuckle end; head (made into brawn); trotters; salt and pickled pork. Also boiling bacon, not necessarily tough, but usually cooked in liquid; ham.

Offal

Offal covers the edible parts of animals such as internal organs, heads, tails and so on. The American name "variety meats" is politer, but not commonly used in this country. Liver is particularly nutritious, as it contains massive amounts of vitamin A and useful quantities of iron as well as protein. Kidneys too are rich in iron. Offal makes a pleasant change from butcher's meat at times.

Here are some of the ways you can cook the most-used types, though I also give some recipes later.

Liver: pig's, lamb's, calf's; grill about 10 minutes, or fry 5-10 minutes. Ox liver has a stronger taste and is tougher, so casserole it or simmer in a brown sauce. Liver can be an ingredient in pâté or pies.

Kidneys: lamb's, calf's, pig's: remove the outside membrane, split with a sharp knife from the outer curve towards the core. Snip out core carefully with scissors, so that you have a circle. Put 2 skewers in at right angles to each other to stop the kidney curling up, then grill; or fry or stew; or use with steak in pies and stews. Ox kidney must be stewed or braised, and is usually just cut into chunks.

Oxtail: stew or make into soup. Needs long slow cooking.

Heart: calf's, pig's, lamb's; can be stuffed and braised. Ox heart needs very long slow stewing to make it tender.

Brains & Sweetbreads: soak in cold salt water to remove blood. Blanch with boiling water, then simmer in a liquid such as stock, wine, milk etc. Serve in a sauce, or with black butter, or egg and crumb and fry them.

Tongue: boil and press, or braise.

Sausages
Sausages are made from minced meat, fat, flavouring and other ingredients. English sausages are usually pork or beef, pork-and-beef, or frankfurter type. They are quick to cook, fairly cheap, fairly nutritious and usually much enjoyed.

To prick or not to prick: opinions vary. I find that if you cook them slowly they do not burst. If you prod them with a fork they are likely to split in the weak place you have made.

They may be fried, grilled or baked, or simmered, after preliminary browning in the frying pan, in brown sauce or other savoury liquid. Mashed potato is the partner in sausage-and-mash.

PORK SAUSAGES OBEY THE RULES FOR ALL PORK: MUST BE THOROUGHLY COOKED.

Timing

Chipolata types (thin sausages, about 16 to the lb.)
Grilled: moderate heat, about 10 minutes. Turn over at half time.
Fried: moderate heat, about 10 minutes. Roll so that they are cooked all over the surface.
Baked: moderate oven, Reg. 4 or 350 °F., about 20 minutes.

Thick sausages (about 8 to the lb.)
Grilled: moderate heat, 10-15 minutes. Turn to cook on both sides.
Fried: moderate to low heat, about 10 minutes. Brown on all sides.
Baked: moderate oven, Reg. 4 or 350 °F, about 25 minutes.

Frankfurters
These are often sold cooked, and need reheating only, in boiling water, or sliced into soup.

III METHODS OF COOKING MEAT

Roasting
Strictly speaking, roasting is cooking by radiant heat, as on a spit in front of a blazing hearth in a medieval kitchen, or, nowadays, on a rotating bar in a specially-made electric oven. The quiet gas-flame or hygienic conventional electric oven are hardly dramatic enough: in fact they bake the meat. But the old name has stuck, and is commonly applied to all meat cooked in the oven without watery liquid. The temperature at which it is cooked varies according to method.

A SEARING METHOD

1 Wipe the meat with a damp cloth. Set it on a trivet or low wire grid if you have one of these, in a meat tin with fairly high sides. Spread the top surface of the meat with dripping or lard.
2 Put it into a pre-heated hot oven, Reg. 8 or 450 °F for 10 minutes. This will seal the outside of the joint. Then reduce heat to fairly hot, Reg. 6 or 400 °F for the rest of the cooking time.
3 Baste at intervals with the fat in the pan.

This is a rather old-fashioned method. It produces meat of very good flavour, but shrinks it considerably. Whatever happened to the joint?

B MODERATE TEMPERATURE METHOD

1 Wipe the meat with a damp cloth. Set it in a meat tin on a trivet and spread it with dripping if the joint is lean.
2 Put it into a pre-heated moderate oven, Reg. 4 or 350 °F for the whole of the cooking period, basting from time to time.

This method is a good general-purpose one. The meat does not shrink so much. It can be kept additionally moist by wrapping in foil—but you must then allow a little longer than the time given for this method below, as the foil insulates the meat to some extent. Unwrap the foil for the last 20 minutes or so to let the meat brown.

Approximate Times for Roasting Meat, which may vary with your particular oven and joint.

N.B. If the joint is stuffed, calculate timing on the stuffed weight.

Beef (Rare or Underdone) and Lamb

Thin joints of meat on bone	Method A	15 mins. per lb. plus 15 mins.
	Method B	20 mins. per lb. plus 20 mins.
Thick joints and rolled joints	Method A	20 mins. per lb. plus 20 mins.
	Method B	25 mins. per lb. plus 30 mins.

Beef (Well Done) and Mutton

Thin joints of meat on bone	Method A	20 mins. per lb. plus 20 mins.
	Method B	25 mins. per lb. plus 25 mins.
Thick joints and rolled joints	Method A	Not recommended
	Method B	30-35 mins. per lb. plus 30 mins.

Internal Temperatures (if you have a meat thermometer)

Beef: rare   140 °F
    medium   160 °F
    well done 170 °F

Lamb & Mutton: 170°-180 °F

Veal

Thin joints	Method A	Not recommended
	Method B	30 mins. per lb.
Thick joints	Method A	Not recommended
	Method B	40 mins. per lb.

Internal Temperature: 165°-170 °F

Pork

N.B.   Pork is always served well done to make sure it is safe to eat.

Thin joints	Method A	25 mins. per lb. plus 30 mins.
	Method B	Not recommended
Thick joints	Method A	Not recommended
	Method B	30-35 mins. per lb. plus 30 mins.

Internal Temperature: 185 °F

Score through the skin on joints of pork to make strips or diamonds, using a very sharp knife, to make it possible to cut through the crackling after cooking. Rub with seasoning before roasting, or, for method B only, with brown sugar mixed with mustard.

Poultry & Game (including *Turkey* if wrapped in foil)

N.B.   Calculate timing on stuffed weight, if stuffing is used.

| | Method A | 15 mins. per lb. plus 20 mins. |
| | Method B | 20 mins. per lb. plus 25 mins. |

Tests for Done-ness

Press the joint with the back of a spoon:

Beef—should produce juice still red for a rare joint

Lamb—should produce reddish-brown juice

Mutton & Pork—should produce brown juice

For *Turkey & Chicken:* prick the thickest part of the thigh with a skewer. The resulting juice should be colourless.

Traditional Accompaniments for Roast Meat

Roast Beef: Yorkshire pudding or popovers, brown gravy, horseradish sauce (grate the cleaned root and mix with cream), mustard.

Mutton: Red currant jelly or onion sauce, gravy.

Lamb: Mint sauce, gravy.

Veal: Gravy.

Pork: Apple sauce, gravy.

Chicken: Grilled bacon rolls, bread sauce, gravy, game chips (crisps), chipolata sausages. Watercress garnish.

Turkey: Cranberry sauce in addition to accompaniments for chicken. If you have no cranberries, use redcurrant or crabapple jelly.

Any of the above may also have a forcemeat or stuffing, and are served with potatoes and at least one other vegetable.

D   Gravy

METHOD

1   Put the roast meat on a hot dish and put it back into the warm oven: the heat is now turned off, but the oven will remain hot for a little while. Letting the joint stand for a few minutes in this way will do no harm; it even makes the meat easier to carve.

2   Strain most of the fat out of the roasting pan into a suitable container. This is valuable dripping. Leave only about 2 teaspoonsful of fat in the pan, but try to retain all the juices.

3 Stir 2 rounded teaspoons of flour into the sediment. Put the pan onto moderate heat on top of the stove, stirring well until the roux turns brown.

4 Take off the heat and stir in 1/2 pint of stock (300 ml.), or water plus stock cube, little by little, blending well. Return the pan to the heat, boil and stir for a few moments. Taste and add seasoning (don't burn your tongue). Strain the gravy into a sauce boat and serve with the roast meat. Some people have been moved to add a dribble of wine to the liquid before boiling: don't let me discourage you.

NOTE: If you prefer thicker gravy, simply increase the quantity of dripping and flour. Gravy browning shouldn't be necessary, but that's up to you.

Now here are a few recipes, so that you can see the theory of roasting put into practice.

Roast Beef with Yorkshire Pudding and Gravy *Joint recipe (sorry about the pun)*
In the days of tradition the batter pudding was cooked under the meat hanging close to the blaze. In consequence the meat juices dripped down to flavour it. In Yorkshire itself I am told that it used to be served before the meat. It helped to fill a hungry hole, so that one would eat less of the expensive roast. You might try the same thing, perhaps, if your budget is tight. More usually, though, it goes with the slices of reddish-brown beef, and plenty of gravy.

The secret of a light, puffy, crisp Yorkshire pudding is simple: make the fat thoroughly hot, in a hot oven, before you pour in the batter.

D *Roast Beef*

INGREDIENTS
1 joint of beef suitable for roasting: e.g. wing rib or rump, or middle, top or forerib (slow method)
dripping or lard
Oven: Hot, Reg. 8, 450 °F to start, then Fairly Hot, Reg. 6, 400 °F
   or Moderate, Reg. 4, 350 °F

D *Gravy*

INGREDIENTS
pan sediment
2 rounded teaspoons flour
1/2 pint brown stock, or water plus stock cube (300 ml.)

M *Yorkshire Pudding*

INGREDIENTS
Plain batter made with 4 oz. flour etc. (page 144)
1 oz. dripping or lard (30 g.)
Oven: Hot, Reg. 7, 425 °F

METHOD
D 1 Light the oven. Weigh the joint to calculate the timing. Wipe the meat over with a clean damp cloth and let it reach room temperature before it goes into the oven. If you have one, put it on a trivet or rack so that the bottom does not fry in the oven, and use a deep-sided meat

roasting tin. If you prefer you can use a bed of root vegetables to lift it off the bottom of the pan.

2　Spread the top of the joint with dripping or lard, especially if the joint is lean, paying particular attention to exposed red surfaces. Usually 2 oz. (50 g.) is about enough for an average joint.

3　Put the joint in the oven, on a middle shelf if it is a large one, but in any case not jammed up against the top of the oven. Baste it occasionally—say every 20 minutes—by scooping up some of the fat in the pan and pouring it back over the joint. Take care not to burn yourself as you lift the hot and heavy pan out of the oven in order to baste the meat.

M　4　Prepare the batter for the Yorkshire pudding as directed on page 144.

5　Arrange with the meat cook to shift the joint down to the bottom shelf of the oven about 25 minutes before it is ready, so that you can adjust the heat to hot, Reg. 7 or 425 °F. Put the dripping in another meat tin and let it heat through in the oven for about five minutes. When it starts to haze pour in the batter and return quickly to the oven.

6　Bake for about 20 minutes in the hot oven on a shelf near the top. The Yorkshire pudding should be golden brown and well-risen, particularly at the edges. Serve it at once on a hot flat dish when it is ready. It should be the last thing brought to table.

D　7　Meanwhile, when the meat is ready put it on a hot meat dish, removing any string that may be round it. Keep it hot.

8　Prepare the gravy as directed in the previous recipe, then serve it with the meat. (A green vegetable and roast potatoes go well with roast beef too.)

D　NOTE: *Popovers* are fun to make. They are simply tiny Yorkshire puddings baked in bun tins. Put a knob of dripping in each compartment, heat for 5 minutes in the oven and fill the tins only 1/2 full of batter. Bake as above, but for only 10-15 minutes. They can be served with savoury things, or with jam sauce as a pudding. Batter made with 4 oz. flour makes about 20 popovers.

D　Roast Pork with Lemon Stuffing

In this recipe the stuffing is baked separately and served as an accompaniment to the meat. Don't attempt to make all these things unless you are already on the way to being an experienced cook; but if you are, this will give you practice in doing a lot of things to serve all together.

INGREDIENTS
1 joint of pork
brown sugar
mustard
salt & pepper
Oven: Hot, Reg. 8, 450 °F to start, then Fairly Hot, Reg. 6, 400 °F (Method A)
　or Moderate, Reg. 4, 350 °F (Method B)
Sage & lemon stuffing (recipe follows)
Apple sauce (page 32)
Gravy (page 107)

METHOD
1　Heat the oven.
2　Wipe the pork with a clean damp cloth. Score the skin neatly with a very sharp knife, then rub it all over with brown sugar mixed with a little dry mustard and sprinkle with salt and pepper. Weigh the joint and calculate the time it will take to cook.

3 Put it in the oven and bake it according to the directions for method A or B according to the thickness of your joint (see pages 106-7). Don't forget to baste the meat at about 20-minute intervals.
4 Meanwhile prepare the stuffing. Bake it on a shelf just below the joint for the last half hour of cooking time.
5 Make the apple sauce.
6 Make the gravy.
7 Serve all hot: if you are very skilled, with a green vegetable and perhaps potatoes steamed in their jackets.

D Sage & Lemon Stuffing

INGREDIENTS
3 oz. fresh white breadcrumbs (100 g.) or use 3 medium slices of bread, crusts removed, cut into dice
1 egg
1 rounded teaspoon chopped fresh sage, or 1 level teaspoon dried sage
grated rind and squeezed juice of 1/2 lemon
1 level teaspoon salt
1/4 level teaspoon white pepper
pinch cayenne pepper
1 medium onion
2 oz. margarine (50 g.)
Oven: Moderate, Reg. 4, 350 °F

METHOD
1 Put all the ingredients except the onion and margarine into a basin.
2 Chop the onion, then fry it gently in the margarine until it is soft but not brown.
3 Add the onion and fat to the other ingredients and beat and mash all together until well mixed.
4 Use for stuffing pork and lamb, or bake in a greased pie-dish covered with foil for about 30 minutes in a moderate oven, Reg. 4 or 350 °F (or on the shelf immediately below roasting meat), and serve as an accompaniment.

Roast Chicken with Accompaniments *Joint recipe*
8 servings with luck

INGREDIENTS
D Sage & onion stuffing (recipe follows)
1 roasting chicken, approx. 4 lbs. (2 kg.)
2 oz. lard or chicken dripping (50 g.)
watercress

For giblet stock
1 onion
1-2 cloves
bay leaf
water

To accompany
M bread sauce (page 31)
M bacon rolls or chipolata sausages (page 112)

M *Gravy* (method on page 107)
pan juices

1 level tablespoon flour
1/2 pint giblet stock (300 ml.)
a little yeast extract or chicken stock cube
seasoning
Oven: Moderate, Reg. 4, 350 °F

METHOD
1 Wipe the chicken with a clean damp cloth, and if it is a frozen one make
   sure that it is thoroughly defrosted. The cavity should be rinsed out with
   cold water.
2 Remember to remove the giblets! Put them into a pan with a peeled onion
   into which you have pushed the pointed ends of a couple of cloves. Add a
   bay leaf too, then cover with water: should be about 1/2 pint. Bring slowly
   to the boil, skim, then leave, covered, to simmer.
3 Stuff the bird with the sage and onion stuffing. This may be done by
   spooning it into the large cavity, or if you don't mind washing a forcing
   bag, squeeze it in with this. No need for a piping tube. But if you have any
   doubt at all about the state of the chicken, don't stuff it: cook it as it is to
   make sure of sterilizing it right through. You can always bake stuffing
   separately.
4 Skewer the bird or tie it into a neat shape if this is not already done. Put it
   in a roasting pan and smear it all over with fat. Put any excess of dripping
   into the pan with the bird. Start off with the breast side down and turn
   over at half time to brown evenly all over. This prevents the breast drying
   out during roasting.
5 Roast in a moderate oven, Reg. 4 or 350 °F and allow 20 mins. per lb. plus
   25 minutes, or until the bird is pleasantly browned and the thigh, when
   pricked, gives only clear juice. Baste from time to time.
6 Remove skewers or string before serving on a hot dish. Garnish with a
   bunch of watercress fore and aft (or parsley if you prefer), and bacon rolls
   or chipolatas. Serve with bread sauce and gravy.

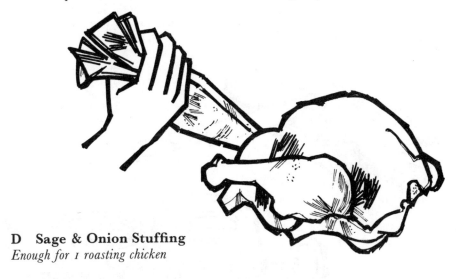

D Sage & Onion Stuffing
Enough for 1 roasting chicken

INGREDIENTS
3 slices bread
3 tablespoons milk
1 level teaspoon salt
good shake black pepper
1 rounded teaspoon chopped fresh sage, or 1 level teaspoon dried sage soaked
   in 1 tablespoon boiling water

1 medium onion
1 oz. butter or margarine (30 g.)
finely grated zest of 1 orange (optional)
Oven: Moderate, Reg. 4, 350 °F

METHOD
1 Cut the crusts off the bread, and then cut into cubes. Put these into a bowl.
2 Heat the milk and pour it over the bread cubes. Add salt, pepper and sage. Leave to soak.
3 Peel the onion and chop it finely.
4 Melt the butter in a small pan (the rinsed milk pan, for instance), stir in the chopped onion and cook gently for a few minutes, just until it starts to turn golden brown.
5 Stir the onion and any butter remaining into the bread mixture. Sprinkle over the grated orange zest if used, and stir vigorously until the mixture is well blended.
6 Either spoon or press the mixture through a forcing bag into the large cavity of a roasting chicken, or alternatively bake it separately in a greased oven-proof dish covered with foil, in a moderate oven, Reg. 4, 350 °F for about 30 minutes.

Bacon Rolls

INGREDIENTS
2 rashers of streaky bacon per person

METHOD
1 Cut the rinds off the rashers. Run the blade of a knife along each rasher to flatten and stretch it. Cut in half.
2 Roll each half rasher and impale the rolls on skewers.
3 Grill under moderate heat for about 7 minutes, turning over once, until crisp on the outside.
4 Pull the skewer through the tines of a fork to remove the bacon rolls. Arrange them round chicken or turkey as a garnish.

Chipolata Sausages
These are very good served with roast chicken or turkey, and they help to "stretch" the birds, if that is what you want. Directions for cooking them are on page 105.

M   Pot Roasting

There is some confusion about the exact definition of this term. Some people use it to mean the cooking of a small joint in a covered saucepan or casserole, with a little fat, over low heat on top of the stove or in a slow oven. This is a gentle baking process. Other people add some liquid, and possibly vegetables, to the pan, so that extra steam will be formed, which adds up to a simple braising process. My own view is that small joints of meat, perhaps on the tough side, would be better properly braised anyway; but as it is a simple method that might be useful to you, here are directions.

INGREDIENTS
1 small joint of beef, wiped and with excess fat removed
2 oz. dripping (50 g.)
1 tablespoon water

METHOD
1   Seal the meat all over the surface in hot dripping (or lard), using a pan just large enough to hold the joint comfortably. Take care, as the pan gets very hot and the joint tends to stick.
2   Reduce the heat. Add a tablespoonful of water, carefully to avoid splutters. Put on the lid and cook gently over low heat for 30-40 minutes per lb. weight of the joint.
3   Dish up the meat, remove excess fat from the liquid in the pan and make gravy as usual.

Grilling

This is an excellent method of cooking small thin pieces of tender meat, especially chops, cutlets and steaks. The rules are simple, as these typical recipes will show you.

D   Grilled Lamb Chops

INGREDIENTS
1-2 lamb chops per person
oil or melted butter
1 pat maître d'hôtel butter for each chop, chilled
a little watercress to garnish, washed and dried

METHOD
1   Light or turn on the grill, and put the grill pan under with its grid to heat.
2   Wipe the chops with a damp cloth and trim off excessive fat if necessary. Brush them over with oil or melted butter on both sides, but don't season them: salt would draw out the juices of the meat which you want to keep inside the chop.
3   When the grill is hot, brush over the grid with oil or butter, too, before laying the chops on it. This prevents the raw meat from sticking to the wires and tearing when you turn it over.
4   Put the chops under the heat to seal the surface, then turn to the other side, using tongs or spoons to do so. Never use a fork, as this pricks the sealed surface, letting the juices run.
5   When both sides of the chops are sealed, reduce the heat to moderate and continue cooking, turning the chops once more, until they are done to your satisfaction: I can only give an approximate time of 8-12 minutes, as the thickness of the chops and the heat of the grill will vary on different occasions. If you press the chop gently in the meaty part, a little juice will

escape: if it is very red, the chop is still not cooked; turning brown means that it is medium-well done, and if there is no juice the chop is overcooked. The surface should be browned but not burnt.

6   Arrange the cooked chops on a heated dish, put a pat of chilled maître d'hôtel butter in the centre of each, and some watercress at the ends of the dish to garnish it. Serve hot, and at once. The savoury butter should not be completely melted by the time the chops are on the table.

D   Steak with Peppercorns   *(Steak au Poivre)*
Steak is perhaps most often grilled quite plain, in exactly the same way as chops, but you may like to try this way too.

INGREDIENTS
Steak
2 tablespoons black or white peppercorns to each rump steak or equivalent smaller ones.
butter to grill
maître d'hôtel butter, shaped into pats and chilled, for garnish

METHOD
1   Let the steak reach room temperature. Heat the grill.
2   Put the peppercorns in a paper bag, then roll over them with a rolling pin so that they are coarsely crushed. If you leave them in comparatively large pieces they taste spicy rather than fiery.
3   Brush the steak with butter, then press the pepper into the surface. Brush over the grill grid with butter.
4   Grill for 1 minute on each side under fierce heat, then reduce heat slightly and cook for a further 2-6 minutes on each side, depending on thickness and your preference for rare meat or otherwise. Don't overcook.

M   Marinaded Steak

INGREDIENTS

For each rump steak or 3 smaller steaks allow:
1 1/2 tablespoons red wine or wine vinegar
1 tablespoon olive oil
1 clove garlic, crushed (optional)
bay leaf
a few peppercorns
butter to cook if necessary
maître d'hôtel butter to garnish, chilled

METHOD
1   Mix the wine or vinegar with the oil and flavourings.
2   Lay the steak(s) in this mixture and baste and turn occasionally. Leave for the very minimum of 1 hour, but better for up to 24 hours to give the meat time to tenderize.
3   Grill for between 3-7 minutes on each side. The marinade may supply sufficient fat, or you may need a little extra butter for grilling. Whatever is left of the marinade can be strained and added to a sauce or gravy on another occasion: but don't keep it very long.

D   Mixed Grill
The only difficulty in this is the timing, because the different items cook at different speeds.

INGREDIENTS

For each person allow:
1 thick pork sausage
1 lamb cutlet
1 lamb's kidney
1-2 large open mushrooms
seasoning
oil or melted butter
1 medium tomato
1 rasher back bacon
watercress, washed and dried, for garnish
1-2 pats maître d'hôtel butter, chilled

METHOD

1   Prepare all the ingredients for grilling, putting them in order on a board
    as you do so. Separate the sausages. Wipe the cutlets and if necessary trim
    away surplus fat. Brush the cutlets with oil. Remove the skin from the
    kidneys, then partially split them with a sharp knife to make a circle of
    each one. Cut out the core in the middle with kitchen scissors. Brush with
    oil. Take out the mushroom stalks (use them for something else), then
    rinse the caps, drain, sprinkle the black sides with seasoning and brush
    with fat. Wash and cut the tomatoes in half, cut a cross in the centre of
    the cut surface, sprinkle with seasoning and brush with oil. Snip off the
    bacon rind with kitchen scissors.

2   Heat the grill and grill pan. Brush over the grid with oil or butter. Turn the heat to moderate, then go on like this:
Grill the sausages for 2 minutes, then start cutlets and kidneys.
Grill for 2 minutes, then start the tomatoes and mushrooms.
Grill for 2 minutes, turn the cutlets, kidneys and sausages, then start the bacon.
Grill for 2 minutes and turn the bacon over.
Grill for 2 more minutes—and hey presto! Everything should be ready. (If not, remove the cooked items and continue to grill the rest until ready.) Dish immediately on a hot serving dish or individual plates, garnish with watercress, put a pat of maître d'hôtel butter on the cutlet and/or kidney and serve at once, perhaps with fried potatoes.

M   Kebabs
4-6 portions

INGREDIENTS
1 1/4 lbs. any lean and tender meat: lamb, mutton, veal, etc. (600 g.)
seasoning
1 onion, minced or grated, or 1 clove garlic, crushed
2 tablespoons olive oil
2 tablespoons wine or lemon juice
bay leaf
1 medium-sized green pepper, flesh only, cut into 1″ squares
4 large tomatoes, cut into quarters
8 or more button mushrooms, or equivalent larger ones cut into quarters
oil or melted butter
boiled rice to accompany

METHOD
1   Cut the meat into 1″ cubes and rub in some seasoning.
2   Put into a basin and sprinkle over the onion or garlic, oil, lemon juice or wine. Give it a stir to make sure things are well distributed and bury the bay leaf in the middle.. Leave in a cool place to marinade for 12-24 hours.
3   To cook, impale cubes of meat onto 4 or more long skewers alternately with pieces of the vegetables. Brush over the top with oil or butter and grill under medium heat for about 5 minutes. Turn the kebabs and brush the other side with oil; grill again for about 5 minutes.
4   Serve on a bed of rice.

NOTE: Kidneys and liver can also be used in this way, but these don't need marinading. Bacon rolls, slices of onion, bay leaves and even pineapple chunks are possible additions or variations. The green pepper may be blanched before use if you prefer.

Frying
Cuts of meat that are tender enough to be grilled can, alternatively, be fried. Don't let the fat get too hot or the outside of the meat will burn before the inside has had a chance to cook. Always serve fried food as quickly as possible after it's done.

D   Fried Liver & Bacon
For 4 people

INGREDIENTS
1 lb. calf's, sheep's or pig's liver (450 g.)
seasoned flour

4-8 rashers any sort of bacon, though streaky and back cuts are especially
  suitable
fat for frying
1/4 pint brown stock, or water plus 1 level teaspoon yeast extract (150 ml.)

METHOD
1 Rinse the liver under the running cold tap and remove any large tubes
  and obvious membranes. Cut it into 1/2″ slices if this has not been done,
  then into convenient pieces.
2 Put one or two pieces at a time into a paper bag with some seasoned flour—
  say a tablespoonful—and shake until evenly coated. Cut off the bacon
  rinds.
3 Heat a little dripping in the frying pan, and when just starting to give
  off a heat-haze put in the bacon and fry it on both sides. I like it crisp,
  myself. Take it out and keep hot.
4 Fry the floured pieces of liver on moderate heat, both sides, for a total of
  about 8 minutes, depending on the size of the pieces. Take them out and
  arrange with the bacon on a hot serving dish. Don't overcook: liver gets
  tough. Don't have the pan awash with fat, either. You need only just
  enough to stop the liver sticking to the bottom.
5 Quickly stir a teaspoonful of seasoned flour into the fat and juices remaining
  in the pan. Stir in the stock, a little at a time, bring back to the boil and
  cook for a minute. Strain the gravy into a sauceboat and serve with the
  liver. Plain boiled, steamed or mashed potatoes go well with this dish.

M Wiener Schnitzel
For 4 people
This is a famous and delicious Austrian dish. Opinions vary as to how it should
be garnished: simply, with lemon; or elaborately, with lemon, egg white and
yolk, parsley, anchovy fillets and olives. The important thing is to beat the
escalopes very thin with a rolling-pin or other suitable banging implement,
and not to overcook them.

INGREDIENTS
4 escalopes of veal, cut from the fillet
seasoned flour
egg beaten with a teaspoonful of olive oil
white breadcrumbs for coating
2-3 oz. butter (75 g.)
a little oil
Garnish: (lemon essential, the rest optional)
lemon slices, butterflies or wedges
2 hardboiled eggs, whites chopped finely, yolks sieved
1 tablespoon chopped parsley
4 anchovy fillets
4 stoned olives or a few capers

METHOD
1 Beat the escalopes until thin. Trim them to a neat shape if necessary.
2 Dust them with seasoned flour, egg and crumb them and firm up the
  crumbs by pressing with the flat of a knife.
3 Heat part of the butter and add a little oil. Fry one or two escalopes at a
  time; about 2-3 minutes on each side, on moderate heat. The crumbs
  should be golden brown only. Use the rest of the butter to fry the
  remaining escalopes.

4   Arrange the schnitzel on a hot dish. Lemon is always served with them. The full garnish consists of bands of yellow sieved egg yolk, chopped white of egg and chopped parsley arranged down the sides of the dish, and a slice of lemon with an anchovy fillet wrapped round an olive or a few capers in the centre of each escalope.

D   Fried Gammon Rashers
or Bacon Chops with Fried Apple Rings
For 4 people

INGREDIENTS
1 lb. gammon rashers, thick cut (450 g.) or bacon chops
lard or dripping
2 large cooking apples
seasoning
parsley

METHOD
1   Remove the rinds from the rashers with a sharp knife or scissors. Make little snips at 1″ intervals through the fat part of the rashers, so that they won't curl up when cooked.
2   Heat a little lard or clarified dripping in a frying pan. Put in the rashers and cook on moderate heat for 3-5 minutes on each side. Bacon chops need about 10 minutes all together.
3   While the bacon cooks gently, peel the apples, cut out the cores using a potato peeler, then cut the apples into rings 1/2″ thick. Sprinkle them with seasoning.
4   When the rashers or chops are done, put them on a dish and keep them hot. Add a little more fat to the pan if necessary and fry the apple rings quickly until light brown on both sides. Put them on top of the rashers or chops and serve at once, hot, garnished with parsley. Tomatoes, grilled or fried, and mashed potatoes go well with this dish.

M   Piquant Pork Cutlets
Serves 4 people
I find that a non-stick sauté pan is the ideal utensil for this kind of dish.

INGREDIENTS
1 1/2 oz. lard (50 g.) or 1 1/2 tablespoons cooking oil
1 1/2 lb. approx. pork cutlets or chops (1 piece per person at least) (700 g.)
1 rounded teaspoon horseradish sauce
2 teaspoons lemon juice
3 tablespoons water
1 scant teaspoon finely-grated orange rind and juice of 1 large orange
shake of pepper
scant level teaspoon salt
parsley or watercress for garnish

METHOD
1   Melt the lard or heat the oil in a shallow pan which has a lid. Put in the cutlets or chops and fry over moderate heat for 5 minutes on each side, until the meat is nicely browned on both sides.
2   Mix the other ingredients together and pour over the meat in the pan. Cover with a lid, turn the heat down somewhat and allow to cook gently for a further 20 minutes, turning the pieces of meat over from time to time.

3   By the end of this time the juice in the pan should have all but disappeared. Dish onto a hot platter, pouring or scraping any residual sauce over. Garnish and serve at once.

Braising

This is a good and economical way of cooking poultry, rabbit, even large pieces of fish, and any stuffed or slightly tough joints. It is a combination of stewing and baking. Meat must be sealed in hot fat first, otherwise much of its flavour will leak into the liquid in which it is cooked. For the same reason it is kept up above the liquid by being placed on a bed of vegetables, called a "braise mirepoix". Meat is usually uncovered for the last part of the cooking to let it brown attractively.

A braise is close cousin to a casserole: in fact, if you have a heavy enamelled iron casserole this is a splendid utensil for braising, as it can go from the heat of the top of the stove to the oven. If you use a saucepan, choose one whose handle and knob will not come to harm in the oven's heat or protect them with brown paper. The pan must have a tightly-fitting lid, otherwise the liquid may evaporate and the vegetables begin to burn, as there is comparatively little liquid.

When the joint has been cooked, it is often cut into slices before being served, though, of course, you may also carve it at table if you prefer. The gravy, which some people think is the best part, is strained and served with the meat, being either poured over it or handed in a sauceboat. There is a division of opinion as to what ought to happen to the vegetables. Perhaps they have served their purpose and can be thrown away; perhaps they are too good to waste and should be piled neatly on the meat dish, or rubbed through a sieve and mixed with the gravy. Anyway, be sure to remove the bouquet garni and also any string that may be around the joint before you serve it up.

D   Braised Beef

INGREDIENTS

1 joint of beef, weighing between 2-4 lbs. (1-1 3/4 kg.) Suitable cuts are topside, silverside, flank, brisket, chuck steak or any large pieces of stewing steak.

Braise mirepoix (i.e. vegetables in season to thickly
  cover bottom of casserole, and bacon optional):
e.g.

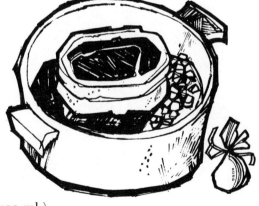

4 oz. carrots (125 g.)
1 large onion
2 sticks celery
1 small turnip
a few mushroom stalks
3 rashers streaky bacon, cut into dice
dripping

Liquid:
1/4 pint red wine (optional) (150 ml.)
1/2 pint stock; or 3/4 pint stock if no wine is used (300 or 425 ml.)

For flavouring & seasoning:
1 clove garlic
1 level teaspoon salt
3-4 peppercorns

1 dessertspoon tomato purée
bouquet garni

Garnish : chopped parsley
Oven : Warm, Reg. 3, 325 °F

METHOD
1 Wipe the joint with a clean damp cloth. Cut off some of the fat if it is very fatty and re-tie the string if necessary.
2 Clean and peel the vegetables and cut them into rough pieces if you are using them merely as flavouring. If you intend to serve them with the meat cut them into neat pieces.
3 Melt some dripping in a frying pan. Brown the vegetables and bacon lightly in this, then transfer them to the casserole with a draining spoon or fish slice. Seal the outside of the meat also in the hot fat, then lift the joint carefully onto the bed of vegetables.
4 Pour in the wine, if used, and enough stock just to come up to the bottom of the meat. Add the flavouring and seasoning ingredients. Bring to the boil on the top of the stove, covered, then transfer to a warm oven, Reg. 3 or 325 °F to cook for a minimum of 2 hours, or 20 minutes per pound of meat and 20 minutes extra for very large joints. For the last 20 minutes take the lid off to let the meat brown.
5 Take the meat out and slice it if you like, arrange it on a hot dish and keep it in a warm place, such as the oven with the heat turned off.
6 Strain the gravy. If it is on the watery side boil it up on the top of the stove to reduce its quantity and concentrate the flavour. Taste it and re-season if necessary. Pour it over the meat or serve it in a sauceboat.
7 Serve the meat hot, with or without the vegetables. Garnish with parsley.

Braised Tongue   *Joint recipe*
Serves up to 12 people

M INGREDIENTS
1 ox tongue, about 4 lbs. weight (up to 2 kg.)
2 onions
3 carrots
1 small turnip
2-3 oz. margarine or dripping (75 g.)
1 tablespoon tomato purée or 2-3 fresh tomatoes
bouquet garni
1-2 cloves garlic
up to 1/2 bottle red wine (optional, but very good)
water

D   *Brown sauce to accompany*
2 oz. dripping (60 g.)
2 oz. flour (60 g.)
liquid from the braise, made up to 1 1/4 pints with water if necessary (700 ml.)
vegetables from the braise
seasoning
Oven : Warm, Reg. 3, 325 °F

METHOD
M 1 Wash the tongue. If you are using the pickled kind, soak it in water overnight to remove excessive saltiness.

2 Prepare the vegetables (except tomatoes) and cut them into rough pieces. Melt the fat in a large pan (enamelled casserole is ideal) and brown the vegetables. Scoop them out and keep them. Then turn the tongue over in the hot fat until the outside is sealed and slightly browned. This will take some time.

3 Remove the tongue from the pan. Pour off excess fat, arrange all the vegetables in the bottom of the pan, put the tongue on top of them, add garlic and bouquet garni and pour in the wine and/or enough water to come half-way up the side of the tongue.

4 Cover, bring to the boil on top of the stove, then transfer to a warm oven, Reg. 3 or 325 °F. Cook for 3 hours or more, until the tongue is tender, turning it over at half time. If you use wine, this will help to tenderize the meat, and so it will not then need cooking quite as long as it does without wine.

5 Skin the tongue and trim it, removing any small bones at the root. Cut it into neat slices to serve hot, with the boiling brown sauce poured over.

D 6 As soon as the tongue is removed from the oven, you take over the rest of the contents of the casserole. Make a brown roux with the dripping and flour.

7 Strain the liquid from the braise, make it up to 1 1/4 pints if necessary with water or stock and use this to make a smooth sauce.

8 Rub the vegetables through a sieve, removing the bouquet garni and stir the purée into the sauce. Reheat if necessary, taste and season well. It may not need much salt. Pour the sauce over the slices of meat.

M   Braised Chicken with Mushrooms
At least 4 portions

INGREDIENTS
Braise mirepoix:
1 small turnip
1 large onion
2-3 sticks celery
2 medium carrots
dripping
1 boiling chicken, weighing about 4 lbs. (1 3/4 kg.) or equivalent chicken joints
1 pint stock approx. (550 ml.)
1 level teaspoon salt
1 clove garlic
1/2 level teaspoon grated zest of lemon
1 bouquet garni
8 oz. mushrooms, chopped (225 g.)
1 rounded dessertspoon cornflour, mixed with 2 tablespoons water
Oven: Moderate, Reg. 3, 325 °F

METHOD
1 Prepare the vegetables and cut them into rough pieces. Brown them lightly in a little dripping and transfer them to a flameproof casserole or suitable saucepan.

2 Brown the chicken in dripping on all sides, and put it on top of the mirepoix. Add all the rest of the ingredients except mushrooms and cornflour. There should be enough liquid to cover the vegetables, but no more. Bring to the boil on top of the stove and simmer for 15 minutes.

3 Transfer the casserole or pan to a moderate oven, Reg. 3 or 325 °F. Cook

for 1 3/4 hours, turning the chicken over at half time. Then remove the lid to let the chicken brown for a further 1/4 hour approx.

4 When the chicken is cooked, transfer it to a serving dish and keep it hot. Rub the vegetables and cooking liquid through a sieve, discarding the bouquet garni. Replace the sauce in the casserole, add the mushrooms and cook on top of the stove for five minutes. Skim off any fat on top and thicken the sauce with the cornflour mixture. Pour a little of the sauce round the chicken, and serve the rest separately.

Casseroling, Stewing, Boiling

In cookery, very often, one process shades off into another. Thus casseroling means cooking slowly in some liquid in a covered casserole in the oven—or on top of the stove. Stewing means slow cooking in some liquid in a covered pan on top of the stove—or in the oven. Boiling means not boiling at all, where meat is concerned, but merely gentle simmering, or the meat will be spoiled: in a pan, generally covered, on the top of the stove. All these have two things in common. The food is cooked in liquid and for a long time. This tends to break down the tough connective tissue and gristle in meat, making it tender, which is why all these methods are used to cook the tougher cuts of meat. Often, though, the meat's surface is browned in a little hot fat first, to stop all the flavour escaping into the liquid.

D   Liver Casserole
4 portions

Ingredients
dripping
3 rashers streaky bacon, cut into dice
1 large onion, diced
1 lb. liver, cut into slices, tubes and membranes removed (500 g.)
1 oz. flour (30 g.)
8 oz. tomatoes, peeled and sliced (250 g.)
4 oz. mushrooms, sliced (125 g.)
1 level teaspoon salt
good shake of pepper
1/2 pint boiling stock or water plus half a stock cube (300 ml.)
Oven: Moderate, Reg. 4, 350 °F

Method
1 Melt some dripping in a frying pan, and lightly brown the dice of streaky bacon and onion. Transfer them to a casserole.
2 Dip the liver into flour to coat it, then seal it in the fat on both sides. Put this on top of the onion and bacon.
3 Put the tomatoes and mushrooms evenly over the liver, sprinkle with salt and pepper and pour over the boiling stock.
4 If your casserole is flameproof, bring the pan to the boil again on top of the stove, and simmer for 10 minutes. Then transfer to a moderate oven, Reg. 4, 350 °F for a further 30 minutes. If your casserole is not flameproof, put it into the oven after adding stock and leave for 45 minutes.

M   Curry
For 4 people
The recipe for this curry was given to me by a Swedish friend married to a Srilankan living in London. I think it can fairly claim to be an international curry! Of course, "curry" is a very vague term in any case: you can have

meat, fish, chicken, vegetable curries ranging from mild to so hot that tropical heat is cool by comparison. The mixture of spices sold as curry paste or powder varies from brand to brand. I can only suggest that you experiment to find your favourite.

INGREDIENTS
1 oz. margarine (30 g.)
2 medium onions, sliced finely
2 rounded teaspoons desiccated coconut
1 lb. stewing steak or shin of beef (450 g.) cut into cubes
3 level teaspoons curry powder, or to taste
1 level teaspoon powdered chillies if available, or to taste
1 fresh or 2 dried chillies
1 scant level teaspoon salt
1 tablespoon vinegar
1/4 pint water (150 ml.)
2 tablespoons milk
boiled rice to accompany

METHOD
1 Melt the margarine in a large saucepan or heat-proof casserole with a tight lid. Sauté the onions and coconut until both are lightly browned.
2 Add the meat cubes and stir over moderate heat until they no longer look raw.
3 Stir in all the rest of the ingredients except of course the rice. Bring to the boil, then simmer covered on low heat for 3-3 1/2 hours, until the meat is tender. Check from time to time that it is not boiling dry. There should be just a little succulent and spicy sauce, which should not require any further thickening.
5 Serve in a border of boiled rice, with more boiled rice to accompany. Serve also chutney, a selection of relishes and poppadums if you can.

NOTE: If you prefer, the curry, like stew, can be cooked in the oven; heat should be cool, Reg. 2 or 300 °F.

D Brown Stew of Beef

For 4 people
This can be cooked either in a saucepan on top of the stove or in a casserole in the oven.

INGREDIENTS
1 oz. dripping (30 g.)
1 medium onion, peeled and sliced
1 medium carrot, scraped and sliced
1 small turnip, thickly peeled and cut into pieces
1 lb. stewing steak (500 g.), most fat removed, cut into 1″ cubes
1 oz. flour (30 g.)
3/4 pint stock (425 ml.)
bouquet garni
bay leaf
1 level teaspoon salt
good shake of pepper
Oven: (if used) Cool, Reg. 2, 300 °F

123

METHOD

1 Having prepared the vegetables and meat as directed, melt the fat in a saucepan (frying pan if you are going to use the oven method). Put in the vegetables and fry them quickly until they begin to brown at the edges. Put them on a plate (or into the casserole).

2 Roll the meat in the flour. Brown this, too, in the hot fat.

3 Put meat and vegetables together into the saucepan or casserole. Pour in the stock, add bay leaf, bouquet garni, seasoning.

4 Either bring to simmering point on the top of the stove and cook for 2 hours, stirring from time, or put the casserole, covered, into the oven and leave for 2 1/2-3 hours; until the meat is thoroughly tender in either case. Remember to take out the bouquet garni and bay leaf before serving the stew.

NOTE: If you are afraid that the thickened gravy may burn in the saucepan, you can leave out the flour until the end, then stir it in mixed with a little cold water; bring to boil and boil for three minutes.

Dumplings (page 141) may also be added to brown stew 15 minutes before the end of the cooking time. A hearty dish.

M Sweet and Sour Pork
Serves up to 6 people
This is a version of the famous Chinese dish.

INGREDIENTS

1 piece streaky salt or fresh pork about 1 1/4 lbs. (1/2 kg.)
2 tablespoons soy sauce
1/4 pint white wine (150 ml.)
shake of pepper
1/2 level teaspoon salt if fresh pork is used, none if pork is salted.
1/4 pint water (150 ml.)
1 medium can (up to 1 lb. or 450 g.) pineapple chunks or pieces
1 rounded tablespoon cornflour
a little water
1 rounded tablespoon sugar
2 tablespoons vinegar
boiled rice to accompany

METHOD

1 Put the pork into a saucepan with a closely fitting lid, and pour on the soy sauce, wine, seasoning and water. Bring to the boil, cover and simmer gently for about 45 minutes. Add more water if it looks like boiling dry, and cook until the meat is tender. Allow it to get cold. Remove fat from the liquid.

2 Cut the meat first into slices, then into chunks, removing any bone but leaving on the rind and fat.

3 Put these chunks back into the liquid in which they were cooked. Add the contents of the can of pineapple, liquid and all. Heat to boiling point.

4 Mix the cornflour with a little cold water. Stir it into the meat mixture quickly. Add the sugar and vinegar, stir well and simmer for 10 minutes to cook the cornflour thoroughly and flavour the meat. Stir often to prevent lumps and burning. Taste and adjust seasoning if necessary. Serve with plenty of plain cooked rice and vegetables such as carrots, peas or buttered cabbage. This is a very rich dish. The sauce helps to offset the fattiness of the pork, but you need to serve only small portions.

Boiled Beef, Carrots & Dumplings   *Joint recipe*
Serves 6

INGREDIENTS

M *Boiled beef*
1 medium-sized boned joint of salt or pickled beef such as brisket, say about
  2 1/4 lbs. (1 kg.)
1 onion
3 cloves
bay leaf
1/2 level teaspoon black peppercorns
1 1/2 lbs. old carrots (700 g.)

D *Dumplings:* suet pastry made with 6 oz. flour etc. (page 140)
chopped parsley for garnish

METHOD
M 1 If you suspect that the beef may be very salt, soak it overnight in
         cold water.
     2 In any case, blanch before cooking. Put it into a pan with cold water
        and bring slowly to the boil. Pour off the water and start again, using
        fresh water. N.B. You need a large saucepan for this recipe to give
        the dumplings room to swell.
     3 Add the flavouring onion, cloves, bay leaf and peppercorns to the
        meat and water. Cover the pan and simmer slowly for 2-2 1/2 hours,
        or until the meat starts to become tender.
     4 While the meat cooks, prepare the carrots. Cut them into two or four
        pieces lengthwise if they are very thick. Put them in with the meat
        and simmer for a further 30 minutes.
D 5 While the meat is cooking, prepare the suet pastry recipe on page 140.
        Divide the pastry into ten or twelve balls of equal size.
     6 Ten minutes after the carrots have been put in, drop the dumplings
        into the liquid in which the beef is cooking and let them simmer, too,
        for 15-20 minutes. They will fluff out considerably.
     7 The meat should be cooked for a total of about 2 1/2-3 hours, but a
        few minutes extra should do no harm if you have under-estimated the
        cooking time of carrots or dumplings. When it is really tender,
        remove the meat from the pot, take off any string and carve it into neat
        slices. Lay the slices down the middle of a large serving dish. Pile the
        carrots into two bundles at each end, and sprinkle chopped parsley
        over. Arrange the dumplings down each side of the meat. Spoon a very
        little of the cooking liquor over the meat, and serve some more
        separately, strained into a sauceboat. (The rest of the liquid is stock.)

IV MISCELLANEOUS RECIPES

D Shepherd's Pie
For 4 people

INGREDIENTS
1 oz. dripping or lard (30 g.)
1-2 onions, sliced
1 lb. lean minced beef (450 g.)

1 oz. flour (30 g.)
1/4 pint water (150 ml.)
1 rounded teaspoon Bovril
1 beef stock cube
pepper
salt if needed

Mashed potato for the topping:
1 1/4 lbs. potatoes, peeled (600 g.)
salt water
3 tablespoons milk
1 1/2 oz. butter or margarine (45 g.)
salt & pepper

METHOD

1 Melt the fat in a saucepan and cook the onions gently until they begin to brown. Stir in the minced beef and continue to cook and stir until it has lost its raw look.

2 Sprinkle over the flour, stir it in and go on cooking for a minute. Then pour in the water carefully, add the Bovril, crumble in the stock cube, sprinkle with some pepper and a little salt (remember there is also salt in Bovril). Stir well.

3 Simmer over very gentle heat, stirring from time to time to prevent sticking, for 20 minutes.

4 While the meat cooks, boil the potatoes in enough salt water to cover them. When they are cooked, after about 20 minutes, drain them and return to the pan.

5 Add milk and 1 oz. (30 g.) of butter or margarine; let these heat through, then mash the potato, using a masher or wooden spoon.

6 Grease a pie dish and put the hot cooked mince in it. Beginning at the sides of the dish and working towards the centre, put spoonsful of mashed potato over the whole surface. Smooth it over, preferably with a palette knife, and then with the point of a knife or with a fork make a design over the top. Dot the surface with little pieces of the remaining 1/2 oz. (15 g.) margarine, and put the pie under a medium-hot grill to brown. Serve hot, with fresh vegetables.

NOTE: Cooked beef can also be used in shepherd's pie, which is a good way to use up left-overs. In this case mince the meat and carry on as above, but cook the mince for only ten minutes.

For *Mince*, cook exactly the same mixture as the bottom of the pie, and serve potatoes separately. It is also often garnished with sippets of toast.

M   Ham Mousse

6 portions

This is a cool and delicate dish, especially suitable for summer. A much cheaper, though still very good mousse can be made by substituting cooked lean boiled bacon for the ham, and evaporated milk for the cream. In any case, serve it with a crisp salad.

INGREDIENTS

1 rounded teaspoon (1/2 envelope) gelatine
3 tablespoons stock or water
8 oz. cooked lean ham, minced (225 g.)
1/4 pint single cream, lightly whipped (150 ml.)
1 rounded tablespoon mayonnaise
pepper to taste
salt if necessary
1/4 clove garlic, crushed, or to taste
2 egg whites, whipped stiffly
lettuce or watercress to garnish

METHOD

1   Soak the gelatine in the stock or water.
2   Mix together the ham, cream, mayonnaise and seasoning: the ham may provide enough salt. Distribute the garlic evenly.
3   Heat the gelatine enough to dissolve it, then fold it into the mixture with the well-beaten egg whites.
4   Turn into a loaf tin 3 1/2″ × 7″ or a ring mould, and leave in a cold place to set.
5   Just before serving turn out and garnish with lettuce or other green salading.

D   Meat Loaf

Serves up to 6 people

INGREDIENTS

1 lb. lean minced beef (450 g.)
1/4 lb. pork sausage meat (100 g.)
1 large or two medium onions, finely chopped
1/2 oz. dripping or lard (15 g.)
1 rounded teaspoon Marmite or other yeast extract
2 tablespoon boiling water
2 oz. mushrooms, finely chopped (50 g., optional)
2 oz. white bread crumbs or very finely diced bread (50 g.)
1 level teaspoon salt
pepper
2 eggs, beaten
1 level teaspoon or more chopped herbs of your choice (optional)
Oven: Fairly Hot, Reg. 5, 375 °F

METHOD

1   Grease a medium-sized loaf tin or large pie-dish, and line it with greased greaseproof paper, e.g. butter paper, with the butter side facing you.
2   Put the mince and sausage meat into a large mixing bowl.
3   Gently fry the onions in the dripping or lard until they are soft and just starting to colour. Add them to the meat.
4   Dissolve the yeast extract in the boiling water and pour it over.

5 Add the mushrooms, breadcrumbs, salt, pepper, eggs and herbs if you like them and if they are available.
6 Now mix all together thoroughly. It takes a little time. I find that a (very clean) hand is the best tool to use, but you can, of course, use a fork or spoon if you would rather.
7 Pack the well-mixed ingredients into the loaf tin, smoothing over the top.
8 Bake in a fairly hot oven, Reg. 5, 375 °F for about 45 minutes, until browned lightly at the edges. Pour off any excess fat, run a knife round the edges to free them and turn out. Remove the paper.
9 This loaf can be served cold, with salad, or hot with hot vegetables and brown gravy.

M Chicken Liver Pâté
8-10 portions

INGREDIENTS
2 rashers streaky bacon
1 medium onion
2 oz. butter or margarine (50 g.)
8 oz. chicken livers (225 g.)
1 egg
3 tablespoons top-of-milk
3 juniper berries, crushed (optional)
large pinch rosemary or thyme, chopped if fresh, or dried
1/2 level teaspoon salt
pepper to taste
melted butter (optional)
bay leaf (optional)
Oven: Cool, Reg. 2, 300 °F

METHOD
1 Remove bacon rinds, dice rashers and slice onions. Sauté in butter or margarine.
2 If a liquidizer is available, put all ingredients up to and including seasoning into the goblet and run the machine until everything is well blended. Otherwise, mince all the solid ingredients finely and mix in the liquids.
3 Pour into a well-greased pie-dish, cover with foil and bake in a cool oven, Reg. 2 or 300 °F for an hour.
4 Allow to cool in the dish, and if the pâté is to be kept for any length of time pour over enough melted butter to cover the sides and top. Put a bay leaf in the middle to garnish. Store in the fridge.

Pastry, Pies & Batters

Now it's time for another story.

Once, long ago, before the Welfare State or anything of that kind, there was an old king, who, one spring morning, was in his counting-house, counting out his money:

"...six pence and eleven is seventeen, and eleven is twenty, er, twenty-eight and fourteen is thirty-something; no, forty-something: oh bother! Now I've forgotten."

He had open in front of him three enormous ledgers, written in green and red and purple ink, and several huge piles of bills, each one longer than the last. They came from the Royal Tuck Shop, the Royal Football Boot Fitters to Their Highnesses the Princes and (the king groaned) the Royal Boutique for the Supply of Party Gear to Their Highnesses the Princesses. There was one from Bee Farms Inc., for one hundred and eighty-three pots of honey for the queen. There was only one for which the king himself was responsible, and that came from the doctor: "To finding the royal pulse, temporarily mislaid..."

The king looked out over the courtyard. He could see into the queen's apartments: there she was at the parlour window, a large lady, with a loaf of bread on the table in front of her and a jar of honey too. It was evidently time for her elevenses, or was it her tenses or twelveses?

Down in the courtyard the six princes were playing four-a-side football. This was difficult, because two of them had to be on both sides—or was it four of them? The king could never add it up. It wasn't easy to think in any case, because there was a loud pop-session in progress in the princesses' room, just below the counting-house. The only thing that pleased the king at all was that the pretty young maid-of-all-work was carrying a basket of laundry out into the garden. He would be able to put on a clean shirt tomorrow, anyway.

Suddenly there was a loud scream from the garden beyond the courtyard. The king thankfully left the bills and went downstairs to investigate.

In the garden he found the princes, princesses and the queen, a honey sandwich still in her hand, crowding round the palace maid, who was sitting on a pile of damp clothes, both hands clutched to her nose.

"Whatever is all the fuss about?" asked the king.

"A blackbird pecked off her nose," explained the queen calmly, as if it happened twice a day.

"Send for the doctor again," sighed the king.

The doctor was the cleverest young man in the kingdom, and in a moment he had covered the maid's damaged nose with sticking plaster.

"You'll be prettier than ever soon," he assured her kindly.

One of the princesses sniffed jealously. The doctor turned. The royal assembly didn't look good. The king's face was lined with worry; the queen had burst yet another button off; and the youngest princesses looked as if they had been up at a party all night (they had). Only the oldest princess and the footballing princes looked healthy.

"You are suffering from too much arithmatic, Sire," said the doctor. "Send the princes to school, so that they'll be able to do your sums for you."

"Hurrah! What a good idea!" said the king, though the princes looked glum.

"The princesses would sleep better if they did some work," continued the doctor. "Perhaps they could cook the dinner, instead of the poor maid, just for today at least?"

"We'll do it if you will stay too," agreed the oldest princess.

"Thank you," said the doctor, "but that reminds me: I suggest, Your Majesty," (he turned to the queen) "that if you ate only three small meals a day, and no snacks, you would turn back into the beautiful slim queen that the people remember."

"Do you really think so?" asked the queen, and dropped her honey sandwich on the grass as they moved indoors again.

At last dinner was announced. The four princesses came into the banqueting hall carrying a large pie, one at each corner.

"Dinner," sighed the king, thinking of money.

"Dinner," murmured the queen, trying to see her feet, but not succeeding.

"Dinner!" anticipated the princes, hungry after exercise.

"Dinner," thought the clever doctor. "I wonder if the oldest princess can cook?"

"Dinner," giggled the princesses, as the king cut into the pie—and a cloud of blackbirds flew out. "They were eating the honey sandwich on the lawn," explained one of the girls. "What a joke!"

"Very funny," laughed the king, thinking how inexpensive it was. (He counted the birds: was it twenty-three or twenty-five?)

"Very slimming," sighed the queen in resignation.

"Not bad," said the princes, tucking into the pie crust. "It's different. What's it made of?"

"All we could find was a packet full of rye," said the oldest princess. "Do you like it?" she asked, and smiled at the doctor.

"A very dainty dish indeed," he said with enthusiasm; but he wasn't really thinking of the pie.

*
* *

I don't know which of the princesses made the pastry, or who caught the blackbirds for the filling. But all pies and flans can easily be made by two people working together: one makes the pastry while the other prepares the filling; in other words all these can be "joint recipes".

I SHORTCRUST PASTRY AND ITS VARIATIONS

Shortcrust pastry is the most useful and versatile of all the pastries. If you knew only how to make this one you would still be able to bake something different with it twice a week for a year. It isn't difficult to make, and when you are expert at rubbing-in it can be made quickly by hand; or if you have one, a food mixer does the job fast and well.

To give yourself practice in rubbing-in, make a crumble mixture before you try shortcrust pastry proper.

D Crumble Topping

INGREDIENTS
6 oz. plain or self-raising flour (200 g.)
pinch of salt
3 oz. fat (100 g.); margarine and lard mixed are good
3 oz. granulated sugar (100 g.) for sweet dishes
1 level teaspoon baking powder if plain flour is used
1/2 level teaspoon spice of your choice (optional)
Oven: Fairly Hot, Reg. 6, 400 ⁰F

METHOD
1 Sift the flour and salt into a wide shallow bowl.
2 Put in the fat and cut it up into half-walnut sized pieces with a knife.
3 Using your finger-tips only, not the palms of your hands, rub the fat and flour together. Lift the mixture a little as you work, so that it dribbles lightly back into the bowl. Give the bowl a shake every now and again so that you mix its contents a bit, and don't go on rubbing in the same lumps.
4 When the mixture looks like fine breadcrumbs, with no large bits left in it, stir in the sugar, baking powder if used and spice.
5 Use to sprinkle over sweetened fruit in a greased pie-dish. Dredge the top with a little caster sugar and bake at Reg. 6, 400⁰, a hot oven, for about 20 minutes, or until the top is just starting to turn colour. If fruit is not yet cooked, reduce heat to warm, Reg. 3, 325 ⁰F and continue baking.

D Suggestions for making Crumbles
Use about 1 1/2-2 lbs fruit (700-900 g.) and 1 1/2 pint capacity dish to serve 4 people.

Almost any fruit can be used: fresh, canned, bottled, dried-and-soaked. Apples, apricots and blackberries, separately, or blackberry-and-apple are all especially good. The fruit must have some juice; if it is of a dry kind add a few tablespoons of water. Also mix sugar with the fruit to taste.

Savoury crumbles are another possibility. Any meat that you would make into a pie can be made into a crumble: perhaps when you haven't time to make a conventional pie (see meat pie fillings, page 137). You need to have a good gravy with the meat, as some of it is soaked up by the topping. Substitute some finely-chopped herbs for the spice in the crumble mixture, or leave it plain.

You can also use this crumble mixture to make a quick flan, pressing it into a plain flan ring (about 7″ diameter) set on a greased baking sheet. Then cover with a neat pattern of any firm fruit, almost drained of syrup or liquid. Dredge with sugar (spice too?) and bake in a fairly hot oven, Reg. 6, 400 °F for about 30 minutes.

All sweet crumble dishes are pleasant served with cream or any custard sauce.

D Shortcrust Pastry

Two things will help to make you .pastry light and "short". The first is not to use too much water, the second (not everyone agrees about this) is to use plain flour, not self-raising; but if self-raising flour is all you have in the house of course that's what you must use.

If you want to make up a big batch of shortcrust pastry and keep it for another day, store it at the rubbed-in stage in a screw-topped jar put in a cool place. This keeps much better than pastry with water added. Simply take out some of the crumble and mix with water when you need it.

Basic proportion: 1/2 fat to flour

INGREDIENTS

1 lb. plain flour (500 g.)

1 level teaspoon salt

1/2 lb. fat (250 g.) which may be butter, margarine, lard or dripping. If possible use a combination of any two.

4-5 tablespoons cold water

Oven: Fairly Hot, Reg. 6, 400 °F

METHOD

1 Sift together the flour and salt if there is time. It isn't completely essential unless the flour is very lumpy, but it helps to make the pastry light. Sift into a fairly large bowl.

2 Cut the fat into small pieces in the bowl of flour, using a round-ended table knife. Then, with a rubbing movement of your thumbs against the fingertips, work the flour and fat together. With practice the movement becomes very light and deft. If you are a beginner try to remember that only the tips of your fingers and thumbs are used, never the palms of the hands. When it is ready the mixture will be in little even lumps like crumbs. There should be no dry flour and no large pieces of fat left.

3 Sprinkle in the water, about a couple of teaspoonsful at a time. Stir and press the pastry together with the round-ended knife between each addition. It helps if you tilt the bowl towards your right hand so that you press lightly against the side of the bowl with your knife.

4 Finally press the pastry together gently with your fingers. The bowl ought to be clean enough for you to wonder (only wonder!) whether it is worth washing it up.

5 All pastries benefit from being left to "rest" for a time in a cool place; say half an hour or so.

6 Using even strokes away from you, roll out the pastry on a lightly floured, dry and smooth surface. Press the edges together to keep them neat if they crack in the rolling.

7 For baking, in general use a fairly hot oven, Reg. 6 or 400 °F. Length of time depends on the thickness of the dish you are making with pastry: tartlets only a few minutes, deep pies very much longer.

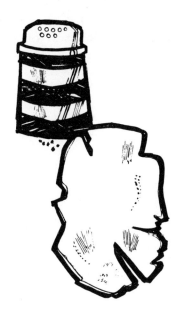
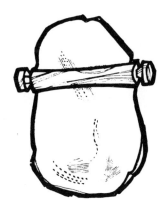

D   Flan Pastry

For 2 flan cases, 7" or 8" diameter

This is a useful variant of ordinary shortcrust. Because it is mixed with egg, not water, it is harder and less likely to break when cooked. The sweet version is sometimes called biscuit crust.

INGREDIENTS

8 oz. flour (250 g.)
pinch of salt
4-5 oz. butter or margarine (125-150 g.)
2 oz. icing or caster sugar (50 g.) for sweet flans only
1 small egg, or 2 yolks, or 1 yolk beaten with 1 tablespoon water
Oven: Fairly Hot, Reg. 5, 375 °F

METHOD

1   Sift the flour and salt into a bowl. Rub in the fat until blended evenly and mixed into fine crumbs.
2   Stir in the sugar if used. Caster sugar gives a more interesting texture, icing sugar a slightly better appearance to the finished pastry.
3   Mix to a smooth dough with the egg, using a round-ended knife. Not all the egg may be needed; or, depending on the flour you are using, it may not be quite enough. In the latter case use a little water. Knead the dough lightly.
4   Leave to rest in a cool place—refrigerator for instance.
5   Roll out thinly and use to line flan rings, or for small tartlet cases, or to cover sweet pies, or even to make small plainish biscuits. Prick them with a fork before baking, to make sure no air-space is left under the pastry. See page 135 for details.
6   If you are baking an empty shell to be filled later, bake it "blind": i.e. prick the base, cover with a circle of greaseproof paper and weight this with a few bits of dried macaroni or haricot beans, etc. Remove the paper and beans a few minutes before baking is complete to let the pastry dry thoroughly. The object of doing this is to keep the pastry flat during the baking: it may otherwise bubble up.
7   Baking in general is in a fairly hot oven, Reg. 5 or 375 °F for about 10 minutes. Don't let it get over-brown. The sugar in the sweet pastry can burn.

NOTE: I have given quantities for two flan cases. If you want one now, it is not much more trouble to make two. An empty flan case will keep well in an airtight tin for several days, or may be crisped in a cool oven for a few minutes. It is often useful to have a spare flan-case by you.

D   Cheese Pastry

This is a useful variant of shortcrust, with several uses. It can be used to make savoury biscuits or cheese straws, as an unusual pie-crust, or to make savoury flans and small canapés.

INGREDIENTS
8 oz. plain flour (250 g.)
1/4 teaspoon salt
shake of pepper
pinch of cayenne
1/4 teaspoon dry mustard
4 oz. fat (125 g.): margarine and lard, or butter and lard mixed.
4 oz. finely-grated cheese, Parmesan for preference but Cheddar will do (125 g.)
beaten egg or egg-and-water to mix
Oven: Fairly Hot, Reg. 6, 400 °F

METHOD
1 Sift the flour and seasonings together into a bowl large enough to hold them comfortably.
2 Using the fingertips only, rub the fat into the flour as for shortcrust pastry.
3 Stir in the finely-grated cheese until well mixed. Sprinkle a dessertspoonful of egg over the mixture, then stir and press against the side of the bowl, using a round-ended knife. Repeat until the pastry can be gathered together into one lump.
5 Knead very lightly until there are no longer any cracks in the ball of pastry.
6 Roll out lightly on a floured board, cut out as you need and bake in a fairly hot oven, Reg. 6 or 400 °F, for seven minutes or more according to thickness. The pastry should be only gently browned.

NOTE: To make *Cheese Straws*, roll out to an oblong, trim all edges and cut into strips about 2 1/2″ wide. Hold a sharp knife as for chopping and guillotine off the straws. Make some rings to hold the baked straws in bundles, using two cutters one larger than the other.

Suggestions for Making Small Tartlets, Large Flans & Pies

Flan, pie, tart, tartlet—name this dish! There is a lot of overlapping, but a flan has pastry underneath the filling and is open on top. A pie is covered with pastry, and may or may not have pastry underneath as well. A tart may be almost the same as a flan, though some people call a fruit pie a tart, too. A tartlet is a small open pastry case, filled for example with jam; savoury tartlets are also known as bouchées when they are made from flaked pastry.

Use shortcrust, sweet flan or a flaked pastry for sweet dishes, shortcrust, unsweetened flan, cheese or flaked pastry for savoury things.

D   Tartlets

1 Always cut as many shapes as possible from the first rolling of pastry, because the more the trimmings are re-rolled the tougher the pastry gets.
2 Use a cutter that seems a size larger than the diameter of your patty tins, to allow for the curve.

3   Prick the bottom with a fork several times, especially if baked empty.

Fillings:
Mincemeat, covered with a pastry lid (damp the edges to make it stick and skewer a small hole for the steam to escape) for *Mince Pies*. Dredge with sugar, caster or icing, after baking.

Jam, added before or after baking.

Lemon curd, added after baking.

Fruit and a glaze, as for large flans.

Fruit and whipped cream.

Any *savoury sauce* (e.g. cheese sauce with cheese tartlets) with minced or chopped *ham*, *chicken*, *tongue*, diced *vegetables*.

Flaked *cooked fish* or shrimps or shellfish, with a sauce or with aspic jelly.

Caviar and mayonnaise.

Hot *scrambled egg* in hot tartlet cases.

Garnish savoury tartlets with parsley, paprika pepper, grated cheese or aspic jelly.

M *or* D   Flans & Tarts
For 4 portions use a 6″ diameter ring, for 6 portions an 8 1/2″ diameter one. If you have both, use a plain ring for savoury flans, a fluted ring for sweet ones.

To line a flan ring
1   Roll out the chosen pastry a little larger than the ring, allowing for the sides. Put the ring on a baking sheet.
2   Lift on the rolling pin, or fold into four, and ease the pastry from the centre of the circle towards the sides and up, pressing with your fingers or a little ball of pastry to exclude air from the angle at the bottom and sides.
3   Trim as illustrated, with rolling pin or knife.
4   Prick and bake blind.

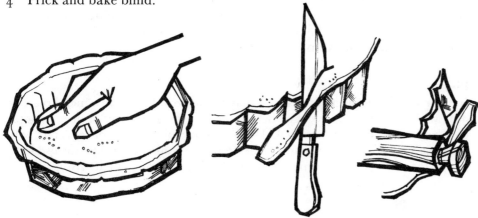

D   Sweet Flans, made from shortcrust or flan pastry, or from a whisked sponge mixture baked in a special mould (well worth buying) are often, but not invariably, filled after baking.

Fillings:
Jam, put into the flan before or after baking, *marmalade* or *lemon curd*.

A thin layer of jam, covered with a *cake mixture*, baked with the pastry, to make a *Bakewell Tart* type of sweet.

Treacle or *golden syrup* and fresh white breadcrumbs, filled into an uncooked flan or tart. Put twisted strips of pastry across the top to make a lattice.

M   *Mousse mixtures*, put in after baking and allowed to set.

Fruit, fresh, frozen, canned, etc. Cherries, raspberries, strawberries, blackberries, peaches, mandarins, pears and apricots are all particularly suitable.

D *Glazes for fruit flans:*
1 Use liquid from canned or stewed fruit to make up 1/4 of a packet jelly of suitable flavour, or use jelly made with water for fruit without juice.
2 Thicken canned or stewed fruit juice with arrowroot: 1 rounded teaspoon to 1/4 pint liquid (150 ml.), using blending method.
3 Clear glaze for fresh fruit: mix together 1 tablespoon lemon juice, 1 rounded tablespoon sugar, 1 rounded teaspoon arrowroot and water to make up 1/4 pint (150 ml.). Boil, stirring, for 3 minutes; pour or brush over fruit while still warm, then leave to set.

Assembling flan
1 Shortly before serving arrange the fruit in the case neatly. Several different colours can look most attractive.
2 Pour the glaze via the back of a spoon so that the arrangement is not disturbed; or brush it on if appropriate. If the glaze is jelly, use just on the point of setting.
3 When set, serve with cream or perhaps curd topping.

Savoury Flans, made from shortcrust, plain flan or cheese pastry, may also be filled before or after baking, and eaten hot or cold.

Fillings:
D Suitable *sauce* with chopped or minced *meat, vegetables* or *fish*, put into baked case. Herbs often enhance flavour.
M *Eggs*, beaten, and mixed with such things as *ham, bacon, cheese, fried onion* and seasoning, baked with the pastry, to make *Quiches* of various kinds. Cream is sometimes used too, to improve texture.
D Curd *cheese*, cottage cheese or cream cheese mixed with minced or chopped *meats* and filled into the baked case. A little tomato purée, garlic, chives and so on may be an improvement.

Pies
In their savoury or sweet forms, pies may be shallow, baked on a metal plate or dish, with the filling sandwiched between two layers of pastry; or deep, in a pie dish with only the top covered. Deep savoury pies are often covered with flaky pastry, though shortcrust or cheese pastry is also used. Do not use flaky pastry for the bottom of a plate pie: the filling will prevent its rising.

D Deep Pies

Fillings:
Meat, such as steak, steak and kidney, chicken, veal. Meat pies can be cooked with a raw filling, but for beginners I recommend that the meat should be stewed first. If you use raw meat the pastry may be overcooked, and you cannot easily tell when the filling is tender. Use 1 1/2 lbs. (700 g.) meat for a 1 1/4 pint pie dish, to serve 4-5 people. Add flavouring vegetables to taste: 1 onion and a few chopped mushrooms for a *Steak and Kidney Pie* for example; season well, and thicken the gravy by the blending method when the meat is cooked.

Fish, mixed with any white, cheese or béchamel sauce, or just moistened with stock or milk. Flavour with herbs perhaps? Particularly good with flaky pastry.

Fruit, such as apples, apricots, berries or mixtures of fruits. Use 2 1/2 lbs.

approx. (1 kg. plus) for a 2 1/4 pint pie dish to serve 6, 1 1/2 lbs. (700 g.) fruit for a 1 1/4 pint pie dish to serve 4. Sweeten to taste, sprinkling the sugar between the layers of fruit as you pack the dish: say 1 rounded tablespoon to each lb. of apples used, for example, and sprinkle with a little water. Add a few cloves to an *Apple Pie*, other spices such as cinnamon, nutmeg, etc. to other fruits as you wish.

To cover a deep pie

1 Make the pastry for a meat pie while the meat is cooking. For a fruit pie make the pastry first and let it rest while you prepare the filling. If two people are working they can start off together. You will need: for shortcrust, 8 oz. flour, etc. for 2 1/4 pint dish, 6 oz. flour, etc. for 1 1/4 pint dish; for flaky pastry 8 oz. flour, etc. for the smaller dish.

2 Roll the pastry into a neat oval rather larger than the pie dish. Put the dish on top and use it as a guide to cut out the shape, but about 1/2″ bigger all round. You should have some trimmings left over.

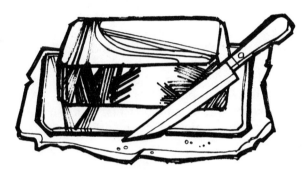

3 Pack the pie dish with the filling. *Meat* should be allowed to cool somewhat; include some gravy but not necessarily all there is—this can be served separately. Put a pie funnel in the middle. *Fruit* should be packed in neatly, and piled into a dome above the level of the dish. No pie funnel is used.

4 Dampen the rim of the dish and put the trimmings, cut side outwards, onto **this. The double thickness** of pastry prevents the edge burning. Dampen this pastry with water, too.

5 Now raise the nearest edge of the lid and ease the rolling pin under until you can lift the whole thing. Put one end into position and ease away the pin so that the pastry falls into place, as illustrated.

6 Press the pastry down firmly all round the rim, pick up the dish and trim away excess pastry from the edge, sharp knife sloping outwards.

7 Put your bent left forefinger on the rim of the pie and, using a small knife, make little cuts from the bottom of the thickness of the pastry to the top, to flake the edge neatly. This is called "knocking-up". Make sure no little burnable bits remain at the edge of the dish.

8 Finally mark scallops as illustrated, 1/2″ or more apart for savoury pies, 1/10″ apart for sweet pies.

9 Decorate a meat pie with pastry leaves (like a raised pie) if you like. Glaze with egg.

10 Sweet pies may be brushed with a little water or egg white and dredged with caster sugar before baking, or baked plain and dredged afterwards. Bake shortcrust pastry for 15 minutes in a fairly hot oven, Reg. 6, 400 °F, then turn down to moderate, Reg. 4, 350 °F for another 10-15 minutes or until the filling is cooked. (Glass pie dish useful?) Flaky pastry is baked for 10 minutes in very hot oven, Reg. 8, 450 °F; then reduce to fairly hot, Reg. 6, 400 °F until the pie is cooked. Allow about 1/2 hour total time when the meat is pre-cooked.

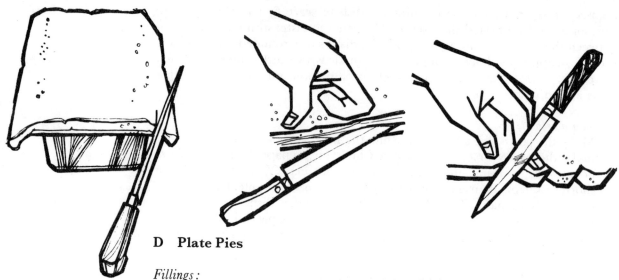

D   Plate Pies

Fillings:

Left-over *chicken*, *game*, minced *ham*, minced *beef* or flaked *fish*, moistened with stock or a little sauce or gravy. Season well, and add herbs if you like. Egg is sometimes mixed in to bind the ingredients together. The meat should be already cooked, as the pastry will not take very long to bake.

Quiche mixtures as for savoury flans.

Fruit, especially berries, apples and apricots. Thicken the juice by mixing a little cornflour, arrowroot or potato flour with the sugar used to sweeten: say 1-2 level teaspoons.

To shape a plate pie:

1   Make the pastry and let it rest while the filling is prepared. Pastry made with 8 oz. flour, etc. is enough for an 8″ pie plate, and 1 1/2 lbs. approx. (700 g.) fruit will be needed to serve 4.
2   Divide the pastry in half. Roll out one part into a circle not more than 1/4″ thick, lift it onto the pie plate with a rolling pin, then press down firmly. Pick up the pie in the left hand and trim the edge level with the plate, sloping the knife outwards and cutting from underneath.
3   Roll out the second half of the pastry. Let it rest while you pack in the chosen filling neatly into a dome shape, remembering that fruit will shrink considerably.
4   Brush the pastry rim with water, lift on the lid and press down. Trim as before.
5   Knock-up the edge as for a deep pie, and make narrow or wide scallops according to whether the pie is sweet or savoury.
6   Decorate if you like, and glaze a savoury pie with beaten egg.
7   Bake in a fairly hot oven, Reg. 6, 400 °F for 10 minutes to set the pastry, then turn down to moderate, Reg. 3, 325 °F until the filling is cooked.
8   Dredge a sweet pie with caster sugar before serving. Good with custard or cream.

II   PLAIN PASTES

D   Hot Water Crust also known as Raised Pie Crust

This is the simplest pastry, and probably the oldest. It is necessary to have it warm for shaping, so you must work quickly. It's important to keep the pie walls thin: a huge wedge of any pastry is unappetizing. Bake it well too, as it is best when crisp and brown.

INGREDIENTS
8 oz. plain flour (225 g.)
1/2 level teaspoon salt
1/4 pint water (150 ml.)
2 oz. lard (50 g.)
egg beaten with 1 tablespoon milk to glaze top

Raised Pie Fillings
For pie to serve 6 portions

INGREDIENTS
1 lb. (450 g.) raw tender meat or game: e.g. pork, veal & pork mixed,
   veal & ham mixed, pigeon, sausage meat.
1-2 teaspoons finely chopped herbs
seasoning to taste
1 egg, hard-boiled and shelled (optional)

Jellied stock:
1 rounded teaspoon gelatine
1/4 pint stock or water (150 ml.); if water is used add 1/2 stock cube and
   1/4 teaspoon yeast extract
Oven: Fairly Hot, Reg. 6, 400 °F to start

METHOD
1   Prepare the chosen filling by chopping or coarsely mincing the meat.
    Mix in the herbs and seasoning. If you have any bone with the meat,
    simmer this for stock. Prepare the boiled egg if you are going to use one.
2   Sift the flour and salt into a basin.
3   Boil the water and lard together. The fat must melt completely. Then pour
    this onto the flour, mixing all together quickly. As soon as your hand can
    bear the heat give the paste a light kneading to make it completely smooth.
4   Cut off about 1/3 to use as the pie lid and put this in a warm place.
5   Quickly roll the rest into a circle about 10″ in diameter.
6   Put the prepared filling in the centre and shape it into a neat cylinder.
    The hard-boiled egg goes right in the middle. Now lift and mould the
    edges of the circle to form the outside wall of the pie. Try to gather the
    edge rather than pleating it.
7   Roll out the lid to fit, dampen the underside and put it on top of the pie.
    Press the edges together, then seal by snipping off a sliver all the way
    round, using kitchen scissors. Crimp the edge with your fingers or with the
    handle of a teaspoon.

8   Re-roll the trimmings. Cut first into strips, then into diamonds. Mark these with a knife to represent leaf-veins, and curl them over your finger. Make a hole in the centre of the lid and arrange the leaves round it, sticking them on by dampening the under surface.

9   Transfer the pie carefully to a baking sheet. Brush over the top and sides with beaten egg or egg-and-milk.

10   Bake in a fairly hot oven, Reg. 6 or 400 °F for 20 minutes. Then reduce heat to moderate, Reg. 4 or 350 °F for a further 1 1/2 hours approximately. You may need to cover the top of the pie with a foil hat after the first hour to stop it getting too brown.

11   Let the pie get cold.

12   Make the jellied stock: soak the gelatine in the liquid, then heat until dissolved. Using a funnel, fill up the pie so that all the cracks where the meat has shrunk will be filled with jelly. Refrigerate to set the stock.

13   Serve cold with salad, for packed lunches or picnics, etc.

NOTE: I think the above method is the simplest way of raising a pie, but there are others. The pastry can be shaped round the bottom and sides of a straight-sided jar about 4″ in diameter. It makes the jar easier to remove if you warm it first. Then pack the meat and egg into the hollow space and proceed as from step 7 above.

    If you have one of the special hinged raised pie moulds the business is of course easier, though the pie will taste the same.

D Suet Pastry or Suet Crust and associated Puddings

INGREDIENTS
3 oz. beef suet (100 g.)
6 oz. self-raising flour, or plain flour plus 1 rounded teaspoon baking powder
    (200 g.)
rather less than 1 level teaspoon salt
5 tablespoons approx. cold water
filling—see below

METHOD
1   If you are using butcher's suet, bought in a lump, cut it first into slices, then into strips and then chop it with a little flour. Remove any bits of papery tissue. If you are using prepared suet it is ready as it is.

2   Put the flour into a bowl and stir in the suet and salt.

3   Mix to a fairly stiff dough with the cold water, using a round-ended knife to stir and press against the side of the bowl.

4   Lightly grease a 1 1/2 lb. size pudding basin (a smaller basin does not allow for enough filling).

5   Cut about 1/3 off the ball of suet pastry for the lid of the pudding. Roll out the rest to a circle about 11″ diameter, to fit inside the basin. Fold it in half so that it is easy to handle, ease it into the basin, then unfold and mould to the sides, avoiding pleats if possible. Some people cut a wedge-shape out of the circle, but this makes a weak place inclined to split.

6   Pack in the filling, adding a little water—say 2 tablespoons.

7   Roll the remaining pastry into a circle to fit the top. Dampen the underside, put on top of the filling and press down firmly at the edges to seal to the pastry lining the basin.

8   Now prepare the covering. Make a pleat across a large piece of greased greaseproof paper, e.g. butter paper. Put this grease side down over the pudding. Take an even larger square of aluminium foil, pleated in the

same way, and mould it closely to the side of the basin, finishing with string tied tightly under the rim to hold the foil in place. The pleats will let the pudding expand as it cooks; if it has no room to do so it will be heavy and unappetizing.

9 Put into a saucepan with water to reach half-way up the sides of the basin. Bring to the boil, put on a tight lid and simmer for 3 1/2 hours for a meat pudding, 2 hours for a fruit one, replenishing the water with more (at boiling point) if much boils away. You need to check this from time to time.

10 To serve, remove the basin from the pan, take off the foil and paper cap, wipe the basin and for a savoury pudding wrap a linen or paper napkin round the outside, with the point of the folded triangle sticking up above the pudding. Serve with a brown sauce and green vegetables, but you won't need much potato, if any. A fruit pudding is turned out onto a heated dish and served with custard sauce.

Suggested Fillings for Puddings
To serve 4
Steak and kidney is the classic, and probably best one. Use 3/4 lb. good quality steak cut into cubes (350 g.) with 4 oz. kidney also cubed (125 g.). Add a chopped onion, a rounded tablespoonful of flour, seasoning and half a beef stock cube. Mix well together. Sprinkle in 2-3 tablespoons water.

Steak or lean *minced beef*, 1 lb. (1/2 kg.) approx. Season well.

Left-over *ham* or *boiled bacon* with skinned sliced *tomatoes* and a few *mushrooms*. If meat is pre-cooked, boil pudding for 2 hours only.

Sliced *apples*, with cloves and sugar to taste.

Blackcurrants with plenty of sugar and a little water.

Apple, rhubarb and a little grated orange zest. Sugar too.

D Dumplings
Makes 12
Cut suet pastry made with 6 oz. flour etc. into about 12 equal-sized pieces. Roll each into a ball between the palms of your hands and drop them into boiling soup, stew or the liquid round a simmering joint. Cook for 15-20 minutes, covered.

III FLAKED PASTRIES

These pastries are the light, crisp and golden ones that melt into flakes in your mouth. This effect is achieved by having alternate layers of flour paste and fat. All the flaked pastries need a lot of rolling to make the layers thinner and thinner but not squashed together. For this reason, though they aren't really difficult, it would be best to become expert at shortcrust pastry first, particularly in rolling it out neatly, with even pressure, into a sheet without ragged edges.

There are more kinds than flaky and rough puff pastry, but these two are enough for most purposes. Though they are to some extent interchangeable, flaky pastry is often used for savoury dishes, rough puff for sweet things.

D Flaky Pastry

Basic proportion: 3/4 fat to flour
INGREDIENTS
1 lb. plain flour (500 g.)

1 level teaspoon salt
3/4 lb. fat (375 g.), i.e. margarine, butter, lard or preferably a mixture of two
2 teaspoons lemon juice
iced or cold water: 8 tablespoons very approx.
Oven: Very Hot, Reg. 8, 450 ºF

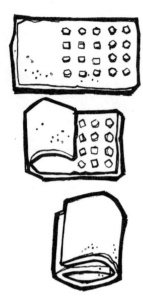

METHOD
1 Sift the flour and salt into a bowl.
2 Put the fat onto a plate and cream it with the blade of a knife until it is fairly soft. Divide this into four portions.
3 Rub one quarter of the fat into the flour.
4 Sprinkle in the lemon juice and mix with enough water to make a smooth and pliable dough. The fat and the dough should be as far as possible of the same consistency. If the fat is too hard it will poke through the dough instead of spreading sideways into even flakes.
4 Roll out the dough, making as neat an oblong as possible, with long sides and short bottom and top.
5 Put little dabs from the second quarter of fat over the top two-thirds of the dough. Space them evenly, not too close to the edge, like buttons on a card.
6 Fold the plain bottom third of the dough over the middle section, then fold the top piece down over it. You should now have a double-decker sandwich of pastry, fat, pastry, fat, pastry. Press the edges together with the rolling pin to keep the air in. Turn the pastry so what was the right-hand side becomes the bottom edge. (This is done before each rolling.)
7 Now repeat the rolling out and dabbing and folding and so on, but before you roll out the next time leave the dough, covered, on a plate in the refrigerator for half an hour or so.
8 When all the fat has been rolled into the dough, fold once more, but in half this time. Rest in the fridge again, then roll out and use.
9 Baking in general is in a very hot oven, Reg. 8 or 450 ºF.

NOTE: When you re-roll trimmings, don't squash them into a ball, but lay out with the grain going the way it did before cutting. Roll out gently.

You can cut strips about 3/4″ × 6″, brush with beaten egg and twist them like barley sugar to make sticks to eat with soup, or cut out little crescents with a fluted cutter to use as a garnish: these are called "fleurons".

D Rough Puff Pastry

Basic proportion: 1/2-3/4 fat to flour
INGREDIENTS
1 lb. plain flour (500 g.)
1 rounded teaspoon salt
8-12 oz. fat (250-375 g.), mixed margarine & lard for preference
1 tablespoon lemon juice
water, iced if possible
Oven: Very Hot, Reg. 8, 450 ºF

METHOD
1 Sift flour and salt into a bowl.
2 Put in the fat, which should be at room temperature, neither very soft nor hard from the fridge, and cut it into walnut sized pieces in the flour, using a round-ended knife.
3 Sprinkle over the lemon juice and about seven tablespoons water, mixing lightly with the knife to make a pliable but not sticky dough. Don't mash up the lumps of fat.

4 Now roll out exactly as for flaky pastry, but of course not adding any more fat. To remind you, it is folded, turned and rolled three times after the first rolling out, and finally folded in half, turned and rolled to the thickness you need. Let it rest between each two rollings in the refrigerator, as for flaky pastry.
5 Brush the baking sheet with water, as this helps the pastry to rise.
6 Baking in general is as for flaky pastry: in a very hot oven, Reg. 8, 450 °F.

Suggestions for Using Flaked Pastries

D   Deep Pies

Flaky pastry is very good as the crust of a meat pie: steak and kidney, rabbit, game and so on. After the final rolling, proceed as for shortcrust pastry. Glaze before baking.

Rough puff or flaky may be used as the crust of a rich fruit pie. Dredge with icing or caster sugar after baking.

D   Mince Pies

Some people use thinly-rolled flaky pastry instead of shortcrust for mince pies. (See page 141)

D   Sausage Rolls

Roll out a thin rectangle of flaky pastry. Turn it over and trim edges. Then put a long thin cylinder of sausage meat across the width. Roll up, sealing pastry overlap by brushing with water. Press firmly to join. Cut into even pieces, as illustrated. Pinch back into shape if necessary, glaze the tops of the rolls with beaten egg, then slash two or three times with a knife, or snip with kitchen scissors. Bake in a very hot oven, Reg. 8, 450 °F for 10 minutes, then reduce heat to moderate, Reg. 4, 350 °F for another 15 minutes or so. (Shortcrust pastry may also be used for sausage rolls if you prefer it.)

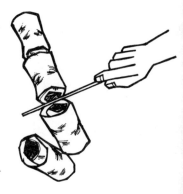

D & M   "Slices" and Gâteaux

If you are fond of flaked pastries, instead of baking a filling between layers of pastry, which causes the bottom layer to remain heavy and squashed, the trick is to bake flat sheets of pastry. Decorate one sheet with shallow cuts and egg glaze, for the top. Then sandwich the cooked sheets of pastry with filling, and cut into portions.

Fish in a very thick sauce is particularly good as a filling, or you can use minced beef with enough thickening to make it stiff, or ham or chopped hard-boiled eggs bound with a panada. The important points are to make the filling stiff enough to be cut with a knife, and to season and flavour it well. Herbs are an improvement very often.

Sweet slices are delicious. For example, to make *Mille-feuilles* bake three thin sheets of rough puff pastry, then spread one with thick whipped cream, one with jam. Assemble them all into a double-decker sandwich. Cover the top sheet with lemon glacé icing or sprinkle with icing sugar. Cut into oblong portions with a sharp warmed knife.

M Use this principle to make other kinds of slices, or pastry gâteaux of many sorts: bake thin rounds of rough puff pastry and cool them carefully. Sandwich several layers together with such things as whipped cream, ice-cream, jam, confectioner's custard, thickened fruit purées, whole strawberries/raspberries, sliced peaches or other fruit, then decorate the top with icing, chocolate, nuts, cream—and serve only to your thinnest friends, for goodness' sake.

IV   BATTERS

D   Plain Batter

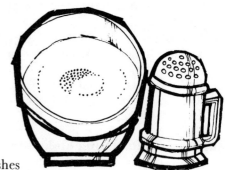

INGREDIENTS
4 oz. plain flour (125 g.)
1/2 level teaspoon salt
pepper for savoury dishes only
1 egg
1/2 pint milk (300 ml.)
Oven: Hot, Reg. 7, 425 °F for baked dishes

METHOD
1   Sift the flour and salt into a basin (with a little pepper, too, for savoury things).
2   Make a hollow in the centre of the heap of flour in the bowl. This is called a "well". Beat the egg in a cup and drop it into the well, then add a little of the milk, too.
3   Using a wooden spoon begin to stir the egg and milk together, but do not attempt yet to mix in the flour. Gradually, as you stir, some of the flour will be drawn into the bit you are mixing. Now add a little more milk.
4   Continue to draw in the flour little by little from the sides of the well until all the flour and about half the milk are mixed smoothly together. If you do it carefully there won't be any lumps. Now tilt the bowl and beat vigorously for several minutes. This will help to make the batter light.
5   If possible, set the bowl aside for an hour, covered. Beat again and then stir in the rest of the milk and use. But if time is short you can add all the milk the first time and carry on with the dish you want to make. This may be plain pancakes, Yorkshire pudding, popovers or perhaps toad-in-the-hole.

NOTE: If you have an electric mixer, use it to make a very good batter. Add the egg and a little milk to the flour, switch on and pour in the rest of the milk gradually while the machine is running.

D   Toad-In-The-Hole
For 4 people

INGREDIENTS
Batter made with 4 oz. flour, etc.
1 oz. dripping or lard (30 g.)
1 lb. sausages of any kind, though pork are perhaps nicest (1/2 kg.)
Oven: Hot, Reg. 7, 425 °F

METHOD
1   Make the batter as usual.
2   Put the dripping and sausages, separated from one another, into a meat tin, and put this into the pre-heated oven for 5 minutes.
3   When the fat is thoroughly hot, pour in the batter quickly, return the tin to the oven, and bake for 20 minutes or until the batter is puffed and golden and the sausages are brown.
4   Serve hot, immediately, with a brown or tomato sauce perhaps.

NOTE: Left-over meat, cut into strips, can take the place of sausages.

M   Rich Batter
Enough for 10-12 pancakes

INGREDIENTS
5 oz. plain flour (150 g.)
pinch of salt: more seasoning for savoury pancakes
1-2 tablespoons oil
1 egg and 1 yolk
1/2 pint milk (275 ml.)

Method is the same as for plain batter. The oil is added with the egg.

M *or* D   Pancakes
10-12 pancakes

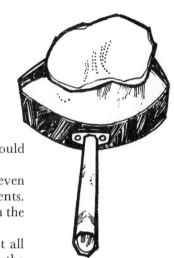

INGREDIENTS
Plain or rich batter, made with 4 or 5 oz. flour, etc.
fat for frying: lard, clarified dripping or oil
lemon cut into quarters
caster sugar

METHOD
1   Having made the batter, heat a knob of fat in a frying pan. There should be just enough to grease the bottom of the pan.
2   Pour in a little batter, swirling the pan so that it is coated with a thin even layer all over the bottom. Leave on the heat undisturbed for a few moments. Then lift one edge with a palette knife to judge if the pancake is done on the underside. It should be striped and freckled with brown.
3   Shake the pan, and slide the palette knife under the pancake if it is at all stuck. Jerk the pan until the pancake is half hanging out of the pan on the side opposite the handle. Take a deep breath and flip!—jerk the pan quickly away from yourself and back to toss the pancake. With practice this becomes easy. If you don't want to risk it, turn the pancake over with a palette knife: coward. Cook on the other side, about 1 minute total.
4   Roll up the pancake, starting from the pan handle. (You can toss it again first, if you like, to get the "best" side outwards.) Put onto a heated dish and keep hot until all are ready; or, better still, serve immediately, but less politely, to each person in turn. A squeeze of lemon and sprinkling of caster sugar goes with each.

D   Suggestions for Pancake Fillings
Any savoury mixtures of minced or chopped meat and/or vegetables and/or sauces may be used to fill pancakes, either plain or rich; e.g. cooked mushrooms with cream; minced chicken, parsley and béchamel; fried onions mixed with grated cheese; left-over fish with chopped tarragon and soured cream.

Similarly you might like to try sweet mixtures: jam, of course, and I particularly recommend a filling of Seville marmalade for the pancakes, with accompanying chocolate sauce. Try also toasted or grated nuts with honey to fill the pancakes, maple syrup poured over, and, of course, hot cooked fresh or dried fruit in pieces or as a thick purée, with fruit syrup to accompany.

Whatever filling you choose, spread it on the half of the pancake nearer the handle, then roll it as usual.

M   Crêpes Suzette
These are thin pancakes made from rich batter. Prepare a filling of butter, sweetened and flavoured with grated orange zest. (Flavour the pancake batter too, if you can, with an orange liqueur.)

Fold the filled cooked pancakes into quarters, lay them in a hot dish with two or three spoonsful of warm rum, brandy or orange liqueur poured over, and set them alight; or if you prefer warm the spirit and light in the pan, then pour over blazing; but either way let your family or guests see the spectacle of the flaming.

The variations on this theme are tremendous. Do invent a few for yourself.

D Fritter Batter

INGREDIENTS
4 oz. flour (125 g.)
2 yolks of egg
5 tablespoons water
1 tablespoon oil
2 egg whites
pinch of salt

METHOD
1 Sift the flour into a basin. Beat together the egg yolks and water in another bowl.
2 Make a well in the middle of the flour, add part of the yolk mixture, and blending gently from the centre draw part of the flour into the liquid, as for plain batter. Continue to add liquid and to stir gently until the flour is all smoothly mixed in.
3 Now beat the mixture well, and when it becomes sticky, fold in the oil.
4 Beat the egg whites with a pinch of salt to a stiff foam, then fold this into the batter mixture just before you want to use it.
5 Dip small dry pieces of food into the batter, drain them for a moment over the bowl, and fry in medium-hot deep fat until golden and puffed. Serve with lemon juice or lemon wedges, and caster sugar if appropriate.

D Fritters

Vegetable and fish fritters have already been described in previous chapters, but fritter batter can be used in other ways too.

For *Savoury Fritters:* use fingers of cooked meat, ham, boiled bacon and so on.

For *Sweet Fritters:* use slices of fruit, for example:

Bananas, peeled and quartered. Serve with lemon and sugar. Allow up to 1 banana per person.

Apples: peeled, cored and cut into slices or rings. 1 lb. (450 g.) to batter made with 4 oz. flour, etc.

Plums: halve and remove stones.

Puddings

Pudding? That's something stodgy, boiled or baked, perhaps with steak and kidney in it, isn't it? Well, a sweet then. Do you mean barley-sugar and jelly babies? Try dessert. That's nuts, figs, grapes—all that kind of thing. Afters? That sounds like something very second-rate and unimportant, and everyone likes a good pudding!

No wonder there are different names, because the variety of sweet dishes is enormous, and difficult to classify. There are other recipes for dishes suitable for the sweet course scattered in other chapters of this book: fruit soups in Chapter 1, sweet sauces in Chapter 2, sweet omelets and soufflés in Chapter 4, crumbles, tartlets, flans, pies, pastry gâteaux, pancakes and fritters in Chapter 7, and in addition many of the cakes in Chapter 9 can be served as puddings.

I FRUIT DESSERTS

D Fresh Fruit

The best dessert of all, and certainly the easiest, is to have a bowl of fresh fruit ready to put on the table. Like vegetables, fruit contains essential minerals and vitamins. Most people like it and although it tastes sweet and has some natural sugar in it, it isn't in general excessively high in calories. It is an especially good choice to balance a rich main dish.

All you need do to hard fruit is to wash it in cold or perhaps just-warm water in case it is dusty or contaminated by insecticide sprays. If the fruit is certainly peeled before eating, like bananas, this isn't necessary. Polish apples and hard kinds of pear with a soft cloth. Don't wash soft fruits though, unless you are sure they really need it, in which case rinse them quickly under the cold tap in a colander, then drain and serve quickly, as dampness makes them mushy.

Berries may need a sprinkling of sugar, not to mention cream or top-of-milk to offset an acid taste. Use caster or icing sugar; granulated is too gritty and doesn't dissolve quickly enough in the mouth for its sweetness to be appreciated.

Arrange fruit such as apples, pears, oranges, bananas and peaches on a large dish or in a big bowl so that the colours go pleasantly together; then let everyone help himself. Soft fruit is probably best put into individual bowls.

Perhaps for a special occasion, you may want to dress up fresh fruit a little more, so here are a few suggestions.

Peaches: blanch them and remove the skins. Cut into neat slices and sprinkle with caster sugar and 1 teaspoon of brandy or rum or liqueur to each two peaches. Let the fruit stand a little while to absorb the taste, then serve it with whipped cream.

Strawberries: hull them, sprinkle with sugar, a little lemon juice or Cointreau and serve with cream.

Raspberries: sprinkle with orange juice, icing sugar and serve with ice cream.

Bananas: peel and cut into circles. Sprinkle with a very little rum or lemon juice and sugar. Serve with cream or yoghurt.

D   Stewed Fruit

Like fresh fruit, this, too, can be a most refreshing dessert, and suitable after a solid first course.

Whether served hot or cold though, the fruit should not be the mushy pulp that might be ideal for a fruit sauce. The secret is to poach the fruit gently in sugar syrup, rather than to boil it. Take care it isn't overcooked, too. Several different fruits can be arranged prettily in a glass dish to make a cold cooked fruit salad—you might try cherries, plums and apple slices for example.

INGREDIENTS

To each 1-1 1/2 lb. fruit (1/2 kg. approx.) allow:
2-4 oz. granulated sugar, amount depending on sweetness of fruit (50-125 g.)
1/4 pint water (150 ml.)
1 teaspoon lemon juice

METHOD
1   Put the ingredients into a saucepan and bring to the boil, stirring until the sugar has dissolved.
2   Put in the prepared fruit and put on the lid. Just heat enough to have the odd shiver in the liquid. Don't let it boil. Cook berries only 2-3 minutes, apples for an average of 5 minutes, hard pears 20 minutes or even more.

NOTE: Of course, for sweet fruits you will cut down on the sugar, while sour ones may need more. Soft, watery fruit may not need so much water and lemon juice can be left out if the fruit is already acid-tasting.

D   Stewed Dried Fruit

Dried fruit can be a valuable addition to the diet, especially in winter when fresh fruit tends to be costly. Prunes, dried apple rings, dried pears, dried peaches and apricots as well as desiccated fruit salad are generally available, especially in health food stores and the more expensive kind of grocer's. They are useful to keep in the store cupboard, though they should not be kept for more than, say, three months, or they get very hard and leathery, even in storage jars.

Before cooking, dried fruit must be soaked in water to bring it back to an approximation of what it was when fresh. It will need a minimum of three hours' soaking, but better still soak it overnight. If you want it quickly, put the fruit in a heatproof bowl and pour enough boiling water over to come an inch above the level of the fruit. If you soak it overnight, there is no advantage in using boiling liquid.

Water is not the only thing you can use for soaking. Prunes are very good soaked in tea, and apple rings soaked in cider or cider and water.

To cook the soaked fruit, put it, and any soaking liquid left, into a saucepan or into an ovenproof dish which owns a cover. Add a little more liquid if most of the soaking liquid has been absorbed, and sugar to taste—between 1-2 oz. (30-60 g.) per lb. (450 g.) of dried fruit. Prunes do not usually need any added sugar in my opinion, but not everyone would agree.

Bring to the boil, then simmer gently for about 20 minutes on top of the stove, or cook in a cool oven, Reg. 1, 300 °F for about 3/4 hour. Dried fruit does not break up as readily as fresh, and should be cooked until it is reasonably tender.

It can be served hot or cold, with custard sauce of any type, or cream.

D   Fruit Salads

These are only one stage more elaborate than plain fresh fruit, as the only addition is a sweet syrup. There are two schools of thought about this syrup. One says that it should be cold, so that the fruit tastes absolutely natural, the other that you should pour it boiling hot over the prepared fruit to stop it going brown.

Fresh Fruit Salad
For 4 people

INGREDIENTS

Sugar syrup:
4 oz. sugar (100 g.)
1/4 pint water (150 ml.)
2 teaspoons lemon juice
1 large firm orange
1 banana
1 apple
1 pear
a few glacé cherries for the sake of colour (optional)

METHOD

1   Put the sugar and water into a pan and bring to the boil, stirring until the sugar is dissolved. Boil for two minutes. Let it cool, then stir in the lemon juice.
2   Using a very sharp knife, cut off the peel of the orange, taking the pith and inner skin, too. Start by cutting off the top, then go round and round, taking off a thin strip as you go. Now cut carefully down next to the skin of each section, so that you get pieces of orange flesh in segments completely free of skin. Put them into a bowl and squeeze the empty skin when you have finished so as not to waste any juice.
3   Peel the banana and cut it into thin rings. Put them with the orange segments.
4   Peel the apple and cut into thin slices or into dice; do the same with the pear and add both to the other fruit. Add cherries.
5   Mix in the cold syrup. Serve within an hour or two, slightly chilled if you like, with cream or curd topping.

M   Citrus Fruit Salad

This one makes a pleasant change, or is useful for winter when other fruits are expensive.

Use 1 grapefruit to every 2 large oranges. Peel them down to the flesh with a very sharp knife, then cut away the sections. Squeeze the remaining skin to extract all juice. Add sugar and Cointreau to taste. Serve chilled with a little grated chocolate on top.

D Baked Apples

These are quick to prepare and are usually popular. The most difficult bit is taking out the core. Use a potato peeler and scoop out a quite generous amount from the middle of the apple. Finding a bit of hard core can remind people of toe-nails!

INGREDIENTS

For each person allow:
1 cooking apple such as Bramley
2 teaspoons any sugar, or honey or golden syrup
1/2 oz. sultanas, raisins or chopped dates
pinch of grated lemon peel (optional)
water
knob of butter or margarine
Oven: Moderate, Reg. 4, 350 °F

METHOD
1   Wash the apples and remove the cores carefully. Slit through the skin with a sharp knife all the way round the equator.
2   Put the fruit on a lightly-greased tin or ovenproof dish. Pack the cavity in the middle with a mixture of sweetening and dried fruit, adding a little grated lemon peel if you like.
3   Put a tablespoonful of water for each apple into the dish, a knob of butter on top of each fruit and bake in a moderate oven, Reg. 4 or 350 °F for 3/4 hour, or until the apples are tender all through (prod with a skewer to find out). Serve with cream or custard sauce.

NOTE: *Apple Dumplings* are a variation of baked apples. Peel the apples whole, remove the cores and stuff them as above. Then wrap neatly in a circle of shortcrust or thinly-rolled flaky pastry, sealing the edges with water and pressing firmly round the apples. Glaze with beaten egg and milk. Bake in a fairly hot oven, Reg. 6 or 400 °F for shortcrust, very hot oven, Reg. 8 or 450 °F for flaky pastry for the first 10 minutes in each case, then reduce the heat to moderate, Reg. 4, 350 °F and continue to bake for a further 35-40 minutes. Serve these, too, with cream, curd topping or custard sauce.

M Brown Betty
Serves 6
The fruit can be varied for this pudding: try apricots as well as apples for instance. The crumbs can be made from left-over plain cake, broken biscuits or even bread.

INGREDIENTS
1 1/2 lbs. cooking apples (700 g.)
8 oz. cake, biscuit or bread crumbs (225 g.)

2-4 oz. sugar (50-100 g.)
large pinch of spice, e.g. cinnamon, powdered cloves, mixed spice
grated rind and juice of 1 lemon or orange
2 oz. butter (50 g.)
3 tablespoons water
Oven: Fairly Hot, Reg. 5, 375 °F

METHOD
1 Prepare and slice the apples and pack half of them into a greased pie dish.
2 Sprinkle over half the crumbs.
3 Mix together the sugar, spice and lemon or orange zest. Use half to sprinkle on top of the crumbs. Dot with half the butter.
4 Now repeat with a second layer of apples, crumbs, sugar mix and butter. Sprinkle over the fruit juice and water.
5 Bake in a fairly hot oven, Reg. 5 or 375 °F for 3/4 hour approx. or until the apples are soft and the top pleasantly brown. If the top seems to be getting brown too quickly, cover with a piece of foil after half time. Serve with cream, top-of-milk or custard, etc.

II MILK PUDDINGS & CUSTARDS

D Hot Milk Puddings

These are all right unless they are lumpy; most of us can remember the paper-hanger's paste concoction that was sometimes sloshed out in institutions, but that is not what I mean at all. A proper milk pudding is creamy and hot, delicately flavoured with nutmeg perhaps, or lemon, or a real vanilla pod. It should be nice enough to make you forget that milk is also Good For You, because it has a lot of calcium for tooth and bone growing, as well as some vitamins and protein.

Rice Pudding (Sago or Tapioca too)
To serve 4

INGREDIENTS
1 1/2 oz. round rice, sago or tapioca (50 g.)
1 pint milk (600 ml.)
1 oz. sugar (30 g.) or to taste
flavouring: choose from vanilla pod, a little grated lemon or orange zest, bay leaf or sprinkling of spice
Oven: Cool, Reg. 2, 300 °F

METHOD
1 Grease a pie-dish which will hold a little more than 1 pint.
2 Put the rice, etc. into a sieve and rinse under the cold tap. This helps to separate the grains a little before cooking, so that they are less likely to stick together in lumps.
3 Put the rice in the pie-dish and pour in the milk, which can be fresh or reconstituted canned evaporated, which tastes extra creamy if you use more of the milk than you should to make up the pint. Add the sugar, stir and add flavouring. Nutmeg is just sprinkled on top, but grated lemon peel should be stirred in.
4 Put the dish on a baking sheet (in case it should boil over) and bake for 1 1/2-2 hours in a cool oven, Reg. 2, 300 °F. The pudding should be stirred

151

from time to time. If you like the crust that forms, stir the pudding with a fork, slipping it underneath the crust.

5   Before you serve the pudding, scrape the side of the dish with a knife and clean off any burnt splashes with a very clean piece of damp muslin. Cream, jam or golden syrup is appreciated with milk puddings by some people.

NOTE: If you have used a vanilla pod to flavour the pudding, remove it carefully before serving, rinse it and dry thoroughly. It can be re-used many times.

Semolina or Ground Rice Pudding
For 4 people

INGREDIENTS
1 pint milk (600 ml.)
1 oz. sugar (30 g.)
1 1/2 oz. semolina or ground rice (50 g.)
vanilla, etc. to flavour
Oven: Cool, Reg. 2, 300 °F if used

METHOD
1   Grease a medium-sized pie-dish if you want to bake the pudding.
2   Heat the milk and sugar in a saucepan and drizzle in the semolina or ground rice a little at a time when the milk boils, stirring constantly.
3   Turn down the heat and continue to cook and stir for 5 minutes.
4   Stir in the flavouring you choose and transfer to the pie dish to bake in a cool oven, Reg. 2, 300 °F for 3/4 hour, or go on cooking the pudding very gently on top of the stove for about another 20 minutes, stirring frequently.

NOTE: All milk puddings can be cooked simply by heating the grain in the milk on top of the stove. Although you can do this on direct heat, it is much better to use a double saucepan for large grains, as there is then no danger of their sticking or boiling over. Allow up to 2 hours for these puddings to cook, and stir occasionally.

M   Low-Fat Yoghurt
Yield: 1 pint (550 ml.)
Yoghurt is not at all difficult to make, though you do need patience. Home-made, it costs much less than the bought kind. Fresh milk can be used, but I find a very acceptable alternative is to use instant milk, made up to 1 1/2 times the strength of reconstituted milk. You need to buy some yoghurt to start off with, but if you continue to make it you can save a little from one batch to start the next.

INGREDIENTS
3 oz. (75 g.) instant milk granules
water
1 good tablespoon yoghurt, bought or previously made at home

METHOD
1   Put the dried milk granules into a measure and make up to 1 pint (550 ml.) with cold water. N.B. Check that this is 1 1/2 times the strength of your brand of reconstituted milk.
2   Stir well. Heat to lukewarm.
3   Pour a little of the warm milk onto the yoghurt in a cup. Stir, then blend into the bulk of the warm milk.

4 Pour into convenient containers such as cups or glasses, cover each with foil and leave undisturbed in a warm place for up to twelve hours. When the milk has solidified store in a refrigerator, or the coolest place you have.

D Proper (or Egg) Custard

As a sauce, 4 portions. On its own, 2 portions.

INGREDIENTS
1 egg
1 oz. sugar (30 g.) or to taste
1/2 pint milk (300 ml.)
few drops vanilla essence, or use vanilla sugar

METHOD
1 Break the egg into a 1 pint capacity basin, add the sugar and whip together with a fork until they are well mixed.
2 Warm the milk and when it is hot, but not boiling, pour it gently onto the egg mixture, continuing to whisk with the fork. Add the vanilla essence if used.
3 Pour the custard back into the saucepan and return to very gentle heat. Stir with a wooden spoon until the mixture thickens a little and coats the back of the spoon. It must not boil or the egg will harden too much and appear to curdle the milk. If you prefer, you can heat it in a double saucepan, stirring as before. In any case, don't expect this custard to become as thick as the packet kind.
4 Serve hot as a sauce for baked puddings, etc., or hot or iced with biscuits as a sweet in its own right.

NOTE: For a richer custard use an extra egg yolk, or an extra whole egg.

For baked custard, use 2-3 eggs, 2 oz. (50 g.) sugar and 1 pint milk (550 ml.). Mix as above, pour into a greased baking dish and cook in a meat tin half full of water in a cool oven, Reg. 1, 300 °F for about 40 minutes or until just set.
M For *Confectioner's Custard*, useful for filling cakes, use 3 egg yolks, 3 oz. sugar (75 g.), 1 level tablespoonful each of plain flour and cornflour, 1/2 pint milk (300 ml.) and vanilla essence to taste. Blend the starches with the eggs, and make as for ordinary custard, except that this one must be brought to the boil. The starch prevents curdling.

M Trifle

Serves 4-6
This is the real thing, expensive and delectable, not the imitation you can make with any old cake and packet custard.

INGREDIENTS
4 sponge cakes (the oblong kind, sprinkled with sugar)
raspberry jam
3 tablespoons sherry or any liqueurs
2 tablespoons sugar syrup (page 149)
proper custard made with 3 eggs, 1 oz. sugar, vanilla and 3/4 pint milk
fruit such as 1 large ripe pear, a few strawberries or pitted cherries (optional)
1/4 pint whipping cream (150 ml.)
caster sugar to taste
tiny pieces of cherries and angelica for decoration

METHOD

1   Cut the sponge cakes in half, then sandwich them together again with a thick layer of raspberry jam. Cut each of them into four or five slices and spread these over the bottom of a decorative glass serving dish.

2   Mix the sherry and sugar syrup. Sprinkle over the sponge cake and let it soak.

3   Make the custard and let it cool.

4   Prepare the fruit according to the kind you choose. Cut into small pieces unless you have berries. Scatter over the cake.

5   Pour over the cold custard, letting it flow slowly over the back of a spoon so that the cake is not disturbed.

6   Whip the cream and sweeten to taste—not too much sugar though, or it will be sickly. Using a forcing bag and small star pipe cover the whole surface of the custard with cream stars.

7   Decorate very daintily and with restraint, using cherries and angelica. Chill and serve cold.

III CREAM & GELATINE DESSERTS

D Curd Topping

4 portions

This is a refreshing replacement for whipped cream to be served with many sweets, particularly with fruit. (It is also less expensive.) Use the smaller quantity of milk, or even less, if you want to pipe it as a decoration; use more milk to get a pouring consistency.

INGREDIENTS

2 oz. curd cheese (60 g.) as fresh as possible

2-4 tablespoons milk or top-of-milk

2 rounded teaspoons caster sugar

2 drops vanilla essence (optional)

METHOD

1   Put the curd cheese into a bowl and beat in the milk a little at a time, keeping the mixture smooth.

2   Beat in the sugar and vanilla.

NOTE: This mixture is also pleasant as a sweet in its own right, or with a few raspberries or strawberries folded in—colouring too if you like. Double or treble the recipe for four people in this case.

M Chantilly Cream

Chantilly cream is vanilla-flavoured whipped cream. You can use whipping cream, beaten to a foam with a little caster sugar and a drop or two of vanilla essence, or better still use vanilla sugar. Double cream can be used as it is, or "stretched" like this:

INGREDIENTS

1/4 pint double cream (150 ml.)

2 rounded teaspoons caster sugar or vanilla sugar

a few drops vanilla essence if plain sugar is used

3 tablespoons single cream or top-of-milk, or 2 egg whites, whipped

METHOD
1 Whip together the double cream, sugar and flavouring until smooth and thick.
2 Beat in the single cream or top of the milk little by little, continuing to whip until the mixture stiffens again, or beat the egg whites to a stiff foam and fold them lightly into the whipped double cream.

NOTE: This is a versatile form of whipped cream, useful for sandwiching together meringue shells, as a filling for sponge cakes (very good in chocolate sponge and with jam in fatless sponges), and to decorate or serve with cold puddings, hot or cold fruit pies and so on.

D Fruit Fools

Fools are a mixture of fruit purée, proper custard and whipped cream. Probably the most distinctive is gooseberry fool, but you can adapt this recipe very easily to your favourite fruit. A sweet fruit, though, will probably not need quite as much sugar.

Gooseberry Fool
For 4 people

INGREDIENTS
8 oz. gooseberries (225 g.)
2-3 oz. sugar (50-75 g.)
1 tablespoon water
1/4 pint milk (150 ml.)
1 egg
1/4 pint whipping or double cream (150 ml.)
a few drops green colouring (optional)

METHOD
1 Wash the gooseberries, cut off their tops and tails with scissors and put them into a saucepan with the sugar and water.
2 Cook quite gently until the fruit is soft. Then rub it through a sieve with a wooden spoon to make a purée.
3 While the fruit is cooking, warm the milk in another saucepan. Beat the egg in a bowl, pour on the warm milk, stir and return to the milk saucepan. Stir over very low heat just until the custard begins to thicken. It must not boil, and will not be as thick as custard-powder mixture would be.
4 Mix together the gooseberry purée and the custard. Allow it to get cold.
5 Whip the cream and fold it into the gooseberry custard. Stir in some green food colouring if you like. Pour into a pretty serving dish and decorate with tiny sweet biscuits such as ratafias if you want to.

M Fruit Creams
Serves 4-5
For these you need fruit with a decided flavour. You can use fresh soft fruit, canned fruit, or stewed fruit. Apricots, peaches, raspberries and strawberries all make delicious creams. The jelly run over the top improves the appearance of the dish but can at a pinch be omitted.

INGREDIENTS
1 rounded teaspoon gelatine powder (1/2 envelope)
1 good tablespoon water
1/4 pint double or whipping cream (150 ml.)

1/4 pint thick fruit purée (150 ml.)
3 tablespoons fruit syrup or juice, or use sugar syrup with fresh fruit
icing sugar to taste
lemon juice (optional)
decoration: reserve a little whole fruit, plus angelica, etc.
1/4 packet jelly, colour and flavour to go with the fruit you use, made up to
   1/4 pint with hot water

METHOD

1   Soak the gelatine in the water.
2   Half-whip the cream. Stir in the fruit purée, fruit juice or syrup, icing sugar to taste (don't sweeten too much) and a little lemon juice if this will improve it.
3   Heat the gelatine until dissolved and stir gently into the mix. Pour into a glass or other serving dish and leave to set in the cool. (Or use individual dishes, or waxed paper dishes for a party.)
4   Decorate the top with a design made from the same fruit that you have used in the cream: e.g. small strawberries sliced in half, dipped into the cold liquid jelly and allowed to set in position on top of the cream.
5   Pouring it over the back of a spoon so as not to disturb the decoration or surface, run the cold jelly over the top of the cream. Finally let this set, too.

D   Absolute Ice-Cream

This is my favourite ice-cream. It isn't cheap, but is so delicious that it is probably worth the money. I won't guess how many people precisely it will serve; so much depends on what you have with it. In my family it will just stretch to 6 portions, with a sauce.

INGREDIENTS

2 eggs
2 oz. caster sugar (60 g.)
1 small teaspoon vanilla essence
1/4 pint double cream (150 ml.)
Refrigerator: coldest setting

METHOD

1   Separate yolks from whites of eggs. Whip whites until very stiff, add sugar and beat again until the mixture is as stiff as before. Fold in the vanilla and egg yolks.
2   Whip the cream separately until it is of the same consistency as the egg mixture, then fold it in.
3   Freeze as quickly as possible in any conveniently-fitting container in the freezing compartment of your refrigerator. There is no need to stir, beat or otherwise disturb the mixture while it is freezing. Serve with wafers.

Variations

Omit the vanilla essence (except for chocolate, which is improved with a little vanilla too) and use one of these flavourings instead:

Strawberry: fold in a few crushed strawberries; colour the mixture pink with cochineal. Serve with whole strawberries or with a sweetened strawberry purée.

Raspberry: as for strawberry, but using raspberries.

Coffee: fold in 2-3 teaspoons coffee essence.

Chocolate: fold in 2 oz. (60 g.) melted plain or bitter chocolate and a drop or two of vanilla.

Ginger: fold in 2 tablespoons chopped preserved stem ginger or crystallized ginger. Use ginger syrup from preserved ginger as a sauce.

Suggestion for Ice-Cream Desserts

The only limiting factor here is imagination. Ice-cream, as many caterers have discovered, goes with anything sweet, and can be used instead of whipped cream with fruit pies or flans, hot or cold, with stewed fruit, with jellies, with fruit salads, inside pancakes, between meringues and underneath sweet sauces. It isn't confined to summertime: some people like their mince pies "à la mode"—an American use of the French phrase meaning "with ice-cream" which is presumably always in fashion. But I think some discretion is called for. If you have a rich pastry sweet, you hardly need a rich ice-cream too, though this is up to you, of course. Here are a few simple ideas anyway.

Ice-cream and biscuits. You don't need to stick to the conventional wafers. Try sponge fingers, ginger nuts, brandy snaps, chocolate biscuits with coffee or vanilla ice-cream, almond biscuits with strawberry ice, digestive biscuits with chocolate ice and so on.

Ice-cream with sweet sauces. Many kinds of sauce mingle pleasantly with the taste of plain or flavoured ices. Serve some sort of biscuit, too, because you need something crisp to contrast with the smooth texture. Try these combinations for a start:
  Vanilla ice with any chocolate sauce, or with sweetened raspberry or strawberry purée.
  Strawberry or raspberry ice with plain chocolate or lemon sauce.
  Coffee ice with any chocolate sauce.
  Chocolate ice with chocolate sauce of any kind, or lemon.
  Ginger ice with chocolate or chocolate rum sauce.

Ice-cream with fruit. Fruit and ice-cream go very well together. Try some of these, for example:
  Vanilla ice with cold stewed apples or apricots.
  Strawberry or raspberry ice with more strawberries or raspberries, or blackberries fresh or stewed.
  Coffee ice with orange segments (skinless).
  Chocolate ice with stewed apples or canned peaches.
  Ginger ice with mashed banana or stewed apples.

Ice-cream sundaes. These are made with fruit, plus ice-cream, plus sauce, with perhaps some chopped or toasted nuts on top—and whipped cream too, if your waist is no worry. The permutations are amazing. Here are just a few:
  Slice a banana lengthwise. Put a spoonful of vanilla or chocolate or coffee ice between the slices. Coat with chocolate sauce and sprinkle over toasted almonds or chopped walnuts *(Banana Longboat)*.
  Put half a fresh skinned peach onto vanilla ice and coat with fresh raspberry purée *(Peach Melba)*.
  Put a spoonful of vanilla ice on top of stewed apples. Coat with sauce made from blackcurrant jam and water and sprinkle with chopped and toasted hazelnuts.
  Now think of about two hundred more for yourself!

M *Ice-cream with cake or pastry.* If you now add the possibility of plain or flavoured sponge, or pastry, to the possible combinations of ice-cream, fruit, sweet sauce and cream, you have an enormous number of ice-cream gâteaux. For instance:

Fill a sponge flan case with fruit and ice-cream and sprinkle with nuts.

Sandwich flaky pastry circles with jam and ice-cream and top with a little glacé icing.

Fill a chocolate sponge sandwich with coffee ice-cream and pour chocolate rum sauce over.

Put a well-frozen block of ice-cream on a round of sponge. Completely cover with meringue (page 181) and bake for 3 minutes in a very hot oven, Reg. 7 or 425 °F to colour the meringue *(Baked Alaska)*.

Fill a meringue flan-case, previously baked, with strawberry ice-cream. Cover completely with fresh strawberries and sprinkle lightly with icing sugar.

M Milanese Soufflé

For 4, perhaps

Here is a delectable recipe. I've used it for years at small dinner parties, though the proportions can easily be doubled or trebled for larger parties or exceptionally greedy guests.

Strictly speaking, cold soufflés should be set in round soufflé dishes with paper collars tied around. When the mixture is set the paper is removed, leaving the just-solid soufflé standing up proudly, as much above the dish as is in it. If you don't want the bother of all this, it looks good in a glass bowl and tastes the same.

INGREDIENTS

2 large eggs

2 oz. caster sugar (60 g.)

1 juicy lemon

1/4 pint double cream (150 ml.)

1 rounded teaspoon powdered gelatine

1 tablespoon (good measure) water

decoration as you like: e.g. whipped cream, chopped nuts, crystallized violets, glacé cherries; not all at once.

METHOD

1   If used, prepare the soufflé dish. Tie a double band of greaseproof paper, twice the height of the dish, round the outside, and grease the exposed inside of the paper.

2   Whisk together the egg-yolks, sugar, grated rind and juice of the lemon over a pan of hot water or in a food mixer until thick and very light. Remove from the heat and continue to whisk until cold.

3   Half-whip the cream and whip the egg whites separately to a stiff foam. Soak the gelatine in cold water, then dissolve over heat.

4   Gently fold the cream, then gelatine, then egg whites into the lemon mixture. Pour into the soufflé dish or glass bowl and leave to set in a cool place. When set, remove paper, if used, like this: untie the holding string. Put a palette knife blade flat against the side of the soufflé, outside the paper. Now start to pull the paper away, pulling against the blade of the knife so that the edge of the soufflé is not torn. Clean the side of the soufflé dish if necessary.

5   Pipe little stars of whipped cream all round the top edge of the soufflé if you like, and decorate as you choose.

IV SPONGE PUDDINGS

Any cake mixture of a straightforward kind can be baked or steamed and served hot as a pudding, usually with a jam, custard, chocolate custard, lemon or other sweet sauce. I think, though, that a fairly plain mixture is best, as the richer ones are cloying and may be indigestible when hot.

D Baked or Steamed Sponge
For up to 6 portions

INGREDIENTS
3 oz. margarine (100 g.)
3 oz. caster sugar (100 g.)
2 eggs
6 oz. plain or self-raising flour (200 g.)
1 level teaspoon baking powder if plain flour is used
pinch salt
milk or water to mix
flavouring such as grated orange or lemon zest, or 1/2 teaspoon vanilla, almond,
    butterscotch essence
sugar for dredging
Oven: Moderately Hot, Reg. 5, 375 °F or steamer prepared

METHOD

1   Grease a large pie-dish or equivalent heat-proof serving dish, or a pudding basin for steaming: 1 1/2 lb. size for this quantity.
2   Cream together the margarine and sugar until light and fluffy. Beat the eggs separately and then beat them in a little at a time.
3   If the mixture "curdles"—i.e. separates, sift in a little of the measured flour and beat again; otherwise sift the flour, baking powder if used and salt, and fold it into the mixture gently, using a metal spoon. Fold in a little milk or water to make a fairly soft but not sloppy consistency. It should just drop off the spoon with a light "plop", and this is called "soft dropping consistency". Stir in flavouring.
4   Scrape the mixture into the pie-dish neatly, smooth over the top with a knife and bake in a fairly hot oven, Reg. 5 or 375 °F for about 30 minutes or until risen and golden brown on top. Dredge with caster sugar (or icing sugar if you prefer) and serve with any sweet sauce you like.
    Alternatively, put the mixture into the greased pudding basin and smooth over. Take a piece of greaseproof paper and grease a circle in the middle. Now make a pleat across the centre and lay it, grease side down, over the pudding. Take a piece of foil, a little larger than the greaseproof paper, and pleat that in the same way. Put on top of the greaseproof. Press the foil down firmly round the side of the basin and tie with string under the rim. Make a loop of string from one side of the basin to the other so that you can lift the pudding. Put it into the steamer over boiling water and steam, lid on, for 1 1/2 hours. Alternatively you can put the pudding basin into a saucepan with water coming half-way up the side of the basin. Simmer gently for 1 1/4 hours. In either case check from time to time that the water is not boiling away. Replenish if necessary from a boiling kettle. Turn out onto a hot dish and serve with sauce, which can be poured over the pudding or handed separately.

Variations of Sponge Puddings

Currant, Sultana, Cherry Pudding, etc.: mix in 2-3 oz. (50-75 g.) any dried fruit such as currants, sultanas, chopped mixed peel, glacé cherries, glacé pineapple and so on, when folding in the flour. Bake or steam. Serve with lemon or custard sauce.

Chocolate Pudding: use only 5 oz. flour and add 1 oz. cocoa powder, sifted with the flour. Add a drop or two of vanilla. Serve with sweet white sauce, custard or chocolate sauce. Bake or steam.

Syrup Pudding: put 2-3 tablespoons of golden syrup into the greased pie dish or pudding basin. Cover with lemon-flavoured sponge mixture. Bake or steam.

Eve's Pudding: half-fill the pie dish with apple slices and a little sugar. Sprinkle with 2 tablespoons water. Make half quantity of basic mixture and spread it over the apple. Bake for 30 minutes in a fairly hot oven, Reg. 5, 375 °F then reduce heat to warm, Reg. 3, 325 °F for another 10 minutes or so to cook the apples thoroughly. Serve with cream or custard.

Upside-Down Pudding: arrange in a shallow greased baking tin enough fruit to make a pleasant design: apricot halves, pineapple rings with cherries in the middle, peach slices etc. Cover with half quantity of basic mixture and bake for about 30 minutes in a fairly hot oven, Reg. 5, 375 °F. Turn out onto a hot serving dish, carefully, with fruit on the top. Serve with cream, custard or lemon sauce.

M   Lemon Sponge Pudding
Serves 4
This mixture makes its own lemony sauce at the bottom of the baking dish.

INGREDIENTS
2 oz. margarine (50 g.)
4 oz. caster sugar (100 g.)
2 eggs, separated
grated rind and juice of 1 lemon
2 oz. plain flour, sifted (50 g.)
1/4 pint milk (150 ml.)
Oven: Warm, Reg. 3-4, 350 °F

METHOD
1   Cream together the margarine and sugar, starting with only half the sugar and adding the rest as the mixture gets soft.
2   Beat in the yolks of the eggs and lemon zest, then fold in flour, lemon juice and milk.
3   Whisk the egg whites to a stiff froth. Fold them into the mixture.
4   Pour into a greased ovenproof dish, set in a baking tin half-full of water and bake in a warm oven, Reg. 3-4, 350 °F or a little less, for 1 1/2 hours approx.

M   Plum Pudding also known as Christmas Pudding
Makes 3 × 1 1/2 lb. basin sized puddings
This recipe comes from an old book I have, published in 1826. The only alteration I have made is to increase the sugar a little: the original had only 4 oz! Sugar used to be more expensive and not as generously used as it is now. The recipe produces a pleasant pudding which is not too rich. Like all Christmas puddings it tastes better if made a month or two in advance. If you wrap a cooked pudding in several thicknesses of greaseproof paper and store in a cool, dry place, it should keep from one Christmas to the next.

INGREDIENTS

1 lb. large stoned raisins (450 g.)
1 lb. currants "well washed and picked" (450 g.)
1 lb. beef suet, shredded (450 g.)
2 oz. unblanched almonds, chopped finely or put through a nut mill (50 g.)
1 lb. plain flour, sifted (450 g.)
6 oz. white bread crumbs (175 g.)
6 oz. chopped mixed peel (175 g.)
2 rounded teaspoons ground nutmeg
1/2 level teaspoon powdered mace
8 oz. soft brown sugar (225 g.)
1 level teaspoon salt
10 eggs
1/2 pint cream or top-of-the milk (300 ml.)
1 wineglass white wine
1/2 gill brandy or rum (75 ml.)

METHOD

1 Have ready a large bowl. I use a basin from a Victorian washing set. A preserving pan would also do. As you weigh out the various dry ingredients put them in even layers into the bowl.

2 Beat the eggs with the cream or top-of-milk before you add them to the bowl. Sprinkle over the wine and rum.

3 Take a deep breath, and a large spoon, and stir and stir and STIR! Traditionally every member of the family should have a stir and a wish. Even if the wishes don't come true, at least your arm will have a rest.

4 My book says that the consistency "must not be thin, as the fruit would then settle at the bottom; tie it carefully in a cloth and boil it 4 hours: serve up with melted butter and white wine." It is probably more practical to pack it into pudding basins, cover with greased greaseproof paper and then a circle of foil secured with string, and simmer in a saucepan with water half-way up the side of the basin. Cook for about 4 hours.

5 Store wrapped in greaseproof paper, then simmer it again as in step 4 for another 2-3 hours before serving.

6 If you want to flame the pudding on Christmas Day, warm 2 tablespoons rum or brandy in a small saucepan, pour over the pudding and light with a match within sight of the family.

7 Serve with brandy or rum butter, custard sauce with brandy added, plain custard or sweet white sauce.

Bread, Biscuits & Cakes

I BREAD

Once bread was such an important part of what people ate that to speak of "bread" was to speak of food in general, as in the prayer "give us this day our daily bread".

Flour is a starchy food, so perhaps you might expect that I'm not much in favour of it: but of course everyone needs some carbohydrate for the energy it produces; it is only bad for you in excessive quantities. Flour, too, is not only starch: it has in it as well a useful if comparatively small amount of protein, many necessary mineral salts and vitamins, particularly of the B group in the case of wholemeal flour and brown bread. So let's start straight away and make some absolutely basic bread, the simplest possible, which none the less can be an eye-opener (or mouth opener) if you are used to the shop-bought, pre-sliced kind.

D Bread

2 medium loaves, or 1 loaf plus rolls

Hands are the best tools for mixing the dough, so do make quite sure that yours are clean enough to eat from.

If you can get hold of it, use "strong" flour for yeast cooking. It has a lot of a substance called gluten in it. This combines with water to make an elastic mesh through the dough when it is kneaded, and this helps to make the bread light, spongy and well-risen. Strong flour is also good for the flaked pastries, incidentally. Ordinary general-purpose flour can be used if you have nothing else. Wholewheat flour can also be used with great success, or a mixture of flours. Once you know how to do it, you may like to experiment. Some health-food shops and the more expensive kind of grocer's keep several different sorts of flours for you to choose from.

Yeast is fascinating stuff: it is a primitive plant, alive, and works best in warm dampness. It feeds on sugar and makes carbon dioxide gas and alcohol. When baked, the yeast is killed but the tiny bubbles of the gas expand to make the small holes all through the crumb. The alcohol evaporates: you won't easily get drunk on bread! You can buy yeast by the ounce from some bakers and health-food shops, or dried yeast from the chemist, in small tins. If you use dried yeast follow the directions on the packet as to how much to use, and how to mix it with the liquid. It must be soaked in water before you use it. The quantity of yeast in the recipes applies to fresh yeast.

INGREDIENTS

2 lbs. plain white strong flour, or 1 1/2 lbs. wholemeal and 1/2 lb. white
   (900 g. total)
2 rounded teaspoons salt
2-4 oz. lard, optional (50-100 g.)
1 oz. yeast (30 g.)
1 rounded teaspoon sugar
1 pint water, approx. (550 ml. approx.) at blood heat: mix 2/3 cold with
   1/3 boiling
Oven: Very Hot, Reg. 8, 450 °F to start (light only after the dough has risen the
   first time)

METHOD

1   Put the flour in a large bowl and mix in the salt. If you are going to use fat,
    which makes the bread taste fresher for longer, rub it into the flour and salt,
    as if making shortcrust pastry. Fat is not essential.
2   Put the flour somewhere where it will get pleasantly warm. The lowest
    setting possible in your oven is suitable. This helps to speed up the bread-
    making process, as yeast works best when all ingredients are at blood-heat,
    more or less.
3   When the flour is ready, mix the yeast and sugar together in a small basin.
    Suddenly it will turn liquid. The sugar gives the yeast something to start
    feeding on. Pour about 1/4 of the warm measured water onto the yeast and
    mix.
4   Make a hollow or well in the middle of the pile of warm flour and pour in
    the yeast water. Start to stir the liquid with the fingers of one hand, drawing
    in some of the flour as you stir. Gradually add more of the warm water and
    mix in more flour, until all the flour is mixed into a slightly sticky goo. You
    may need a little more or a little less water, because different flours vary in
    the amount of water they will soak up.
5   At this point you must start to knead the dough. If you are right-handed,
    you will find it easier to knead with your stronger right hand and turn the
    bowl with your left hand. Push your fingers down the side of the bowl and
    hook over the dough in your hand to press it down into the middle of the
    mass. Turn the bowl with your other hand so that you work on another bit
    of the dough. After a while you will find that things are definitely less sticky.
    Rub your fingers as free from dough as possible and wash your hands
    (again).
6   Dredge a clean working-surface with flour. Turn the dough out of the basin
    and flour your hands. Now the kneading movement is slightly different.
    Cup your hands round the ball of dough, then bring your palms over and
    push into the middle. Some people find it easier to use the clenched fist.
    Turn the dough so that it all gets equal attention, and try to work fast so
    that the dough doesn't get too cold.

7 When the dough is quite smooth and soft and no longer sticky at all, put it back into the bowl in which it was mixed, cut a cross on the top to let it expand, cover with a clean damp teatowel or a piece of greased polythene and put it in a warm place, such as an airing cupboard, top of not-too-hot boiler or radiator, or on the plate rack over something cooking on top of the stove. Don't let it get hot, or the yeast will be killed, but don't let it get cold either, or the yeast will work only very slowly indeed. Leave the bread to rise until it is twice the size you left it. The time it takes will depend mainly on how warm it is: it may take from 1/2 hour up to 2 hours. Have patience! In the meantime, clear up any mess in the kitchen.

8 When well-risen, turn the dough out of the bowl onto a floured surface again. Knead again, but very lightly and for only a few moments this time. The second kneading is sometimes called "knocking up" or "knocking down". Grease two loaf tins, medium-sized. Cut the dough in half. Shape each piece into a thick roll on the working surface, then turn it over to fit into the tin, tucking any ends underneath, so that the top is smooth. Leave again in a warm place to rise or "prove" a second time, say for 1/2 hour. If you fill the loaf tins half full they will be ready for the oven when the dough has risen to the level of the rim. The dough also has a fat and bulky look.

9 Bake towards the top of a very hot oven, allowing room for rising, Reg. 8 or 450 °F for 10 minutes. Then reduce the heat to fairly hot, Reg. 6, 400 °F and bake for another 30-40 minutes. When done the loaf is pleasantly browned and slides out of the tin easily to show a golden-coloured base, which sounds hollow if you tap it. Cool the loaves on a wire rack—and distract the family's attention until the bread is cool. If you like, you can rub over the top of the loaves with a butter paper to polish them a little.

NOTE: If you have no loaf tins, use medium-sized cake tins, or shape the bread into one large or two small cottage loaves, like this: mentally divide the mixture into thirds, and cut off one third. Roll into one large and one small ball-shape, put the large one on a well-greased baking sheet, put the smaller one on top and push a floury finger or thumb right through the middle of the top ball to anchor it firmly in position.

If you want to bake enormous quantities of bread at any one time, the proportion of yeast does not multiply in the same proportion as the flour: use 1/2 oz. yeast for 1 lb. flour, 1 oz. yeast for 2 & 3 lbs. flour, then 1 1/2 oz. up to 7 lbs. flour. After that, consult your trade manual: you must be in business as a baker! In fact, the exact proportion of yeast you use can vary, because the yeast grows all the time the bread is rising. Less yeast = longer rising, more yeast = quicker rising.

D   Milk Bread

INGREDIENTS
1 lb. approx. plain white strong flour (450 g.)
1 level or rounded teaspoon salt, as preferred
1/2 oz. yeast (15 g.)
1 level teaspoon sugar
1/2 pint milk (300 ml.)
3 oz. butter or margarine (80 g.)
Oven (when you are ready): Very Hot, Reg. 7, 425 °F

METHOD
1 Mix 1 lb. flour (450 g.) and salt together. The amount of salt you use depends on how you like your bread. Warm the flour through as for plain bread.

2   Cream the yeast with the sugar. Heat the milk to blood heat with the fat and stir until the fat is melted. Mix some of this with the yeast.

3   Make a well in the middle of the flour, pour in the yeast/milk mixture and mix to a softish dough, adding the rest of the milk. (If the dough is too sticky, add a little more flour.)

4   Knead well, first in the bowl then on a floured surface.

5   Leave to rise in a warm place, covered with a damp cloth or greased polythene bag. (You can put the whole bowl into a polythene bag if you like, but remember afterwards to wash the bag and keep it out of the way of small children always.)

6   When risen to double its bulk, knock up the dough, shape it into a loaf or loaves, or rolls, or a large plait if you like. If you want a plait, divide the dough into three. Roll out each piece into a long sausage in your hands. Press them firmly together at the top, then plait them. Press together at the bottom. Put onto a greased tin or baking sheet, prove in a warm place, brush over with milk and bake in a very hot oven, Reg. 7, 425 °F for 10 minutes; then reduce heat to fairly hot, Reg. 5, 375 °F for another 30 minutes approximately, until well-browned. Cool on a wire rack.

D   Vienna Bread
Make as for milk bread, but use a beaten egg in place of part of the warm milk. Shape it into a plait and glaze with a little beaten egg-and-milk.

D   Currant Bread
Make as for milk bread or Vienna bread, but knead in 2-3 oz. currants (50-75 g.), 1 oz. mixed peel (30 g.) and 3 oz. any colour of sugar (75 g.) after the first rising. Bake in a large cake tin or make into several small loaves.

D   Rolls
Any bread mixture can be shaped into rolls, and if you have ever played with plasticine you'll have ideas of your own. Some of the possibilities are illustrated: plain round ones, slashed across the top, a plait, a coil, a double spiral. Try your initials, too, and finger rolls and longer sticks. Shape them after the dough has risen, then leave them to prove on a greased baking sheet, like bread. Bake at the temperature given for the kind of dough you are using, but for less time. Thin rolls may need only ten minutes, ordinary round rolls about 20.

M   Croissants
Makes 2 doz. small croissants

INGREDIENTS
Milk bread dough made with 1 lb. flour, etc.
5 oz. butter (150 g.)
egg-and-milk glaze
Oven: Fairly Hot, Reg. 6, 400 °F

METHOD

1   After the dough has had its first rising, knock it up gently and chill thoroughly in the refrigerator.

2   Roll it out into a long strip.

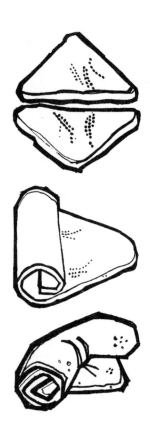

3　Cream the butter until fairly soft and spread this all over the top of the dough.

4　Fold the bottom third over the middle, then the top third down, as for flaky pastry. Turn through 90°, roll out again, fold and chill.

5　Repeat the turning, rolling and folding. Leave, covered with foil, in the refrigerator overnight.

6　Roll out to 1/4″ thickness. Cut into squares about 4 1/2″ sides for small croissants, or if you prefer bigger ones, 7″. Cut each square into two triangles. Turn a triangle over and roll from the long edge towards the point. Twist the roll into a crescent or horseshoe shape and put on a greased baking sheet.

7　Leave the croissants to prove at room temperature for a few minutes. (If you put them in a warm place the butter runs out.) Brush over the top with egg wash and bake in a fairly hot oven, Reg. 6, 400 °F for 15 minutes, or until golden-brown. Serve if possible while still warm, especially for a luxurious breakfast with hot coffee, French style.

D　Currant Buns
Makes 8 large or 12 small buns

Try these once you have practised on bread dough.

INGREDIENTS
1/2 lb. strong plain white flour (225 g.)
large pinch of salt
2 oz. caster sugar (60 g.)
2 oz. butter or margarine (60 g.)
1/2 oz. yeast (15 g.)
rather less than 1/4 pint warm milk (less than 150 ml.)
1 egg beaten
2 oz. cleaned currants
large pinch of mixed spice (optional)
bun wash:
1 rounded tablespoon sugar
1 tablespoon milk
Oven: Very Hot, Reg. 7, 425 °F

METHOD

1　Mix together the flour, salt and sugar. Rub in the fat with your fingertips, as for shortcrust pastry. Put the bowl in a warm place and let the flour warm through.

2　When the flour is warm, put the yeast in a cup (no sugar needed: it will meet the sugar in the dough). Mix it with a little of the warm (not hot) milk.

3　Make a well in the middle of the flour. Pour in the yeast, then the egg and start mixing. Add enough milk as you mix to make a fairly soft dough. Knead well, as for bread, then put it back into the bowl, cut a cross on top, cover with a damp cloth and leave in a warm place, as for bread. When risen to twice its bulk, turn it out gently onto a floured surface.

4　Knead the currants and spices lightly into the dough. Divide into 8 or 12 even-sized pieces. Roll each into a ball and put on a greased baking sheet. Let them prove again until puffy and double the size.

5　Bake in a very hot oven, Reg. 7, 425 °F for 5 minutes, then reduce to fairly hot, Reg. 6 or 400 °F for another 10 minutes, or until decently browned.

6　When the buns are nearly cooked, boil the sugar and milk together to make the bun wash. Brush it over the buns when they come out of the oven, using a pastry brush. It gives them a shiny sticky finish. Cool the buns a bit on a wire rack before trying them.

D Sandwiches

The trouble with sandwiches is bread. How many, too many, times have you been offered two doorsteps of stale, tasteless white stodge, stuck together with paste? Please don't do it yourself. Here are some hints which I hope will help you.

1 Use bread which is fresh, but not so fresh that it is difficult to cut thinly. If this is the case, make open sandwiches.
2 Use different kinds of bread, not just white. Try wholemeal, Hovis, rye, granary, French, milk—even home-made bread! There are so many kinds that you need hardly eat the same one on any two days in the year. Cut off crusts if you like.
3 Use butter, even very thinly spread, in preference to margarine. If you have to use margarine, choose a luxury one, do not have much of it, and use a strongly-flavoured filling. Cream the butter to make it soft.
4 The thickness of the filling should in general equal the thickness of one slice of the bread being used, unless the filling is very rich or highly flavoured.
5 Fillings should be fairly moist. A lettuce leaf may well improve a dry or very stiff filling.
6 Do not leave sandwiches lying about for long. Wrap them in a polythene bag or in foil unless they are intended for eating at once. This will help to keep them fresh as well as away from flies or dust.

Suggestions for Sandwich Fillings

Grate Cheddar *cheese* finely, and mix with tomato ketchup or chutney, or pound to a paste with butter and Worcestershire sauce. Season to taste.

Chop hard-boiled *eggs* and mix with seasoning, a pinch of curry powder and mayonnaise, or with butter and chopped parsley.

Cucumber, sliced thinly, with plenty of salt and pepper. Use very thinly cut white or brown bread.

Mash the entire contents of a can of *sardines*. Add a few drops of lemon juice or vinegar and spread thinly.

Cooked *asparagus tips* with a very little mayonnaise, rolled up like cigarettes in brown bread and butter thinly cut. Crusts must be removed.

Cream cheese mixed with chopped chives, seasoning, spread on fresh, buttered bridge rolls cut in half.

Minced *chicken* spread fairly thickly on bread buttered with curry-flavoured butter—cream just a pinch of curry powder into the butter.

Ham with pickled gherkins, or plenty of mild mustard.

Thinly-sliced peeled *tomatoes* with salt and black pepper on rye bread. Also good with cheese spread.

Watercress with pounded egg.

Lettuce and Marmite: plenty of lettuce and a scrape of Marmite.

II BISCUITS & SCONES

Nice for a nibble, but try to eat biscuits as part of a proper meal instead of having them as snacks; they don't do much for your teeth or figure.

D Sweet Biscuit Dough

Makes approx. 3 dozen 2" biscuits
These are easy to make once you have tried shortcrust pastry.

INGREDIENTS
8 oz. self-raising flour (225 g.)
pinch salt
5 oz. fat (150 g.)
4 oz. caster or light brown sugar (125 g.)
possible additions & flavourings: choose from 1 level teaspoon grated lemon
    or orange rind; or 2 oz. (50 g.) currants or other dried fruit, or 1 oz. (30 g.)
    chocolate chips and/or 1 oz. (30 g.) chopped walnuts or 2 oz. (50 g.)
    toasted flaked almonds; or a few drops of any kind of flavouring essence
1 small egg, beaten
caster sugar for dredging
Oven: Moderate, Reg. 5, 375 °F

METHOD
1 Sift the flour and salt into a bowl and rub in the fat, as if making shortcrust
    pastry. Mix in the sugar and the fruit, nuts, flavouring, etc. that you have
    chosen.
2 Mix to a stiff dough with the beaten egg, pressing against the side of the
    bowl with a round-ended knife as you stir.
3 Roll out on a lightly-floured surface to 1/4" thickness, then cut with biscuit
    cutters or a knife into neat shapes.
4 Lay the biscuits on a greased baking sheet, leaving 1" between them to let
    them spread without touching each other. Prick each one two or three
    times with a fork. Bake at moderate heat, Reg. 5, 375 °F for 10-12 minutes,
    until delicately golden.
5 Let them cool a moment on the tin, then lift with a palette knife onto a
    wire rack. Dredge with a little caster sugar while they are still hot. Store
    when cold in an airtight tin.

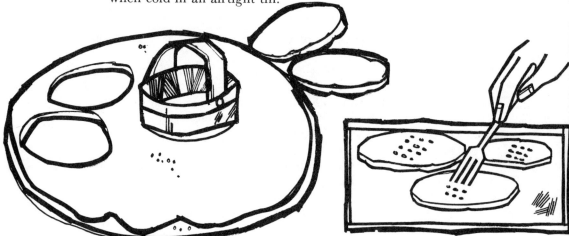

D Chocolate Crispies
Yield: 20 crispies
Quick and simple to make, chocolate crispies always disappear fast at parties.
I remember the first time I had them (at the age of five) was at the wedding of
an aunt of mine. I ate seven of them, I recollect, in spite of being already sticky
from the melting of green adhesive tape that was wound round the stems of
my posy of flowers.

INGREDIENTS
4 oz. plain chocolate or cake covering chocolate, plain flavour (125 g.)
3 oz. approx. rice krispies (100 g. approx.)
paper cases

METHOD
1. Break the chocolate into small pieces and melt it in a bowl that fits safely over the top of a saucepan in which there is hot water, or use a double saucepan if you have one. You need quite a big bowl.
2. Stir in the krispies, gently, not mashing them, until they are evenly coated with melted chocolate.
3. Remove the bowl from the heat.
4. Drop spoonfuls of the mixture into paper cases and leave to harden in a cool place. Store in an airtight tin if they are not needed at once.

M   Chocolate Chip Cookies
Yield: 3 dozen cookies

INGREDIENTS
1/2 lb. self-raising flour (200 g.)
4 oz. margarine (100 g.)
4 oz. caster sugar (100 g.)
1 teaspoon vanilla essence
1 medium egg
2 oz. chopped walnuts (50 g.)
2 oz. coarsely chopped plain chocolate (50 g.)
(Needed later) *Oven:* Fairly Hot, Reg. 6, 400 °F

METHOD
1. Sift the flour and rub in the margarine. Stir in the sugar.
2. Beat the essence into the egg and stir into the flour mixture with the nuts and chocolate to make a stiffish dough, using a round-ended knife.
3. Make into a thick roll 2″ in diameter. Put onto a piece of foil and wrap it up. Refrigerate for several hours or overnight.
4. To bake the cookies, unwrap the foil and cut off thin slices of the mixture with a sharp knife. Put them on a greased baking sheet and cook at Reg. 6, 400 °F, a fairly hot oven, for 7 minutes. Cool on a wire rack, but leave the cookies on the baking sheet to harden for a minute before transferring them with a palette knife.

D   Basic Scones
Yield: about 9 scones

INGREDIENTS
6 oz. self-raising flour (200 g.)
1/2 level teaspoon salt
3 oz. margarine or butter (100 g.)
milk to mix
Oven: Fairly Hot, Reg. 6, 400 °F

METHOD
1. Sift the flour and salt into a bowl, then rub in the fat as if making shortcrust pastry, until the result looks like fine breadcrumbs.
2. Mix to a fairly soft, but not sloppy dough with milk, stirring with a round-ended knife against the side of the bowl.
3. Sprinkle a little flour over a pastry-board or clean working surface and roll out thickly, 3/4″ or more. Cut into 2″ rounds with a plain floured cutter, put onto a greased baking sheet and brush over the tops with a pastry-brush dipped in milk.
4. Bake in a fairly hot oven, Reg. 6, 400 °F for 10-15 minutes, until well risen

and golden on top. Lift one off the sheet to see if they are done: the bottom ought to be just brown as well.

5   Serve warm, with plenty of butter and jam or cream and jam, or with cheese.

D   Cheese Scones

Add 3 oz. (75 g.) grated hard cheese such as Cheddar, 1 level teaspoon dry mustard and a good shake of cayenne pepper to the rubbed-in basic scone mixture. When you have cut them into rounds sprinkle a little more grated cheese on the tops before baking.

D   Herb Scones

Add extra seasoning and 1 rounded teaspoon chopped fresh herbs such as thyme, sage or rosemary to the rubbed-in basic scone mixture. These are good with soup or with cream cheese.

D   Sweet Scones

Add 1-2 oz. (30-50 g.) caster sugar to the basic mixture at the rubbed-in stage. These can be cut out with a fluted cutter if you like.

D   Sultana Scones

Add 1-2 oz. (30-50 g.) caster sugar and the same amount of sultanas to the basic mixture at the rubbed-in stage. Other dried fruit can be used instead if you like, to make currant scones etc.

M   Welsh Cakes

Yield: 3 dozen

These are scones in national dress. Like all plain mixtures they are best eaten on the day you make them.

INGREDIENTS

8 oz. plain flour (200 g.)
1 rounded teaspoon baking powder; or use self-raising flour and omit baking powder
1 level teaspoon salt
4 oz. margarine, cooking fat or a mixture (100 g.)
4 oz. washed currants (100 g.)
4 oz. granulated sugar (100 g.)
1 level teaspoon nutmeg or mixed spice
1 egg
2 tablespoons approx. milk
fat or oil for frying
caster sugar for dredging

METHOD

1   Sift the flour, baking powder and salt and rub in the fat.
2   Stir in the currants, sugar and spice.
3   Beat the egg and milk together and use it to mix the dry ingredients to a dough. If very stiff use a little more milk; it should be just softer than short-crust pastry.
4   Roll out to the thickness of the currants. Cut into rounds with a plain 2″ cutter.
5   Heat a knob of cooking fat in a heavy frying pan, or heat a girdle iron and grease it. Cook the cakes over quite low heat for about 2 minutes on each side, turning carefully. The cakes are apt to burn outside before the middle is cooked, so low heat is important.

6   Dredge the cakes with caster sugar and cool on a wire rack.

III CAKES

Now stop a minute and think: why do you want cake anyway? Perhaps you are young, very active and hard-working physically, slender and hungry. Pass, friend, (from time to time) into this section. Perhaps you want something nice to give to a guest? All right, you too. Perhaps you want something sweet and comforting to eat, even though you are already on the plump side? You would do much better to turn back to the sections on vegetables, salads, fruit, meat, eggs, cheese, fish and perhaps bread. Cakes are, frankly, high in calories. There is nothing against having them occasionally, like the rich puddings which they resemble and can replace, but don't make cakes a way of life. They aren't.

D   Rock Cakes
Makes 18 small cakes
These are made from a rubbed-in mixture, which makes the plainer kinds of cake. They need to be eaten when they are fresh. Try them if you have already made a crumble mixture or scones.

Ingredients
6 oz. self-raising flour (150 g.)
pinch salt
2 oz. margarine (50 g.)
2 oz. granulated sugar (50 g.)
2 oz. sultanas, currants or mixed fruit, washed (50 g.)
1 medium egg, beaten
1/2 teaspoon grated lemon peel or flavouring essence (optional)
a very little milk
Oven: Fairly Hot, Reg. 6, 400 °F

Method
1   Grease a baking sheet. Mixtures that contain sugar must go on to greased tins for baking, or else they stick.
2   Sift the flour and salt together. Rub in the margarine as if making a crumble or shortcrust pastry. When the mixture looks like breadcrumbs stir in the sugar and fruit.
3   Now, using a round-ended knife, mix in the beaten egg, lemon peel and essence, if used. Stir and press against the side of the bowl and add a dribble of milk, too, (2 teaspoons?) if the mixture isn't sticking together. It needs to be quite stiff: too stiff to fall off a spoon even when you jerk it.
4   Scrape heaped teaspoonsful of the mixture onto the baking sheet, using another teaspoon to push them off the first spoon. Leave some space between the little heaps as the cakes spread out a bit when they are baked.
5   Bake in a fairly hot oven, Reg. 6, 400 °F for about 12 minutes, or until they are golden brown. Taking care not to touch the baking sheet with your hand, lift the cakes off with a palette knife and cool them on a wire rack. Serve them soon.

Note: Once you have made these, you might like to try altering the recipe a bit. Add an extra teaspoon or two of milk, and use 2 oz. (50 g.) chopped glacé cherries in place of the other fruit to make *Cherry Buns*. Bake them in greased bun tins.

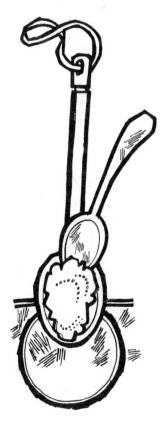

If you prefer *Chocolate Buns*, take out 1 dessertspoonful of flour and put back 1 dessertspoonful of cocoa. Add a few drops of vanilla to the mix and make a little softer in texture than rock cakes by using 2 teaspoons extra milk. Bake on well-greased bun tins.

D   Whisked Sponge Cake

Also known as a fatless sponge, this is one of the most useful recipes I know in the cake line, because it is quick to make and can be baked in so many different ways. I'll give you the basic recipe first, then tell you how it can be used.

Basic proportion: 1 egg to each oz. (30 g.) caster sugar and flour
INGREDIENTS
3 oz. plain flour (scant 100 g.)
3 eggs
3 oz. caster sugar (scant 100 g.)
1 good tablespoon hot water (optional)
few drops flavouring essence, or grated lemon zest (optional)
for chocolate sponge, substitute 1 dessertspoon cocoa for 1 dessertspoon flour
Oven: Moderate, Reg. 4-5, 350°-375 °F depending on the thickness of the cake.

METHOD
1   Get the tins that you are going to use well-greased and dredged with flour. Tap and empty them to remove the surplus. Or grease the tins and line with greased greaseproof paper.
2   Sift the flour with a few grains of salt.
3   If you have an electric mixer, simply beat eggs and sugar together on medium/high speed until they thicken and increase in bulk considerably. An electric mixer makes excellent sponge cake. If you haven't, put the eggs and sugar into a mixing bowl which will fit safely over a large saucepan half-filled with hot water. Turn the heat under the saucepan to moderate. Using a wire whisk, or rotary beater, whip the mixture in the bowl. First it will get foamy, with large bubbles, then the bubbles get smaller, the mixture thicker. You should continue to whisk until the foam "leaves a trail"—that is, you can dribble a bit off the whisk and see the pattern you have made on the surface. Write your initials, for example.
4   Turn off the electric mixer or take off the heat, and very gently fold in the water and flavouring if used, and the flour, using the wire whisk or a metal spoon.
5   Pour gently into the prepared tins and bake at a moderate heat, Reg. 4 or 5, 350° or 375 °F depending on whether you are making a compact cake in a deep tin or a thinly-spread-out one, which needs the higher temperature for a shorter time. Bake until the cake is risen and just starting to turn golden-brown at the edges only.

D   Cream Sandwich
1 small round cake
Make a 3-egg sponge mixture and bake in two sandwich cake tins (7″ diameter), greased and lined on the bottom. When cold, and the paper removed, sandwich the two halves together with a thick layer of whipped cream and your best jam.

D   Swiss Roll

METHOD
1   Grease an oblong baking tin 7″ × 11″. Cut an oblong of greaseproof paper

large enough to fit and overlap the edges a little. Snip carefully down into the corners so that you can make it fit exactly into the tin. If you have enough grease on the tin it will stay in position. Brush over the top surface of the paper with oil or melted fat, not forgetting the sides.

2 If you want an elegant roll, make a 2-egg sponge. If you want a fatter roll, or your tin is a bit bigger than the one I have suggested, make a 3-egg mixture. Spread it evenly into the prepared tin and bake in moderate oven, Reg. 5, 375 °F for 7-10 minutes. Don't let it get more than faintly coloured.

3 While the sponge bakes, spread a clean towel on the table; cover that with a sheet of greaseproof paper larger than the baking tin and dredge the paper with caster sugar all over. Warm 3 tablespoons jam (especially raspberry) until it is easy to spread. Have a sharp knife handy.

4 When the sheet of sponge is cooked, turn it out onto the sugary paper. Tear off the greaseproof paper on the back of the sponge. Quickly trim the sides and far end with the sharp knife and score the end of the cake 1/2" in from the end nearest you to make it easier to roll: take care not to cut right through. Spread all over the surface of the cake with an even layer of jam, but not quite to the end or it will squash out.

5 Working quickly, start to roll up the sponge by lifting the towel to push the edge of the cake away from you. Press down firmly where you scored along the edge of the sponge, then roll as tightly as you can, pushing from behind the towel. The cake should not split—it would mean that you had baked it too long or been too slow—and you should have 2 1/2 turns for a perfect Swiss roll.

D Sponge Flan

For a comparatively modest sum you can buy a sponge flan tin, which turns out a cake with a rim round the edge. If you like sponge flans and have been in the habit of buying them ready to fill, you will save the money spent within a few puddings.

Grease the tin well: I use a brush filled with oil for mine. Make a 2-egg sponge mixture and pour it into the prepared tin. Bake in a moderate oven, Reg. 4, 350 °F, for about 15 minutes. Turn it out onto a wire rack, let it get cold and then fill with fruit, fruit and jelly on the point of setting, cream and so on. See also page 135.

D Trifle Sponge Cakes

You can bake small sponge cakes in patty tins, or, if you have a special tin with oblong moulds set into it, make your own trifle sponge cakes. Young children seem to have a passion for them, either plain or perhaps spread with a little jam in the middle.

Grease the tins and spoon in the sponge mixture; 2-egg mix will make about 8 sponge cakes. Dredge the top with caster sugar and bake at moderate heat, Reg. 4, 350 °F for 10-15 minutes.

M Genoese Sponge

It isn't often that one can follow the evolution of recipes as clearly as in this case. I'm quite sure that some enterprising cook once muttered "I wonder what would happen if I folded a little melted butter into a whisked sponge mixture...?"

INGREDIENTS

3 eggs
3 oz. caster sugar (scant 100 g.)
3 oz. plain flour, sifted (scant 100 g.)
2 oz. butter, melted (60 g.)

icing sugar or glacé icing and decoration to finish (optional)
Oven, Moderate, Reg. 4, 350 °F

METHOD

1 Prepare a large shallow cake tin with a liberal greasing and dusting with caster sugar.
2 Whisk the eggs and sugar together over hot water or by electric mixer until they are thick and very much increased in bulk.
3 Fold in a little of the sifted flour alternately with butter.
4 Pour the mixture into the prepared tin and bake in a moderate oven, Reg. 4, 350 °F for about 25-30 minutes, or until well-risen, golden and firm to the touch. Serve plain, or dusted with icing sugar, or topped with glacé icing and decorated.

NOTE: This cake can be baked in a square tin, cut into squares or diamonds and coated in melted coloured fondant (page 187) thinned slightly with stock syrup. (Hold on a palette knife over the saucepan.) Decorate at pleasure.

D   Glacé Icing
Enough to cover top of 8″ cake

INGREDIENTS

4 oz. icing sugar (125 g.)
1-1 1/2 tablespoons water
flavouring and colouring to taste: e.g. vanilla, coffee essence, cochineal
decoration if liked, such as nuts or cherries or bought sweets such as chocolate beans

METHOD

1 Sift the icing sugar if at all hard or lumpy.
2 Stir in the water to make to the consistency of thick cream.
3 Put into a double saucepan, or into a small bowl over hot water, and heat gently until it becomes liquid.
4 Stir and pour carefully over the cake—or biscuits, etc.—add decorations if used and leave undisturbed to harden.

NOTE: For *Chocolate glacé icing* add 2 rounded teaspoons cocoa powder to the icing sugar before sifting, and 1-2 drops vanilla essence with the water.

D   Creamed Sponge Mixtures
These mixtures are what most people think of immediately when anyone says "cake", and in fact variations of them make the biggest group of English cakes.

Fat, which should be butter or good-quality margarine, can be used in varying proportions with flour, depending on how rich you want the finished cake to be. The amount of sugar is equal to the amount of fat. Thus, you can make a good cake with half fat and sugar to flour: e.g. 4 oz. (100 g.) butter and sugar to 8 oz. (200 g.) flour, and so on all the way up to equal quantities of them all. The richer the cake, that is, the more fat and sugar it contains, the better it will keep.

The classic in this category is Victoria sponge. Hold onto your waistline: here we go!

Victoria Sponge Sandwich
1 × 6 1/2″ sandwich cake

INGREDIENTS

4 oz. butter or margarine (100 g.)

4 oz. caster sugar (100 g.)
2 stardard eggs (2 medium eggs for metric measure)
4 oz. plain flour (100 g.)
1/4 level teaspoon baking powder
pinch of salt
flavouring such as: grated lemon zest, orange zest, any essences; or reduce flour
  by 1 dessertspoon and replace with cocoa powder
jam or buttercream for filling
caster sugar, icing sugar, buttercream or any icing to finish top (optional)
Oven: Moderate, Reg. 4, 350 °F

METHOD

1 Grease two sponge sandwich tins, dredge lightly with flour and caster sugar,
   and tap to remove the surplus.
2 Put the butter and sugar into a very slightly warmed bowl and beat
   together with a wooden spoon (or very clean hand) until they are soft and
   fluffy, and the colour has changed from yellow to almost-white. This
   process is called "creaming", and unless you have an electric mixer, which
   does the job admirably, it cannot be skimped if you want a properly-light
   cake.
3 Break the eggs into a basin and beat them slightly with a fork. Add them
   a little at a time to the mixture, beating again after each addition. If you do
   this carefully, and have the eggs at room temperature, the mixture should
   remain smooth. Occasionally you may get an effect of separation, called
   "curdling" because it looks as if the mixture had curdled: it hasn't, of
   course, but needs correcting by beating in a spoonful or so of the measured
   quantity of flour.
4 If all goes well, sift the flour, salt and baking powder into the mixture,
   say about a third at a time, and fold it in using a metal spoon, avoiding
   beating. This is because flour contains gluten, which is splendid for bread,
   but tends to make cakes tougher than necessary if you stir too hard or too
   long. (See page 192 if you aren't sure about "folding".)
5 Spoon the mixture evenly into the two prepared cake tins, smooth over the
   top with a knife, then bake in a moderate oven, Reg. 4, 350 °F for about
   20-25 minutes. Turn the tins round at half time to help the cakes to rise
   and brown evenly.
6 When well-risen and golden coloured and starting to shrink a bit away from
   the sides of the tins, you can consider them done. Leave for a few minutes
   in the tins, then run a knife round the edges. Turn each onto a clean cloth
   held in your hand, then turn onto a wire rack to cool. If you do it this way
   you don't get the top marked with a wire grid.
7 When cold, sandwich the two halves together with jam or flavoured buttercream (recipe follows). Sprinkle the top with caster or icing sugar: you can
   put a fancy d'oyley on top to use as a stencil when you sprinkle with icing
   sugar if you like that kind of thing. Lift it off cleanly so that you don't
   smudge the design. Or ice with glacé or royal icing and decorate. Or even
   leave plain.

Buttercream
Enough to fill and cover a 6 1/2" sandwich sponge

INGREDIENTS
2 oz. unsalted butter (50 g.) or marg. if you can't tell the difference
4 oz. sifted icing sugar (100 g.)
a little warm water or fruit juice
flavouring to taste: see below

1 Cream the butter and icing sugar together until soft and light.
2 Add a little warm water—say 2 teaspoons, or equivalent fruit juice to make a soft but not floppy mixture.
3 Use as a cake filling, or for icing the top, perhaps with a piped design or simply by spreading over and smoothing with a knife. Decorate, too, if you like.

Flavourings:

Lemon: add lemon juice and grated zest. Taste.

Orange: ditto, but orange.

Vanilla: add a few drops essence.

Coffee: 1 teaspoon coffee extract instead of 1 teaspoon water, or use instant coffee to taste.

Chocolate: add melted chocolate (1-2 oz., 30-60 g.) or cocoa powder to taste.

M Sachertorte

1 large cake

This delectable cake, the speciality of a famous Viennese restaurant, has numerous examples of the only true recipe, all slightly different. This one is at least Austrian in origin! More important, it produces a delicious cake. An electric mixer is a help, if you have one, as there is a lot of beating involved.

INGREDIENTS

Cake:
6 oz. caster sugar (175 g.) in two lots of 3 oz.
6 oz. butter (175 g.)
6 oz. plain chocolate, melted over hot water (175 g.)
6 eggs, separated
6 oz. plain flour, sifted (175 g.)
1 teaspoon vanilla essence
apricot jam, warmed and sieved

Icing:
5 oz. icing sugar (150 g.)
2 tablespoons water
4 oz. plain chocolate, melted over hot water (100 g.)
Oven: Warm, Reg. 2-3, 325 °F

METHOD

1 Prepare a moule à manqué or other large shallow round cake tin by greasing it and lining the base with greased paper.
2 Cream together 3 oz. sugar with the butter and melted chocolate, then add the egg yolks and beat for 5 minutes minimum.
3 Beat the whites of egg to a stiff foam, then add the rest of the sugar and beat again to stiffness.
4 Fold the egg white mixture thoroughly into the creamed one.
5 Fold the flour and vanilla essence into the mixture.
6 Transfer to the prepared tin, smooth over the top and bake in a warm oven, Reg. 2-3, 325 °F for at least 1 1/2 hours, until thoroughly firm and shrinking from the sides of the tin.
7 Turn out and cool on a wire rack. Split carefully in half, making a mark

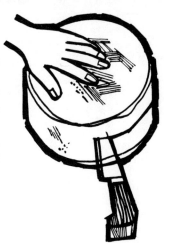

on the side of the cake so that you can reassemble it correctly. Spread with a thin layer of warm jam and replace the top.

8 Brush all over the top and sides with warm jam, then make the icing: stir together the icing sugar and water, bring to the boil and boil for a few seconds (to a thread).

9 Stir in the melted chocolate quickly and spread the icing over top and sides of cake with a palette knife. You must work fast as the icing sets quickly. Sachertorte is not decorated further in any way.

NOTE: If you prefer, use melted plain chocolate cake covering to ice the cake.

M   Rich Fruit Cake
1 large cake
This is suitable for a Christmas, birthday or wedding cake. It is very rich. If you like you can reduce the amount of dried fruit to 1 lb. (450 g.) and omit the cherries, peel and ground almonds to make a more everyday fruit cake that is still very good.

INGREDIENTS
8 oz. butter or good margarine (225 g.)
8 oz. soft brown sugar (225 g.)
3-4 eggs, beaten
2 oz. ground almonds (60 g.)
8 oz. plain flour (225 g.)
1 level teaspoon mixed spice or 1 teaspoon grated lemon zest
1 1/2 lbs. total mixed dried fruits: sultanas, currants, raisins (washed and stoned if necessary) or any one or two kinds (700 g.)
4 oz. glacé cherries, halved (100 g.)
3 oz. chopped mixed peel (75 g.)
1 tablespoon brandy or rum (optional)
Oven: Warm, Reg. 3, 335 °F

METHOD
1 Grease and line a large cake tin with a double thickness of greased greaseproof paper. Also prepare a double circle of paper ready to put on top of the cake while it is baking.

2 Cream together the fat and sugar, beat in the eggs and ground almonds. If you are using an electric mixer, three eggs will probably be sufficient, as you should avoid a very soft consistency.

3 Sift together the flour and spices, and stir these into the mixture with the prepared dried fruits, cherries and mixed peel.

4 Turn into the prepared tin and bake in the lower half of a warm oven, Reg. 3, 335 °F for 1 hour. Then cover the top with a double piece of greaseproof paper to prevent it browning too much. Continue to bake for a further 2 1/2 hours or until a skewer pushed into the middle of the cake comes out clean. Leave the cake in the tin until it is cold, but sprinkle a tablespoonful of spirits over the top while it is still warm if you like, to give a good flavour. Leave the paper round the cake until you want to use it.

NOTE: This cake is a good keeper. If you intend it for Christmas, cover at least the top with almond paste, and ice with royal icing (see later recipes).

M   Dundee Cake
Make and bake as rich fruit cake, but arrange blanched split almonds, in a pattern, liberally all over the top of the cake before baking.

M   Simnel Cake

INGREDIENTS
1 rich fruit cake, baked
almond paste made with 8 oz. ground almonds, etc.
little beaten egg yolk and milk
decorations such as chicken, chocolate eggs, etc.—bought sweets can be used.

METHOD
1   Cover the top of the cooked cake with a thick layer of almond paste rolled out and cut to size, using the tin in which the cake was baked as a guide. Use rather more than half the almond paste for this.
2   Roll the rest of the almond paste into small balls, and stick them in position round the edge of the cake with a dot of the egg mixture.
3   Glaze the surface of the paste with the beaten egg and milk, not too generously, then put it under a medium grill for a few moments, or into a hot oven, watching it constantly. Almond paste can melt or burn easily, so you must be attentive. The top should be merely highlighted golden brown.
4   Decorate as you like with birds, Easter eggs, and so on. Serve at Easter.

D   Almond Paste *(Uncooked Marzipan)*
To cover 1 cake 8″ approx. diameter

INGREDIENTS
8 oz. ground almonds (225 g.)
8 oz. icing sugar (225 g.)
8 oz. caster sugar (225 g.) or use a total of 1 lb. icing sugar (450 g.) and no caster sugar
1 teaspoon lemon juice
a few drops almond essence or vanilla essence
1 1/2-2 small eggs, beaten

METHOD
1   Put the ground almonds into a large mixing bowl. Sift in the icing sugar and add the caster sugar if used. Stir.
2   Sprinkle over the lemon juice and a few drops of almond or vanilla—half a dozen should be enough.
3   Using a round-ended table knife, stir the mixture, pressing against the side of the bowl and adding the egg, a little at a time. Go on mixing and adding egg until the consistency is pliable but not sticky. You may not need all the egg.
4   Use for covering cakes or for making sweets.

D   Royal Icing
To cover a cake about 8″ diameter
This will set rock-hard in time. If you want to decorate a Christmas or wedding cake well in advance, add glycerine to the icing to stop it getting too stony. If the cake is to be eaten in a day or two you need not bother.

INGREDIENTS
1 lb. sifted icing sugar (450 g.)
1 teaspoon glycerine, optional (bought from chemist)
1 dessertspoon lemon juice
2-3 whites of egg

METHOD

1 Put the icing sugar into a large bowl, add glycerine if used, lemon juice and part of the white of egg, unbeaten.
2 Using a wooden spoon, rub and work together gently, trying to avoid a beating movement which causes air-bubbles.
3 Use enough egg white to get the consistency you want: test it on the back of the wooden spoon. To cover a cake by the pouring method the icing must just flow. To cover it by the scraping method, it must just fail to flow. If by chance you make the icing too thin, simply add a bit more sifted icing sugar.
4 Use to ice cakes (see *Christmas Cake* recipe).

NOTE: If you want royal icing for piping, make it a fairly stiff mixture. Add food colouring drop by drop, blending it well. Keep bowls of icing covered with a damp tea towel when they are left for more than a minute or two: this will stop them setting hard on top.

Christmas or Birthday Cake   *Joint Recipe*

This is an assembly job. In my household I usually make the cake, then, when she feels like it, my daughter Pip makes the almond paste, but usually leaves me to apply it to the cake. After it has dried out for a day or two I make the royal icing and pour it over the cake. In another two or three days, when the icing hardens, Pip likes to take over. She sticks the cake to a silver board with a little left-over icing, then prepares some more icing with which to pipe a design on the cake. Sometimes she uses bought cake decorations too; Father Christmas for instance. I prefer a restrained effect, but Pip likes to use lots of colours. Cake decoration is a complete branch of cookery in itself. There is only enough space here to start you off.

INGREDIENTS

M 1 rich fruit cake, baked
D more royal icing made with up to another 1 lb. icing sugar, etc.
   apricot jam
   water
M royal icing made with 1 lb. icing sugar etc.
D more royal icing made with up to another 1 lb. icing sugar etc.
   colouring to taste
   decorations (bought) and cake frill (optional)

METHOD

To cover cake with almond paste:
1 It is often a good idea to turn the cake upside down for icing, as you then get a completely smooth surface.
2 Prepare the almond paste.
3 Put two or three spoonsful of apricot jam in a small saucepan and heat it gently. You want plenty of the runny part of the jam, not the bits of fruit, so strain it when it has melted, and if it is very thick add a very little hot water. Using a clean pastry brush, brush the jam all over the top and sides of the cake.
4 Divide the almond paste into one-third and two-third pieces.
5 Make the small piece into a ball, then roll it out into a circle as if rolling pastry, except that the rolling surface is dusted with icing sugar instead of flour.
6 Lift the circle on the rolling pin and lay it across the top of the cake. Press it onto the cake with a light roll across with the rolling pin. Trim off carefully with a sharp knife level with the sides of the cake.

7 Roll out the rest of the paste into strips which, when trimmed, will exactly fit the height of your cake. Short lengths are the easiest to handle. You can roll the cake like a wheel onto the strips, but take care not to spoil the top; or lift the strips with a palette knife and press them against the sides of the cake by rolling a straight-sided jam jar round the outside. Make sure that the joins between the strips are tight and neat.

8 Leave the cake to dry for a day or so before icing with royal icing.

To cover cake with royal icing:

1 First decide whether you will pour the icing over, or scrape it. I think that pouring gives a better finish, but scraping is easier and perfectly acceptable. Make up the royal icing to suit your method: i.e. thinner for pouring method.

2 *To pour:* tip all the icing out of the bowl on top of the cake, which has been put on a wire cooling tray. Now tilt the cake this way and that, until the icing has covered the top and runs slowly and evenly down the sides. You may need to "help" the sides a bit, with a knife, but don't touch the top, unless there are large bubbles on the surface, which you can burst with a clean hatpin.

To scrape: the icing must be of thicker consistency, and you need a steady hand. Put a large dollop of icing in the middle of the cake, and work it over the top by spreading with a palette knife. Now get a straight edge such as a clean ruler or a knife with a blade long enough. Holding it in the fingertips of both hands, with the cake underneath and between them, draw it steadily across the top of the cake towards you, so that you scrape the icing level. It is difficult to scrape the sides level in this way unless you have a turntable, so I suggest that you rough-ice the sides, swirling and pulling the icing into icicles with a palette knife.

3 Leave the cake undisturbed in a dry atmosphere for a day or two before you lift it onto the cake board. (Put a dab of wet icing in the middle of the board to hold the cake firm.) Excess icing that has dripped off the cake after pouring can be scraped up and used to sweeten puddings and so on.

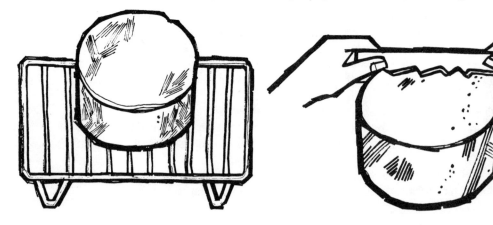

To decorate a Christmas, Birthday or Wedding Cake
This does require skill: on the other hand, once you have managed to pipe even a few stars you can give a professional-looking finish to cakes, and it may well be worth the effort. It is certainly fun.

1 Decide on a design: a large star or a tree perhaps for Christmas, for example. Draw it in pencil on greaseproof paper, using compasses for geometrical designs. Put the pattern on top of the smooth, dry icing, and prick through the greaseproof paper with a sharp hatpin to make guidelines in pinholes on top of the cake. (A small pin is too dangerous to have anywhere near food.)

2 Make up some royal icing and colour it with proper food colouring. Add it only a drop at a time, from the end of a skewer, and keep the bowls of icing covered with a clean damp tea towel to stop them drying. The icing must be just stiff enough to hold its shape.

3 You can use an icing set if you have one, but I think a paper forcing bag is easier to use. Make a triangle by folding a 14″ square of greaseproof paper from corner to corner. Cut along the fold. This will make two bags. Fold the triangle again to make a smaller one, double thickness. Lift point C and curve it round so that the underside lies on top of point A. Lift point B and curve it round so that it lies at the back of point A. Fold these points down together two or three times so that the bag is secure. Snip off the point of the cone you have made and drop in a small star or writing tube.

4 Put a heaped tablespoon of icing into the bag, fold the top over and over and twist the ends to keep the icing in. Hold the filled bag in the "V"s made by your first and second fingers of both hands, pressing down with your thumbs. Practise a little to find out how much you have to press to make stars and whorls of different sizes with the star pipe, or lines and squiggles with the writing pipe. Once you are confident, off you go onto your design on your cake. If you do make a mistake, just gently scrape it off with a small knife.

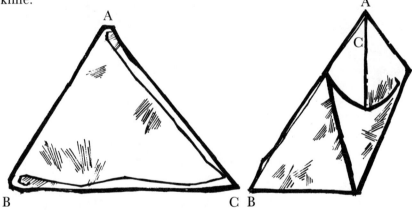

M *or* D Meringues
Makes 10-12 medium shells—i.e. 5-6 (paired) meringues
Is there anything more delicious than a meringue, light, crisp, sweet, filled with slightly chilled thick Chantilly cream? Only another meringue, light, crisp, etc. with real ice-cream and genuine chocolate sauce!

INGREDIENTS
3 egg whites plus pinch of salt
6 oz. caster sugar (150 g.)
little extra sugar for dredging
Chantilly cream or plain whipped cream slightly sweetened
Oven: lowest setting possible

1 Cover a large baking sheet with foil.

2 Put the egg whites into a bowl which has a rounded interior, or into the bowl of an electric mixer. The bowl must be absolutely clean, without a scrap of grease, and the egg whites must have no trace of yolk in them.

3 The next thing is to beat with a wire or rotary whisk or with electric mixer beaters, until the whites are very stiff and dry looking. If you are whipping eggs with a wire whisk have the bowl at a convenient height for you (have the bowl in your lap as you sit down, perhaps). Keep your elbow close to your side and with an easy, loose movement of your wrist and hand holding the whisk, spin it in circles through the egg white. Remember that the object of your movement is to get air into the whites, not to bang the bowl. It is a skill that comes with practice, but it is a very necessary one, as beaten whites of egg are used in so many of the more interesting dishes. Incidentally some people prefer to beat the whites on a plate, using a palette knife in the same way as I describe using the whisk, but I think a bowl is safer for a near-beginner.

4 When the white is stiff enough it will look dry, will easily stand up in high peaks when you pull the whisk away, and (the classic test) the egg whites will not fall out if you turn the bowl upside down: but nobody explains what you should do if you then discover that the whites weren't whipped quite enough, after all.

5 Very gently fold in half the measured quantity of sugar, then start to whip again. The whites will get runnier, then stiffen again. Have patience here, and go on beating until the mixture is really as stiff as it was before. It is easy to think "Oh, that'll do"—but it won't.

6 When it is really stiff again, fold in the rest of the sugar. If you have a forcing bag, fit in a star pipe and fill the bag, turning down the top edge first so that it doesn't get smeared with meringue. Pipe the meringue into whorls or rosettes or fingers with a rosette at the end, always matching two to a pair. Keep all meringues on one baking sheet about the same size, or some will cook before others. If you have no forcing bag, or don't want to use it, drop the mixture into neat piles from a tablespoon, scraping the meringue out with another spoon.

7 Dredge lightly with more caster sugar for a crisp finish.

8 Bake—or dry out rather—on the floor of the coolest oven you can have in

your cooker. Solid fuel cookers, or those with warming ovens, are good, as you can leave the meringues there for hours. I find that my meringues are cooked after 2 1/2-3 hours on the floor of a very cool oven, Reg. 1/4, 250 ºF approx. Don't worry if they are slightly golden rather than pure white: most people prefer them with a light tan.

9 Peel the foil away from the base of the meringues, which should be crisp all through. Store in an airtight tin: they keep well.

10 Just before serving, sandwich them together with slightly sweetened whipped cream or with Chantilly cream. Also very good with cold fruit salads and ice-creams of any flavour. Can be used for a splendid dessert as well as for a special tea.

M Meringue Flan

Meringue can be used to pipe a very decorative flan case, over a circle marked on foil on a baking sheet. Pipe the meringue in a spiral, leaving no gaps, and make a rim by piping a second layer of meringue round the edge, or by piping large rosettes. Bake as for small meringues.

This flan is particularly good filled with a mixture of whipped cream and fresh fruit.

M Suggestions for Making Gâteaux

It is creatively rewarding to devise gâteaux for yourself, and several times in the course of this book I've given some suggestions as to how this can be done. Here is a brief re-cap of ideas, with some new ones:

Basis of gâteaux can be made from one or a combination of these:
shortcrust pastry
flan pastry
flaky pastry
rough puff pastry
whisked sponge
Genoese sponge
Victoria sponge, including chocolate flavour
meringue mixture baked in discs or as a flan

Fillings:
whipped cream, plain or flavoured with chocolate, liqueurs, etc.
buttercream
ice-cream
confectioner's custard
sweet sauces
fruit: raw, canned, stewed or glacé
jam, marmalade, lemon curd

Toppings:
as fillings, or glacé or royal icing, or melted chocolate

Decorations:
nuts, whole, chopped or toasted
fresh or glacé fruits
tiny meringues
piped cream or buttercream
melted or grated chocolate
sweets—and etc. too, if you can think of any more!

Home-made Sweets

You need never have sweets at all, and be perfectly well-fed and happy. If you never eat sweets your teeth will be much more likely to be healthy, and you will be less likely to be too fat. But of course it is all a matter of degree. Occasionally you may want to give sweets as a gift (to someone who already has false teeth?) or to celebrate Easter or Christmas or some other festival. I will tell you then how to make a few of the more popular kinds.

Sugar is curious stuff, and it behaves differently when heated to different temperatures. There is a lot of very skilled handling involved when making many sweets, but the recipes which follow are reasonably beginner-proof. A sugar-boiling thermometer is an asset, but not essential, though if you decide to buy one you may well find it very useful indeed if you make much jam.

Sugar is usually boiled with a liquid: the longer it boils the more water evaporates, the more concentrated the sugar solution and the higher the temperature at which it boils. Here is a table to show you, if you are interested, some of the names given to various sugar-boiling stages:

Water boiling point	212 °F	
Jam setting point	220-222 °F	Jam on cold plate crinkles on surface
Thread	220-225 °F	A cooled drop pulls out to a thread between finger and thumb
Soft ball	240 °F	Mixture can be gathered into a soft lump when dropped into cold water
Hard ball	250 °F	Mixture sets to a harder lump in cold water
Small crack	280 °F	Mixture gets harder still and brittle
Crack	310 °F	
Caramel	345 °F	Sugar turns golden brown
	Above 345 °F	Mixtures taste bitter and burnt. Only use of sugar taken to this stage is to colour gravy brown.

DON'T MAKE BOILED SUGAR RECIPES UNLESS YOU HAVE AN ADULT'S PERMISSION. BOILING SUGAR CAN GIVE A HORRIBLE BURN.

D Basic Fudge

INGREDIENTS
1/2 pint milk (fresh or reconstituted evaporated) (300 ml.)
2 lbs. granulated sugar (900 g.)

2 oz. butter or margarine (50 g.)
1 level tablespoon glucose if available
1 teaspoon vanilla essence

METHOD

1 Grease a shallow tin such as a Swiss-roll tin, about 7″ × 11″ or equivalent. Have a plate ready too, for the scrapings.
2 Put the milk, sugar, fat and glucose into a large thick-based saucepan. The mixture will froth up a great deal when it boils, so use a 5-pint capacity pan, or bigger if you have one.
3 Heat the mixture gently, stirring all the time, until it boils.
4 Continue to boil, stirring from time to time, taking care not to let the mixture boil over. You must adjust the heat to suit your particular saucepan. Cook the fudge for 10-15 minutes, until it is light fawn coloured and when a little of it is dropped into cold water you can roll it into a pliable ball. On a sugar-boiling thermometer it should register 238-240 °F.
5 Remove the saucepan from the heat and let it stand for three minutes.
6 Stir the essence into the fudge. Tilt the pan a bit and work the spoon through the deep puddle of fudge, rubbing the side of the pan to and fro. This process, called "graining", will make some of the sugar turn into crystals: this is the tricky bit, because you want enough crystals to make the fudge set, but not to set too hard.
7 When the mixture starts to thicken pour it quickly into the prepared tin. Don't scrape out the saucepan into the bulk of the mixture, or the last scrapings will probably be harder than the poured fudge. Put them on your "bits" plate instead.
8 Cut the fudge into squares while still warm, using a sharp knife and a ruler if you haven't a steady hand.

Fudge Variations

When you have made a batch of successful basic fudge once or twice, you can try variations like these:

Chocolate: Stir 3 oz. (75 g.) melted plain chocolate into the cooked fudge and continue to grain.

Nut: Use almond essence in place of vanilla if you like, and stir 2 oz. (50 g.) chopped walnuts or almonds or hazelnuts into the cooked fudge and continue to grain. The nuts can be toasted or not, as you like.

Cherry: Stir 2 oz. (50 g.) chopped glacé cherries into the cooked fudge and continue to grain. Cherry fudge is very good if you also add chocolate as above.

Nut & Raisin Fudge: Stir 1 oz. (30 g.) chopped nuts and 1 oz. (30 g.) cleaned raisins into the cooked fudge and continue to stir.

Ginger Fudge: Omit vanilla essence. Stir 2-4 oz. chopped preserved ginger (50-100 g.) into the cooked fudge and continue to grain.

D   Home-Made Chocolates

You can produce very creditable chocolates at home with a little care. I do recommend the use of chocolate cake covering rather than ordinary melted chocolate, because the cake covering, which you can buy at a grocer's, is easy to melt and handle, whereas ordinary chocolate is more difficult to get to exactly the right temperature and may turn a greyish colour if overheated.

I won't give you quantities, but don't use less than 1/2 lb. (225 g.) of chocolate, or you won't have enough depth for dipping.

Chocolate cake covering
centres as you like:
e.g. fondant creams, plain or fruit flavoured
    peppermint creams (very good), coffee creams, etc.
    fudge, plain or any variation
    almond paste, cut into squares or fancy shapes
    whole nut kernels, especially Brazil nuts
    chopped nuts mixed with royal icing, rolled into balls
    glacé fruits, including cherries

decoration (optional):
e.g. little bought silver balls
    "hundreds and thousands"
    nuts
    crystallized violets
    angelica

METHOD

1 Melt the chocolate covering in a double saucepan, or in a basin over hot water. Do not continue to heat the water after the chocolate has melted.
2 While the chocolate is heating, spread a tray with foil.
3 Remove the double saucepan from the heat. Using the back of a fork or the round end of a skewer, dip each centre into the molten chocolate, lift it to drain for a moment, then invert it over the foil so that it drops off the fork or skewer.
4 Decorate the top of the chocolate before it sets, e.g. with a little piece of walnut, or leave it with the mark of the dipping tool on top.
5 Leave the tray of chocolates alone for 24 hours, putting them in a cool place to harden. Peel off the foil and store in boxes or tins. If there is a wide "foot" of chocolate round the edge of the sweet you can trim it off with a small knife. The chocolate recovered may be remelted.

M Rum Truffles
Makes 16-20 sweets
These are my favourite home-made sweets: they are pleasant with coffee after dinner.

INGREDIENTS
1/2 lb. plain chocolate (225 g.)
4 teaspoons top-of-milk or cream or 1 oz. unsalted butter (30 g.)

6 teaspoons rum
chocolate vermicelli, sold sometimes as chocolate flavoured sugar strands
paper petit four cases

METHOD
1 Melt the chocolate in a double saucepan.
2 Stir in the milk or butter and the rum. Blend thoroughly.
3 Remove from the heat. When cool enough to hold its shape, roll into small
   even-sized balls in the palms of the hands. Roll each in chocolate
   vermicelli (alternatively you could use chopped nuts). Put into petit four
   cases and leave in a cool place until set.

D Uncooked Fondant

This is quick to make as an alternative to boiled fondant. It is not quite so
melting in texture, but still very good.

INGREDIENTS
1 lb. icing sugar (450 g.)
1 tablespoon glucose
2 egg whites approx.

METHOD
1 Put the icing sugar into a bowl and mix in the glucose and egg white,
   unbeaten, to make a stiff paste. You may not need quite all the white.
2 Turn out of the bowl onto a smooth clean surface and knead to make
   sure it is well mixed. Flavour and colour as given under variations for
   fondant.
3 Roll out as if it were pastry, but dust the rolling surface with icing sugar
   and cut into small fancy shapes, or squares, diamonds or triangles if you
   have no small cutters.
4 Leave to harden for a day on trays covered with foil or greaseproof paper.
   Pack away in tins, with greaseproof paper between each layer.

M Fondant

This useful substance can be used for icing special cakes, as well as for making
sweets. To ice cakes with it, warm it gently—very gently indeed—in a double
saucepan until it is pourable. A little added water is sometimes needed, and
flavourings such as concentrated fruit juices or liqueurs added. A sugar-
boiling thermometer is desirable for this recipe, though you can do without.

INGREDIENTS
2 lbs. granulated sugar (900 g.)
1/2 pint plus two tablespoons water (300 ml.)
1 tablespoon glucose

METHOD
1 Put the sugar and water into a large saucepan, bring to the boil slowly, add
   the glucose and brush down the sides of the pan with a pastry brush dipped
   in cold water to remove any stray sugar crystals.
2 When all the sugar has dissolved boil without stirring to 240 °F, soft ball
   stage.
3 Rinse out a large shallow tin, such as a meat tin, with cold water so that it
   is just damp. Pour in the fondant. Don't scrape out the saucepan.
4 Leave the syrup to cool to 110 °F: this will take about 15 minutes.

5 Now "turn" the fondant by folding the syrup with a palette knife from the outside of the tin towards the centre, then making a figure-of-8 movement in the middle. Repeat from the outside, turning the tin round to turn all the fondant evenly. Suddenly and spectacularly the syrup will change from transparent stickiness to hard opaque whiteness.

6 Scrape it out onto a suitable surface and knead the lump until it gets less hard and more pliable. If it is very hard, leave it covered with foil and a tea towel for some minutes before kneading.

7 When it softens the fondant can have colouring and flavouring essences kneaded into it.

8 Roll out if it is meant for sweets and stamp out fancy shapes, circles and so on. Leave them for 24 hours in a cool airy place to harden before packing them into boxes, or dipping them into chocolate, or asking your daughter to do so.

Variations for Uncooked and Boiled Fondant

Vanilla creams: add vanilla essence to taste. Leave white.

Ginger creams: add 4 oz. (100 g.) finely chopped crystallized ginger to the fondant before rolling out.

Peppermint creams: add a few drops of oil of peppermint (obtainable from a chemist and *much* nicer than peppermint essence). Taste as you go. Colour green or leave white.

Fruit creams: add best-quality strawberry/raspberry essence or liqueurs, and colour appropriately.

Nut creams: add 4 oz. (100 g.) chopped almonds, walnuts or hazelnuts.

Coffee creams: flavour and colour with coffee essence. Nuts can be added too.

Chocolate creams: knead in 4-6 oz. melted plain chocolate (100-150 g.). Nuts too? Or ginger?

Tips & Terms

An alphabetical list of miscellaneous directions, definitions and opinions. Left-handed people please reverse manipulative directions.

Angelica A plant, the candied stem of which is often used to decorate sweet dishes. Cut it with a sharp knife.

Aspic A clear savoury jelly, brushed over cold foods to add a sparkle or for setting moulds of chopped meat, etc. See also MASKING A MOULD. Sprinkle 1/2 oz. (15 g.) powdered gelatine into 1/2 pint (300 ml.) strained bone or fish stock. Stir and leave to soak for a few minutes. Then add 1 tablespoon sherry and an egg white and heat, whisking. Boil 10 minutes, strain as for consommé and leave in a cool place. Use at setting-point, or chop set jelly with a wet knife for garnishes.

Au Gratin *see* BREADCRUMBS.

Basting Pouring fat and meat juices from the pan with a spoon over meat in the course of roasting, or pouring flavoured syrup over a cake. The idea is to stop the surface of the meat from drying out, or to make the cake soak up the liquid.

Beating A vigorous movement, either to combine two ingredients or to whip air into a mixture. Depending on the recipe use a wooden spoon (creaming), a wire whisk or rotary beater (sponge mixture) or palette knife, wire whisk or electric beater (egg whites). For method of whipping whites see page 182.

Beurre Manié A mixture of two-thirds butter (or margarine) to one-third flour. Add it little by little to boiling soups or sauces, etc. to thicken them at the end of cooking. Useful if you don't know how much liquid there is exactly, so can't calculate how much other thickening to use.

Blanching Dipping vegetables or fruit into boiling water briefly, or pouring it over them, then plunging them into cold water. This makes removal of skins easier. Also done to whiten or disinfect the surface of food.

Boiling Cooking in liquid at boiling point. In practice, SIMMERING is more often used.

Bouquet Garni A little bundle of herbs used to flavour soups, stews and other savoury dishes. It is made by taking a sprig or two of parsley, a small or half bay leaf, 1 clove, a piece of blade mace and if possible a sprig of thyme or marjoram, or a pinch of the dried herbs. Tie them all up in a piece of muslin, lashing it well with cotton thread. Leave a long piece of thread to tie to the saucepan handle; then you won't forget to remove the bouquet before dishing up. The muslin at least isn't edible! Alternatively you can, more expensively, buy little sachets of dried herbs that look like tea-bags. It really is worth the trouble to include a bouquet garni if the recipe calls for one. Once you have tried you will be converted.

Breadcrumbs *White crumbs:* get hold of a two-day old (stale) piece of white bread and grate it on a fine grater. Bread can also be dried a little in a cool oven. Use for egg-and-crumbing (page 89). White crumbs can be fried in a little butter to use as a garnish.

Browned crumbs or Raspings: made from bread baked slowly golden-brown, then crushed (in a polythene bag) with a rolling pin and sifted. Use for sprinkling over food that is to be browned under the grill. This process makes the dish AU GRATIN: cheese is not essential.

Bun Tins *see* PATTY TINS.

Burns *see* FIRST-AID.

Burnt on Splashes Scrape them off and rub with a damp clean muslin before the dish appears at table.

Butter or Margarine? From the point of view of texture of the finished food, and food values, these are generally interchangeable; but not from the point of view of taste. I don't know how important this is to you, nor how much butter you can afford. Margarine generally makes good plain cake and pastry, and can be used in some sauces.

Calories Units of heat. Calorie-values of foods are a way of expressing their energy value only, and to know the calorie value of foods is not necessarily to know how good they are for you, though they are useful in calculations to a nutritionist. FOOD VALUES are really more important.

Chopping Cutting up into small or very small bits. Use a large sharp knife and a firm wooden board. Cut the food to be chopped into pieces if appropriate. Follow directions for chopping herbs, page 49, and see illustration. Keep the food to be chopped in a neat pile.

Clarification of Fat *Dripping:* boil the dripping in plenty of water. Strain into a bowl and let it get cold. Take the cake of fat from the top of the bowl and scrape the bottom clean.

Butter and margarine: melt and pour off the clear oily part, leaving sediment behind.

Coating Covering, as with sauce or egg-and-crumb mixtures. When coating a food with sauce, pour a thin and steady trickle backwards and forwards across the dish, starting at one side and overlapping a little on each journey to and fro. This gives a more even effect than pouring over the middle of the food.

Condiments *see* SEASONING.

Cook's Knife or French Knife A long pointed sharp knife, especially useful for chopping.

Cream The butterfat of milk. It rises naturally to the top of the container of milk if undisturbed, and can be skimmed off. Cornish or clotted cream has been treated with gentle heat to make it thicken and form a crust. You can readily buy different kinds of cream commercially:

Single or coffee cream: will not whip, but is used for pouring over or into food and drink.

Whipping cream is suitable for most cream desserts. It will whip to a fairly thick texture.

Double cream is richer, and whips to a very solid state.

Soured cream has been turned sour by a special culture of bacteria, rather like yoghurt. Delicious and useful in many cold or hot savoury dishes. You can turn cream sour yourself by adding lemon juice or vinegar to it.

Evaporated milk can stand in for cream at a pinch. Also see recipe for curd topping.

Creaming Beating something, such as butter or yeast, until it is soft and like cream. Butter and sugar are often beaten together in this way to make cakes. Illustration page 175.

Croûte A piece of toast, fried bread or pastry used as a base for a savoury mixture.

Croûtons Little dice of fried bread or toast; a garnish, especially for soup.

Cutlet A small piece of meat, sometimes with bone, from the rib region of an animal, or sometimes from the thick part of the leg.

Cuts *see* FIRST-AID.

Dariole Moulds or Castle Pudding Tins Small metal moulds used for puddings, small cakes or custards which are turned out after cooking. The result looks like a collection of sand-castles.

Dividing Mixtures If you want to divide dough or pastry into even-sized pieces, always start by cutting it into halves as equally as your eye can judge, having made it first into a symmetrical shape; then halve and halve again, and so on.

 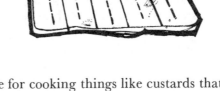

Double Saucepan A useful pan to have for cooking things like custards that should not be boiled, or for melting chocolate. The inner pan fits inside the outer one, which is half-filled with water. The water can boil but the inner pan is never heated above this point. You can improvise a double saucepan by fitting a pudding basin into a larger saucepan half-full of hot water.

Dredger A sprinkler for flour or sugar. I keep one of each. It will dispense just a small quantity of flour for rolling out pastry, or caster sugar for sprinkling over biscuits.

Dried Fruit Currants, raisins, sultanas; often bought now ready-washed and picked over. If not, rinse under the cold tap in a sieve, then pick over to remove stalks or bits of grit. Spread out on a baking sheet and put into a very cool oven. Turn over from time to time until dry. Raisins if large may need to be split with a small knife and the stones removed. Have a bowl of warm water into which you can drop the pips and rinse your sticky fingers.

Eggs *Cracking and separating*: give the egg a sharp tap on the edge of the pan, table or bowl. Then break the shell cleanly in half, using both hands. Drop the yolk from one half-shell to the other, delicately so that you don't break the membrane round the yolk, letting the white fall into a bowl underneath. *Glaze*: egg painted onto pastry, bread, etc. will give a pleasant golden sheen to the finished dish. You can use whole egg, or egg yolk, either plain or beaten with a teaspoonful or two of milk or cream. Left-over glaze can be used up in custards or scrambled egg.
Left-over whites: make meringues, uncooked fondant, royal icing; clear some consommé; make white scrambled egg; add to custards.
Left-over yolks: make any egg custard dishes, mayonnaise, scrambled egg; 2 yolks = 1 egg in cakes; use for glazing pastry.
White v. Brown: as you don't eat the shell except by accident, why pay extra for brown?

Entertaining Don't try out a dish for the first time if you have guests. Better a poached egg on toast, perfectly prepared, than a collapsed soufflé. The food isn't the important factor: the embarrassment is.

Fat for Frying *For shallow frying*, where the fat should reach only half-way up the sides of the food being cooked, almost any fat can be used. Butter and oil mixed are good for foods where the flavour of the fat is important.
For deep frying butter and margarine are unsuitable, because their smoking point is low. Use lard, clarified dripping or cooking oil.

First-Aid for Burns & Scalds Run the cold tap over the burn immediately and for several minutes until the pain is eased, or for large areas plunge into deep cold water. Cover the damaged skin with a clean dry dressing. If more than a small burn, treat for shock: that is keep warmly wrapped all over and have plenty of liquid to drink. Take to doctor or hospital as soon as possible in serious cases. If clothing is stuck to a burn, do not disturb it.

First-Aid for Cuts Wash gently round the cut area to remove grease, etc. Cover superficial cuts with sticking plaster; bandage deeper ones firmly enough to stop the bleeding, lifting up the limb, or press with fingers, and take to doctor or hospital.

Flambé "Flamed" or set on fire with brandy, rum or other spirits. Warm the spirits first, then you won't have trouble getting them to light. Illustration page 161.

Flavouring Essences e.g. vanilla, almond, lemon, ratafia and so on. These are strong, and usually you need only a drop or two. Too much makes food taste synthetic. To add them to a mixture, dip a skewer into and out of the bottle, which will bring one drop of essence with it. Or add from the point of a teaspoon, but never straight from the bottle.

Flour Powdered wheat grain, using more or less of the wheat. There are differences of opinion among nutritionists and cooks as to which kind is best for you or best for baking. You can buy *self-raising flour*, which contains a lot of raising agent or baking powder; I find this best for plain cakes and other occasional uses. *Plain flour* can be used perfectly well for all cakes with the addition of some baking powder or other raising agent such as bicarbonate of soda. Plain flour is definitely better, in my opinion, for pastry. *Wholemeal or wholewheat flour* contains some of the outer covering of the wheat and the germ or embryo new plant, not just the starch, and many people maintain that it is better for you. Other *brown flours* have various other ingredients added in various proportions or are made from other cereals such as rye. *Cake flour* has a low proportion of gluten, and is best for cakes, bad for bread, but *strong flour* has more gluten than ordinary flour and is best for bread, flaked pastries and choux pastry, but bad for sponge cakes. So you see there is quite an art in going and buying just a bag of flour. I keep self-raising, plain, wholemeal and strong flours in my store cupboard and buy others as I need them, but if I had to choose only one I would have plain flour, as this can be used for everything.

Foil, Aluminium or Metal Cooking Foil Most useful to the cook. Can be used to wrap up foods to keep them moist in the fridge, to prevent sticking on baking sheets—e.g. meringues—or to make little heat-reflecting hats for dishes that are browning too fast in the oven. Many other uses given on the box, folks.

Folding A very important term. A gentle mixing movement applied to ingredients which you must not beat or stir vigorously. Sprinkle or spoon whatever it is that is to be folded in, onto the top of the main mixture. Using a metal spoon for delicacy of touch, scrape the bowl of the spoon along the bottom of the basin, draw it up and across the surface of the mixture, and repeat. Then make a cutting movement with the edge of the spoon right through the centre of the mass. Repeat these movements gently and lightly until you have combined the ingredients thoroughly.

Food Values Not all foods are of equal use, or value, to the body. Some are needed because they provide useful "fuel", for keeping you warm and on the move. Even when you are asleep you heart must go on beating, your lungs breathe and your feet be prevented from freezing to the bedclothes, so imagine what a game of football or hockey does to your energy supply. The more physically active you are the more energy foods you need, though different people doing similar work may differ in their needs for energy foods in the same way that some people are tall and others short. The foods that supply warmth and energy are in general the fatty, oily and starchy or carbohydrate ones: for example butter, margarine, fat from meat, flour and things made from it, and sugar.

Then, too, both children and adults wear out some of their cells in the course of living, and these have to be made good again. Children must actually build their bodies from babyhood to adulthood. The extra bone, flesh and so on has to come from the food that is eaten: foods such as milk and cheese for bone-building calcium, and protein foods: meat, fish, eggs, milk and cheese again.

Other foods are needed because they contain traces of complicated substances called vitamins which your body needs to function properly and keep itself healthy. Certain mineral salts are needed in the living process in much the same way. Vitamins and mineral salts are found in many of the foods I have mentioned already, as well as in fruit and vegetables. Water is needed too; and plant fibres, which though not absorbed by the body keep the digestive tube exercised.

Most people need not fuss about whether or not their food is giving them enough of everything they need, provided they are sensible and don't eat too much of any one group of foods at the expense of the others. Generally speaking, if you eat a wide variety of foods, without going hungry and without stuffing just because you like food, you will be all right. If you are in doubt, choose fresh foods first, having protein foods, including milk, and also fruit and vegetables. After that fill up on things like bread, pastry and plain puddings, with biscuits, cakes and sweets last on your list, because only if you follow an extreme and unbalanced slimming diet are these likely to be in short supply in what you eat.

Forcemeat Another word for STUFFING. FARCE is another. A mixture of spices and savoury flavourings, panada or bread, to accompany meat or poultry or to fill the gap left after boning or drawing out entrails.

Forcing Bag A conical bag made of linen or nylon. Has a hole in the bottom into which a metal tube or pipe will fit. *See* PIPING.

Garlic A pungent flavouring. Often only a very little is needed. Squash a clove (the small division of the larger bulb, or head), with a knife-point. A sprinkling of salt makes it easier. Then put this paste into the main mixture. Illustration page 22.

Garnish & Decoration Little pieces of food added to the main part of a dish to make it look more attractive. Often used to add colour, or to contrast in taste or texture. Garnish is the word usually used for savoury dishes, decoration for sweet. Can be overdone. If in doubt, don't.

Girdle Iron, Griddle A large, heavy and flat sheet of metal with a handle over the middle, used for cooking scones and oatcakes and similar things, originally on an open fire. A heavy frying pan can be used instead.

Glaze For many baked dishes, a little polish is a good thing. Egg is often used: see EGGS—*Glaze*. Alternatively you can use cream or top-of-milk. Another way for cakes and pastry is to sprinkle the top with sugar before, or half-way through, baking, or paint with egg white and dredge with sugar. Bun wash is a glaze added after baking.

Grapefruit To prepare grapefruit, use a special curved knife if you have one, otherwise a small vegetable knife. Cut the grapefruit in half first, across the equator. Then cut down, close to the skin, at each side of every segment, but don't pierce the rind. Separate the flesh from the rind by cutting round just inside the white pith. Sprinkle with a little caster sugar and leave the fruit to absorb it before eating. Serve, chilled, with a glacé cherry in the middle, except at breakfast: no-one can face glacé cherries at breakfast.

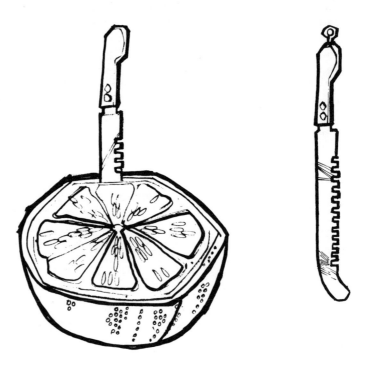

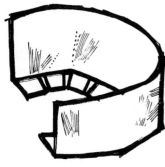

Greasing Tins, Lining Tins Before baking cakes, etc., you must prepare the tin by greasing, so that the food will not stick. For plain cakes it may be enough just to grease the tin; for richer, shallow ones, grease the tin and sprinkle flour over, then tap the tin to distribute the flour evenly. Caster sugar is sometimes used too.

For very rich cakes and large cakes you must also line the tin, after greasing thoroughly, with greased greaseproof paper. Run a pencil round the tin to mark paper to fit the bottom exactly. Cut it out. Cut double thickness into a strip or strips long enough to go round the sides, and a little deeper than the depth of the tin. Make a crease half an inch up along the length, and snip to this line at 1/2″ intervals. Then you will be able to curve the paper round the sides of the tin, with the snipped bits overlapping on the base. Fit in the bottom paper. Brush all over the surface that will be next to the cake with melted fat or oil—or do this before fitting the paper in.

Fat for greasing tins can be lard, butter, margarine or oil. It is ideal to keep a brush especially for use in greasing tins, as it is a quick and easy spreader.

Non-stick bakeware does save a little time.

Herbs Aromatic or highly flavoured plants used in cooking, in small quantities as a rule. Marvellous for varying flavours subtly, but don't overdo them. Experiment, please.

If possible, grow your own; at least a few of the basic ones such as mint, parsley, thyme, sage, rosemary. Some others are bay, basil, borage, dill, tarragon, savory, fennel, chives, marjoram, chervil, oregano. Dried herbs are nowadays readily obtainable, but they don't keep very well: the taste disappears somewhere on the kitchen shelf. Buy in small quantities and replace them from time to time. See also BOUQUET GARNI.

Jelly I usually suggest that you turn out jellies by inverting them over a plate, but you may like to try the professional way. Dip the mould in just-warm water, wet your hand and turn the jelly out onto your palm. Then you can arrange it on the dish as you like. If the dish is damp, too, you will be able to shift the jelly if it is in the wrong position.

Jelly Bag A conical bag made from linen, with two wide hems at the top. Push bamboo canes through the hems, so that you can fill the bag, then support it by the sticks on something like an upturned stool.

Lemon Butterflies A garnish. See illustration on page 117.

Lemon Juice If the recipe calls for rind as well as juice of lemon, use a fresh lemon. If only lemon juice is needed it is more economical to use bottled lemon juice, which is quite satisfactory for most purposes except jam-making, when fresh must be used.

Liaison A thickening for sauce or other liquid: e.g. roux, beurre manié or egg and cream beaten together.

Lining Tins *see* GREASING TINS.

Making a Well Making a small hollow in a heap of flour or other dry ingredients into which you pour a liquid. This enables the liquid to be mixed in smoothly.

Marinade or Marinate To soak food, often meat, in a liquid, which often includes wine, vinegar or lemon juice, to flavour and tenderize it.

Masking a Mould Lining a mould with a gelatine mixture which is allowed to set before another mixture is put in. It is a way of decorating cold food. Aspic is used for savoury dishes, fruit-flavoured jelly for sweet ones. Little pieces of decoration can be set in the masking jelly if you like. Have the jelly on the point of setting and swill out the chilled mould with it, turning it in a bed of ice and salt to speed the process of setting.

Oven Management An important skill in cookery. In this book oven temperatures are given as if you were baking only one dish at a time, and that one as near the top of the oven as is convenient without crowding the dish or cutting off the circulation of hot air; unless, that is, some other part of the oven is specifically mentioned.

But in practice, you may want to cook more than one dish at a time: in fact it is wasteful, often, not to do so. In this case you must remember that the oven temperature or Regulo applies to the top of the oven, and that dishes cooked below are at about 25 °F or a Regulo setting below the maximum temperature for each item as you go down the oven. Thus, if you are baking something at moderate heat, Reg. 4, 350 °F on the top shelf, the middle-oven temperature will be warm, Reg. 3, 325 °F or thereabouts, while the floor of the oven will be cool, Reg. 1-2 or in the region of 300 °F.

If you are baking several trays of pastry, biscuits or cakes, always put them for the first 5-10 minutes of their baking time at the top of the oven at the correct temperature. Then you can shift them to a lower shelf and put in a new trayful on the top shelf. If the oven is very full you may need to increase the setting, or allow longer, or both, to cook all the food satisfactorily.

Palette Knife or Spatula A flexible broad-bladed round-ended tool useful for scraping out bowls and lifting biscuits off baking sheets and so on. Can also be used for whipping egg whites on a plate.

Panada A very thick white sauce, made by the roux method. The proportion is 1 oz. fat, 1 oz. flour (30 g. each), 1/4 pint liquid (150 ml.). Useful for binding together some ingredients in savoury dishes: e.g. egg cutlets, or may be used as the basis of others: e.g. soufflés.

Parsley A herb useful as a garnish, also rich in iron and vitamin C. May be used fresh in sprigs or chopped, or fried.

Pastry Brush A small brush sold as a cooking tool, used for brushing food with water, egg or fat. Much neater to use than fingers for these purposes.

Patty Tins or Bun Tins Baking sheets with small hollows for baking small cakes, mince pies and tartlets.

Paupiettes Little rolled-up pieces of meat or fish. Usually served in sauce. Illustration page 93.

Pinch A small measurement, less than you can measure with a teaspoon. It is as much as you can hold between (adult) finger and thumb. Used for salt and spices and other strongly-flavoured powders.

Piping Pressing a softish substance through a hole in a metal nozzle to achieve a decorative effect. Fun to do, and can give a professional-looking finish to such things as meringues, potatoes, desserts decorated with cream and cake icings, but it is never actually essential: it is literally a frill. Large cone-shaped forcing bags often made of nylon are used for large quantities of mixture, and several different-shaped nozzles, called pipes or tubes, are available in large and small sizes for making rosettes, ropes, leaves or writing. For icing cakes, a small bag of greaseproof paper is the easiest to manage, though there are also icing sets that one can buy. (See page 181.)

Poaching Cooking gently in liquid just off the boil. A term applied most often to eggs and fish.

Preserving Pan A very large saucepan with slightly sloping sides and with handle across the top, or with two handles at the sides to make lifting easier. It looks rather like a wide shallow bucket. It is used for making jam, marmalade and chutney.

Purée *see* RUBBING THROUGH A SIEVE.

Ramekins Little earthenware dishes, useful for baking eggs and other small quantities of mixture.

Rare When applied to steak means underdone, still red in the middle.

Raspings *see* BREADCRUMBS.

Recipes Instructions for making dishes of all kinds. They usually consist of a list of *ingredients* or food components to be used, with weight or quantity of each, and *method*, telling you in greater or lesser detail how to mix together and treat the ingredients to achieve the finished result. Sometimes they are written as a kind of narrative; this is especially true of old recipes (old word "receipts") which go something like this:

"Take enough day-old milk, and put to it three or four new-laid eggs. Let your dish be buttered before you put them in..."

Many people read cookery books for pleasure, as well as using them as a practical help in the kitchen. Old recipe books can often give you a sense of the reality of the past. I personally find it more interesting to imagine what it must have been like to be a housewife or a cook in some past age than to know who was the king or queen at the time, or which political party was in power. What ingredients would have been available? What kind of stove, saucepans, serving dishes? Are modern equivalents better, worse or just different?

Altering recipes: while you are learning the basic things about cooking, it is wise to follow a recipe exactly. But later it often makes cookery very interesting indeed if you try your own adaptations of recipes by substituting one ingredient for another similar one or adding a different flavour and so on.

Remember that recipes are suggestions only. You are the cook and you are in charge.

Altering recipes for larger or smaller numbers. Usually you can do a straightforward multiplication or division of ingredients, though you may have some odd quantities like 3/4 of an egg, but it is terribly easy to forget half-way through, and go wrong. Write a note "×2" or "divide" on a postcard and keep it as a marker by the recipe you are using. The baking time will be longer for double-sized dishes, but not twice as long, shorter for smaller dishes, but not half as short; and of course the timing for small items such as biscuits will be the same.

Reduce Can mean to simmer for a long time so that water evaporates, particularly from a sauce, and taste becomes more concentrated, but can also mean to cut down on the amount of any particular ingredient in a recipe, as "reduce the amount of flour by 1 teaspoon and use cocoa instead."

Refrigerator A valuable piece of equipment for any cook. It will help to keep foods fresh for longer, and also can be thought of as an oven in reverse, making chilled puddings, sweet and savoury jellies, mousses and ice-cream possible even in hot weather—when you want them most. As coldness reduces the apparent flavour, make the mixtures rather stronger and sweeter than you would otherwise do.

The coldest place in the fridge is the ice-making compartment where you also store frozen foods. Your fridge may have a star-rating which will tell you how long it is safe to keep frozen foods. Most households have a little booklet tucked away somewhere giving directions and even recipes using your particular model. It might be worth having a look.

Remember though that even a fridge doesn't keep food fresh for ever, and also that it will work best if defrosted regularly and kept clean. Always cover foods before putting them in, because otherwise they will dry out, and excessive frost will also form on the business part of the machinery.

Rendering Down Fat Don't throw away the bits of fat trimmed from joints of meat, bacon and so on. Cut it into small pieces, put it in a baking tin on a low shelf when you have the oven on for some other reason and pour off the liquid fat which will run out. Clarify as dripping.

Roux A mixture of fat and flour, usually equal quantities of each, cooked together. A common thickening for sauces and soups. *White roux* is cooked for a short time, and the flour does not colour. *Blond roux* is cooked for a little longer, and the flour turns a pale straw colour, while *brown roux* is cooked for longer still until the flour turns a pale brown.

Rubbing Through a Sieve Breaking up cooked vegetables and fruit by pushing through the grid of a wire, hair or nylon sieve to make a PURÉE. Put the sieve, shallow side upwards, over a basin. Pour some of the food to be sieved on top. Holding a wooden spoon at the top of its bowl between your right thumb and first and second fingers, start to push and stroke the food towards you. As the purée collects on the underside of the sieve, scrape it off with a different, clean spoon. Steady the sieve with your left hand as you push the food through with your right. Illustration page 19.

Rubbish, Garbage or Refuse Whatever you don't want any more in the kitchen, like potato peelings, plastic bags, cardboard cartons and cornflake packets, used tea leaves and pieces of string. The jumble can be divided into: *Food rubbish:* peelings, cores, carrot tops and so on. Could some of these things go for pig swill in your district? Or compost in someone's garden? Tea-leaves make good compost I believe. If not, put with *wet and greasy paper*, and burn if possible, or else wrap in plastic or newspaper and put in the dustbin. *Clean dry paper and cardboard:* keep this separate from other rubbish for collection by the dustmen. Waste paper is valuable.

Plastic: put in the dustbin, or possibly burn. Keep plastic film and bags right away from babies and small children.

Tins and bottles: rinse out, so that you won't feed flies, and put in the dustbin.

Some of your problems are solved if you have a waste disposer but otherwise don't put tea-leaves down the sink: you may block it. Some people say coffee grounds are all right, but perhaps you had better not risk it. Blocked sinks are nasty. On this subject, clean the drain occasionally with a handful of soda and kettleful of boiling water poured over. Also empty and rinse out the kitchen pedal-bin every day.

Sauces If you prepare sauces in advance and want to keep them hot, put the pan into a larger one containing hot water. Cover the top of the sauce with a piece of butter paper or other greaseproof cut to the size of the pan. Then you won't get a skin on top.

Sauté or Sweat To fry or at least start cooking food in a little hot fat, sometimes with the lid on, until the fat is absorbed. It is often a preliminary process in making stews and sauces.

The term also refers to a method of cooking meat, partly by frying, partly by simmering in sauce. A SAUTÉ PAN is the kind of straight-sided pan like a modified frying pan with lid in which, ideally, this is done.

Seasoned Flour Flour for coating fish or meat etc. to which a sprinkling of salt and pepper is added.

Seasoning, Condiments Words commonly used to mean salt and pepper. These are absolutely indispensable to the cook. Even sweet dishes are better for a little salt. There are different kinds and qualities of salt, but all are basically sodium chloride.

Pepper isn't just of one kind. The most useful, I find, are white pepper (ground) for pale dishes, black pepper (ground) for other savoury dishes, red cayenne for its strength, and mild red paprika as a garnish. You can buy black and white whole peppers or peppercorns to grind yourself if you have a grinder, and the taste of these is more spicy than bought ground pepper, I find. Tabasco, used a drop at a time, is a very strong peppery sauce.

But there are other kinds of seasoning too: the word can include things like mustard, horseradish, vinegar, garlic, other herbs and all the spices that there are.

Shredding, Slicing, Dicing Cutting up foods into pieces. Shreds are long thin slivers, of cabbage for example. Dice are cut from slices which have been cut across again into strips. Cut up a pile of strips at a time, or you will be up all night. See also pages 47 and 48.

Sifting Sieving of dry ingredients, especially flour, partly to remove lumps and "foreign bodies" (found any dead Chinamen lately?), and partly to aerate the flour and make folding-in easier.

Simmering, Stewing Cooking in liquid just below boiling point, often for a long time.

Sippets of Toast Little pieces of crisp toast served with something sloppy like mince. Cut the crusts off a piece of toast, then cut into strips. Pile up the strips and cut into triangles. Arrange these round the edges of the dish.

Skimming Scooping off froth or foam that rises on soup, jam and other liquids when boiled. Use a large spoon and draw it across the surface. Too much skimming is wasteful. Illustration page 15.

Skins, Removal of *see* BLANCHING.

Soufflé A light, delicate dish which always contains stiffly-beaten egg white. Baked soufflés have a panada base, and may be either savoury or sweet. Cold soufflés are uncooked and hold their foamy texture because they are made with gelatine. Recipes for baked soufflés begin on page 79, soufflé omelet on page 78 and Milanese soufflé on page 158.

Spices Like herbs, these are aromatic, often the seeds or roots of plants. Commonly used to flavour many sweet dishes, but also valuable for savoury ones: e.g. curry powder which is a mixture of spices. Here are some of the well-known spices: cinnamon, cloves, ginger and its relation turmeric, nutmeg and mace from the same plant, aniseed, caraway, cardamom, cumin, saffron, sesame seeds and poppy seeds and allspice, which is not the same as mixed spice, though supposed to taste like a lot rolled into one.

Stewing *see* SIMMERING.

Stirring Moving a soft mixture about, either to blend ingredients or to prevent burning. To stir cold ingredients together, simply move the spoon round the sides of the bowl and through the middle until everything is mixed.

To stir hot liquids in a saucepan, use a wooden spoon, if possible of a kind that has a flat bottom to scrape the base of the pan. Go round, round again, then across the pan, so that the bottom is evenly scraped and the liquid kept in motion. There isn't any need to stir fast as a rule; a relaxed but steady movement is best.

Stock Syrup or Sugar Syrup Sugar and water boiled together. Most useful is 1/2 lb. sugar to 1 pint water. (200 g. to 500 ml.) Use for stewing (sour) fruit, sweetening drinks, making trifle and so on. A higher proportion of sugar can be used if you like. It keeps well.

Sugar Comes either as white, highly refined, or brown, less refined.
White: lump or loaf: compressed sugar in cubes. Main use for sweetening cups of this and that at table.
Preserving: broken or irregular bits of loaf sugar, useful for making jam and marmalade.
Granulated: large crystals of refined sugar. Can be used anywhere where the sugar will dissolve.
Caster: fine crystals of refined sugar. Useful in dishes which don't contain much liquid, and where dissolving is therefore more difficult; or where you want the sugar to dissolve quickly.
Icing: powdered sugar. For making icing, obviously, but also useful for dishes where you don't want a gritty texture: e.g. brandy butter, or for sweetening cold drinks.
Brown: coffee crystals: very large crystals for coffee.
Demerara: rather like granulated, but brown. Some people prefer it to white sugar.
Soft brown: like caster but damper and pale brown or darker. Has a delicious slightly toffeeish taste. Good in some cakes, especially chocolate and fruit cakes.
Barbados, Foot, Pieces: darker sugars that taste more or less of treacle. Also suitable for some cakes and puddings.

Taste The sense that is as important to the cook as hearing to a musician. It is one of the lesser valued senses in our society, sadly, receiving little training or conscious attention. Yet the development of the palate and an awareness of the different nuances of flavours can be an enormous source of civilized pleasure. You must eat in order to stay alive: why not learn to appreciate what you eat, to judge and discriminate? This has only a little to do with the amount of money you spend: you can get a gourmet's satisfaction from savouring an apple or a piece of cheese.

Taste As a direction in a recipe: dip a clean teaspoon into the mixture, cool slightly if hot, then put the specimen into your mouth. Register what it is like, and then try to imagine what it would be like with more salt? pepper? vinegar? tabasco? sugar? spice? extra herbs? a pinch of anything more? If you think any of these things would improve your dish, add them and taste again until you have it right. If you would have preferred less of any of these things, well, too bad this time, but make a note of it, and remember to adjust the recipe next time you use it.

To Taste A note in a recipe meaning that the amount of the ingredient to be added is up to you, and that you must please yourself.

Toast Grilled bread. Have the grill heated evenly before you start to make it, from bread cut into moderately thick slices. Don't go away or start thinking about anything else. Nothing burns more easily than toast. Cut off the crusts if you want to be posh and cut rounds of toast into triangles. Put in a toast rack, not flat on a plate, or it will go sadly soggy. Or butter hot if something is to go on top. Serve quickly. Melba toast is made by splitting a piece of ordinary toast through the middle, then re-toasting it on the raw sides.

Tomato Purée A concentrated Italian kind can be bought economically in tins, tubes or jars. Recommended.

Vanilla Flavouring. The delicately aromatic fruit pod of a tropical orchid, long, thin and black. Keep one in a jar of caster sugar. You will in time have a jar of vanilla sugar, if you top up and shake when you have used some of it. For flavouring liquids such as custards, leave the pod to infuse in hot milk, then take it out, rinse, dry and re-use another day.

Washing-up A necessary chore. Do it fast and well, because otherwise it is as dreary as Cinderella without her godmother. Hot water, detergent, rinsing bowl if possible. Clean tea towel. Glass first, cutlery, pudding dishes, meat plates, eggy plates. Saucepans last. Rinse everything thoroughly, dry well or drain in a rack and put away tidily. Don't dry saucepans on a tea towel though: wipe them with a wrung-out dishcloth and leave to dry in the air. Put hollow-ware (baking tins, etc.) somewhere warm to dry off before putting away. There! That wasn't so bad really. Did you remember to clean the sink and wipe down the draining board—oh, and to hang up the dishcloth and tea towel?

Well *see* MAKING A WELL.

Wine Fermented juice of grapes, or occasionally other fruit, or even vegetable and flower juices and infusions. Praised by poets. The much-prized partner of good food. Like food itself, it can be abused and taken to excess.

Wine, its brothers the liqueurs and its cousins the spirits, beers, ales, ciders, perries, meads, metheglins and cordials, can be ingredients in, as well as companions to many delicious dishes. Wine will tenderize meat and make the sauce taste much better than patent gravy thickening! If you disapprove of alcohol on moral grounds, it may console you that the alcohol content of wine evaporates when it is heated for any length of time, just leaving the taste behind. Generally, too, you don't use much wine. Its use is not extravagantly extravagant.

Another use of wine in the kitchen, I have heard it said, is to encourage the cook.

In this book I have suggested that you use a spoonful of this or a little of that occasionally, but usually you *can* leave it out if you must. You don't know what you're missing.

Zest The coloured part only of citrus fruit peel. Used finely grated or very thinly pared to flavour many dishes.

Also, in common use, a word that means piquancy, enjoyment, gusto. I hope that this book will add zest to your time in the kitchen, relish to your time at table. A good word to end with!

Index